Christianity
and Revolution

Documents in Free Church History

A Series Edited by Franklin H. Littell and George H. Williams

"And now judgment presseth the kingdoms, and of all the heaviest judgments, the sword. . . . I hope this war shall be Christ's triumph; Babylon's ruin."
Samuel Rutherford, *Lex Rex: The Law and the Prince* (1644)

Christianity
and Revolution

**Radical Christian
Testimonies
1520-1650**

**Edited by
Lowell H. Zuck**

Temple University Press
Philadelphia

Temple University Press
Philadelphia 19122
© 1975 by Temple University
All rights reserved
Published 1975
Printed in the United States
of America
International Standard Book
Number: 0-87722-040-9 cloth;
0-87722-044-1 paper
Library of Congress Catalog Card
Number: 74-25355

To Maya and Peter

Contents

Series Foreword

Studies in the Radical Reformation continue to grow in number with each passing year. This fact reflects not only the response of scholars to the quantity of primary sources discovered and published in recent decades but also the shifting center of gravity in world Christianity. On the mission fields and among the younger churches, from which delegates at ecumenical conferences and councils play a much larger role than they did even a generation ago, there is a pronounced sense of recapturing and reliving the life and spirit of the New Testament and Early Church. European "Christendom," whether medieval or sixteenth century, seems far more strange, far more distant in time and space than the congregations to which Paul wrote his Epistles. Thus the scientific effort, whose beginnings might be dated in America with Harold S. Bender's founding of *The Mennonite Quarterly Review* in 1926 and in Germany with the publication of the first volume of the *Täuferakten* (Anabaptist Archives) in 1930, has been sustained by a growing awareness in the churches that in Protestantism, at least, there are two distinct church types and life-styles dating from the earliest years of the movement. One continued in modified form the territorial and parochial patterns of the medieval period, while the other used the New Testament and Early Church as a model. One was essentially concerned for reformation of doctrine and reform of ecclesiastical institutions, the other was devoted to the restitution of pristine Christian polity and faith.

In June 1964 a seminar on the Church in the World brought together a number of Free Church scholars—primarily from the "historic peace churches" (Mennonites, Brethren, Friends) at Earlham School of Religion. In June of 1967 a large number met for a week at Southern Baptist Theological Seminary.*

In late June of 1970 the Second Believer's Church Conference met at Chicago Theological Seminary.† Beginning in 1971 a section of Free Church Studies established itself as a regular feature of scholarly sessions at the annual convention of the American Academy of Religion.

Parallel to this development of cooperation and consultation among American specialists, the work of the German commission sponsoring publication of the *Täuferakten* has gone forward steadily. A Dutch counterpart, *Documenta Anabaptistica Neerlandica*, has been initiated. At the meetings of historical societies held during the holidays in 1964, the suggestion that a comparable American organization be formed was discussed. In April of 1965 the North American Committee for the Documentation of Free Church Origins was launched, and the dates 1525–1675 chosen to bracket the era of concern (including the *TAK* attention to the sixteenth century, but adding also the Polish Brethren, the beginnings of radical Puritanism, and Pietism).

Of first importance among the Committee's publishing projects has been a series of sourcebooks of Free Church materials on themes of contemporary concern, such as the status of women, the genesis of the modern conscience, revolution, war and violence, religious liberty, the mystical basis of religious dissent, mutual aid, and democratic government (both church and civil). These are matters on which the Free Church pioneers took quite different positions from the established churches, both Catholic and Protestant, and on which their testimonies sound strikingly contemporary.

Today Catholics, mainline classical Protestants, and many others are finding in the Radical Reformation principles and motifs of vital importance whose adherents their own spiritual ancestors were liable to punish by fire and sword.

Franklin H. Littell
Temple University
George Williams
Harvard University

---

*The 1967 conference papers, edited by James Leo Garrett, Jr., have been published as *The Concept of the Believers' Church* (Scottsdale, Pa.: Herald Press, 1969).

†The 1970 papers, edited by Clyde L. Manshreck, were published in The Chicago Theological Seminary *Register* 60 (1970): 1–59.

Christianity
and Revolution

Introduction

Both skeptics and believers frequently say that Christianity has little to do with revolution, past or present. Churches are traditional and backward-looking, while revolution demands drastic social and political change. History shows, however, that biblical religion, both Hebrew and early Christian, had profound revolutionary effects upon its societies. Moreover, religious controversy has powerfully shaped social change at least three times during the second thousand years of Christianity—namely, during the eleventh-century Gregorian reform, during the sixteenth-century Reformation, and, perhaps less clearly, during the twentieth-century theological revival and Catholic upheaval.

If we define revolution as a transformation of the constitutive principles of a society with the result that political power is seized by means of popular uprisings,[1] the First (sixteenth-century) Reformation, which transformed the religious institutions of its day, produced a true revolution of religious consciousness. Uneasily contained within that movement, though part of the Second Reformation, were the Anabaptists, who most radically sought to manifest the era's new religious and political forms, as the Puritans did later against the Anglican reformers. As a radical opposition movement, the Anabaptists struggled against Catholics and other Protestants over how to resolve the issue of the ethics of resistance. In facing this problem, early Anabaptism involved itself in the seemingly contradictory activities of pacifist nonviolence and violent revolutionary activity. Violence may be the ordinary means for introducing revolution, but any practical large-scale realization of nonviolent Anabaptist proposals would equally have necessitated a new notion of political power. Consequently, the Catholic mainliners of the First Reformation were as suspicious of the revolutionary implications of non-violence as they were of its seeming opposite, violent resistance.

This collection of sixteenth- and seventeenth-century Free Church testimonies seeks to follow the thread of the Second or radical Reformation as it diverged from the First, conservative Reformation of Wittenberg, Zurich, Geneva, Canterbury, and Rome.[2] The lines between the two are not clear-cut. Indeed, by emphasizing the Second Reformation, we have underplayed the revolutionary significance of the two great figures of the First Reformation—Luther and Erasmus. Erasmus may be compared to Pope John XXIII, a common-sense modernizer of the church, sympathetic to both reformations. So far no twentieth-century Luther has appeared, although Hans Küng and others are candidates. Even in his own time, the great rebel Luther advocated both youthful spiritual reformation[3] and institutional reformation, although his resistance theory against the Catholic emperor stiffened as he grew older, or as the situation changed (see Document 26). Zwingli and Calvin also combined radical theology with conservative ecclesiology in fruitful, inconsistent ways.[4]

Representatives of radical reform during the Second Reformation actually appeared, therefore, in opposition to the leading reformers. George H. Williams has divided them into three groups: Anabaptists (Grebel vs. Zwingli); Spiritualists (Muentzer vs. Luther), called Spiritualizers here; and Rationalists (Servetus vs. Calvin).[5] These movements were many-sided, however, and in some respects the radicals failed to form any movement at all. They went beyond Luther and Calvin in radicalism, but also looked backward for inspiration to medieval Catholicism.[6] Spiritual reformers could be traditional indeed.

Our first section of documents considers social rather than religious history—the great Peasants' War. From the standpoint of social history, the Peasants' War was the culmination of the European peasants' revolts of the fourteenth century. The English peasants' revolt in 1381 and the Hussite wars of Bohemia in the early 1400s came close to becoming national or even international revolutionary movements.[7] Divided Germany, already near social revolution in the early 1500s, found that its knights and peasants had misinterpreted Luther's view of God's justification of the sinner to mean that serfdom and the traditional feudal order were open to attack by revolutionary idealists.[8] The peasant revolutionaries faced firmly backward, aiming to restore the better situations which they imagined had existed in the past. Our first documents, therefore, record the conservative manifestos of the Peasants' War. Only Michael Gaismayr and Thomas Muentzer, who died an outlaw after the failure of his leadership in the Peasants' War, come close to the present-day Marxist ideal of self-conscious social revolutionaries leading an attack on the feudal order in the name of the suffering masses.

Although the evidence is ambiguous, economic agitation among the peasants did find support among Second Reformation religious leaders, especially Hubmaier, Muentzer, and Hut,[9] while the First Reformation leaders, obviously, drew back in horror at the implications of peasant revolt. Tragedy resulted for the peasants. But fanatical as Muentzer was, his theology ought not to be condemned without consideration, and his leadership in the Peasants' War was significant, as Manfred Bensing, a Marxist, has pointed out.[10] The Anabaptists had a more evangelical, church-forming doctrine than did the peasants.[11] But their fates were similar. A martyr movement is likely to be serious and socially sensitive; when the second horror of the age, the Anabaptist Kingdom of Muenster, appeared, economic distress played a still more notable role than during the Peasants' War, even though the Muenster ideology was religious.[12]

Part 2 of this book documents opposition to Luther by spiritualizing prophets from Zwickau and by the apocalyptic crusader Thomas Muentzer.[13] Although he was technically not a rebaptizer, Muentzer's teaching established its politically illegitimate, radical idealism as the center of Second Reformation consciousness. It may not be accidental that a decade later the Anabaptist kingdom at Muenster closely followed Muentzer's program and that the radical Puritan Fifth Monarchists relied upon him ideologically and hoped to realize his program at last in the English Puritan millennium.[14]

The selection of documents in Parts 3–5 reflects the observations of James M. Stayer, who distinguished between moderate apolitical (Luther), realpolitical (Zwingli), and crusading (Muentzer) attitudes within the Reformation regarding the legitimacy of coercive force.[15] Stayer has denied both traditional historiographical stereotypes—the out-group interpretation (Luther's) that Anabaptism was revolutionary and the in-group (Mennonite) interpretation that Anabaptism was nonresistant. He describes instead a basic Anabaptist *apoliticism* that is not fundamentally violent coupled with a basic *radicalism*, an illegitimacy sometimes compatible with violence. Therefore the Anabaptists, whether nonviolent resisters or violent conspirators, or both, developed paradigms of revolution that were abortive in their own time but pregnant with the bases for modern revolutions, beginning with the visions of the perfect society that emerged in the democratic Puritan revolution.

Part 3 considers the Swiss Brethren, the first of the Anabaptist sects, within the revolutionary context. Despite the standard Mennonite interpretation, the documents give tantalizing hints that the Zurich radicals suggested a variety of revolutionary ideas, including Muentzer-like violence (Simon Stumpf) and rapid destruction of Catholic religious order in Zurich (Grebel and Manz), before repression by Zwingli forced them into what became the definitive Mennonite view on separatism and nonresistance.[16] This pacifism, the polar opposite of Muentzer's violent revolution, appeared equally illegitimate in its own day, and continues to raise legal and moral questions in conservative minds; despite its commendable sensitivity, the radically separatist pacifist position seems even today to frighten traditional patriots. The Zurich Anabaptists were insufficiently apolitical in their teachings to prevent their own leaders' involvement in the Peasants' War. Hubmaier, especially, encouraged use of violence on the side of the peasants and against Hapsburg power and, through Muentzer's converts Denck and Hut, transmitted Muentzerite influences to central Germany and Austria.[17] But by 1527, Grebel's disciple Michael Sattler was able to re-establish Anabaptist radical apoliticism in the Schleitheim Confession, which became the definitive Anabaptist policy on rejection of revolutionary violence.

The documents in Part 4 trace the movement of Melchior Hofmann's excited millenarianism from Strassburg into North German and Dutch Anabaptism, culminating in the Kingdom of Muenster.[18] Following Hofmann's imprisonment in Strassburg, John Matthys, a Dutch fanatic, reintroduced Anabaptism, and was permitted by Bernhard Rothmann, pastor in Muenster, to turn that city into an Anabaptist refuge. As publicist for the Muenster movement, Rothmann encouraged Anabaptist resistance to persecution, and under John of Leiden a Davidic kingdom was established at Muenster which introduced polygamy and communism.

After Muenster had fallen to a combined Catholic and Protestant episcopal-princely siege, apocalyptic crusading among Anabaptists was discredited, and a reaction toward stability, conservatism, and church-forming produced the Mennonites and Hutterites, the continuing, normative forms of Anabaptism, as Part 5 documents.[19] To be sure, the Mennonites looked back eventually to Zurich Anabaptism and Schleitheim for their nonresistant norms, but Menno had reasserted the original Melchiorite teachings without chiliasm, and even today the Hutterites have maintained their interpretation of the biblical character of Christian communism without Muenster fanaticism.[20]

Following the lurid failure of the Kingdom of Muenster, formidable revolutionary movements developed elsewhere than in Germany, as Parts 6–8 illustrate. Inspired by First Reformation Lutheran resisters to the Catholic emperor at Magdeburg and based upon Luther's guarded, legally supported resistance theory,[21] Calvinism, like Lutheranism, showed some affinity with the Second Reformation, producing a resistance theory and revolutionary movements based on religious faith, though far more respectable and successful than the egalitarian millenarianism of Muentzer and the Anabaptists ever could be. Its broader social base and more effective leaders (the French nobility, for example) allowed Calvinism to form the first revolutionary political parties.[22] In financial and military resources, in organizational talent, and in political leadership, the Dutch Sea Beggars, the French Huguenots, and the Scottish Lords of the Congregation equalled the governments they opposed. Unlike the Anabaptists, the Scottish, French, and Dutch Calvinists achieved successful political and religious revolutions. Yet they left the social structure of their countries intact. In England, Cromwell (Part 8) did come close to achieving a democratic and egalitarian revolution —the First Reformation using the Second—only to turn against his allies the Levellers, Diggers, and Fifth Monarchy Men at the moment when the revolution had succeeded externally.[23]

Much like their First Reformation Calvinist opponents, such Roman Catholic apologists as Jesuits William Allen and Juan de Mariana (Part 7) in England and Spain encouraged violent resistance to Protestant kings thought to be tyrants by faithful Catholics. Besides defending Catholic resistance in writing, Bishop Allen established a seminary at Douai in 1568 which prepared hundreds of priests abroad for treasonable activity in Elizabethan England.[24] When their work was forbidden in England, Catholics plotted at Douai in the manner of Second Reformation free churchmen, just as Calvinists (and Lutherans) had done before they succeeded in getting their revolutions established in Germany, Scotland, France, and the Netherlands.

The story of Second Reformation revolutionaries ends (in Part 8) when the English Puritans brought into existence the first modern democratic revolution, thereby extending into succesful practice previously successful principles from both Reformations.[25] To be sure, the Puritan Revolution lasted less than twenty years, and the kingship was later restored. Nevertheless, the "Great Rebellion" combined the conservative religious reform methods of the First Reformation with the radical religious goals of the Second Reformation with the result that a modern state appeared in which democratic freedoms triumphed (Revolution I).

Thus far we have emphasized religious and social history, since that approach has dominated the selection of our documents. But we should also consider Christianity and revolution from the standpoint of analytic or intellectual history. Karl Griewank has noted that the cyclical term "revolution," connected with the motions of the planets, was first applied to the year 1660—the *end* of the English Puritan Revolution.[26] Thus the English Revolution, like the French Revolution, may be considered cyclical in Polybius's terms: it moves from the collapse of monarchy and aristocracy through an increasingly democratic republic to military dictatorship and, eventually, to monarchy again.

Modern revolutions do not simply return, however, to their starting points; they have further effects, shaping the subsequent development of nations. The same preconditions lay behind the Dutch struggle for independence from Spain as behind the English Revolution against the king and bishops. Though the English revolutionaries held common goals (like securing the personal rights of individuals), inner conflict blunted the direction of their revolution as First Reformation Calvinists collided with the chiliastic sectarian movements of radical Puritanism. The more socially conservative movements like Cromwell's were able to overcome the chiliastic movements, but powerful forces were unleashed which helped to integrate the English nation and increased personal liberties.

Chalmers Johnson's analysis of six types of revolution distinguishes different goals among them.[27] Johnson begins, as do we, with a reformist-Jacquerie type, the Peasants' War—a traditional, spontaneous, mass peasant rising. The second type, millenarian-eschatological, is found in Thomas Muentzer and the prophets of Muenster, as well as in Puritan Independents like Thomas Goodwin or Diggers like Gerrard Winstanley or Fifth Monarchists like John Spittlehouse. The third type, anarchistic rebellion, idealizes the old order. In some ways the Swiss Anabaptists, Mennonites, Hutterites, Unitarians, and Quakers—most of whom still exist, at least in fossilized form—preserve this method as a New Testament restorationism, although their church ordinances are seldom anarchistic. The fourth—the nation-forming, great-revolution type—Johnson saw as occurring only in the French, Russian, and Chinese revolutions, though Lawrence Stone has objected to Johnson's linking Jacobin and Communist types, noting that the French Revolution was not communist, while the Russian and Chinese revolutions were not Jacobin.[28] But the English Revolution, as we here interpret it, was also a great revolution, and a culmination of the second and third types, with strong religious motivation involved. Johnson's fifth type, the conspiratorial coup d'etat (Nasser and Castro), might have happened under the direction of Thomas Muentzer, the Protestant Spiritualizer, or of William Allen, the English revolutionary traditionalist. The sixth type, militarized mass insurrection (Yugoslavia, China, Algeria, Vietnam), Johnson claims as a twentieth-century innovation, producing guerilla warfare determined by political attitudes.

In addition, analytical models emphasize preconditions and precipitants of revolution, as ways of determining causes. Revolution becomes *possible* when agents repudiating multiple dysfunction meet an intransigent elite: an abortive Second Reformation on the Continent opposing First Reformation and Catholic traditionalists (too strong an enemy); a successful First Reformation in Scotland against queen and church; a partially successful French First Reformation against king and church; a successful Dutch First Reformation against Spanish domination; and, in England, a temporarily successful First *and* Second Reformation opposing the king, the bishops, and each other. But revolution becomes *probable* when circumstance provides a catalyst: an inspired prophet (John of Leiden, John Lilburne), a secret revolutionary organization (Muentzer's covenant groups, Huguenot companies, Dutch Sea Beggars), an extraordinary legislative body (Charles's calling the Long Parliament).

We have not attempted to draw analogies to the present in the selection of documents, preferring to let the sixteenth- and seventeenth-century revolutionaries speak for themselves. Much of this material may have been prematurely revolutionary—stillborn and/or fanatical. A careful reading of the testimonies will show, however, the depth of religious conviction in that age and the strong effect religion had upon personal conduct and the ordering of society. This was true as well of those labeled "visionary," "chiliast," or "other-worldly" by moderns, whose faith is invested elsewhere. In the English Puritan Revolution, Reformation religious ideals were finally realized along with basic human freedoms. Even more than its achievement in actual practice, the English Revolution presents us with some of the finest rhetoric in history concerning human freedom, which was the fruit of that spiritual religious reform we have labeled Second Reformation, dependent as it was upon the First Reformation's concern with theological and organizational renewal and upon the whole cultural and religious tradition of Western Christendom. Revolution I and its successors are the ambiguous descendants of that powerful religious, social, and political ferment that reveals itself to us through the testimonies of radical Anabaptists and Puritans. The testimonies themselves are treasures to be pondered by a generation which today lives in a similar troubled, uncertain age, but which may be still awaiting an era when spiritual and social destiny may be more fully realized.

Part 1

The Peasants' War: South Germany, Austria, and Switzerland

1   The Twelve Articles
of the Peasants

Editor's note

In the same year when Luther's religious reform began, centuries-old secular and religious peasant agitation coalesced in the most widespread unrest thus far—the "Bundschuh" conspiracy of 1517. By 1525 the great Peasants' War had broken out in Germany, close to antiprincely and antinoble Switzerland, where Zwingli's reform was under way.[1] From its beginning near Schaffhausen in 1525, the revolt spread into upper Swabia, where at Waldshut the Anabaptist Balthasar Hubmaier was involved; into Franconia, where at Rothenburg the spiritualizing reformer Andreas Carlstadt vainly tried to moderate peasant excesses, and where the noble knights Florian Geyer, Wendel Hipler, and Goetz of Berlichingen exercised leadership; and beyond the border areas of Hesse into Thuringia, where Thomas Muentzer failed in his effort to lead the peasants.[2] The revolt came to a dismal end at Freiburg in the Breisgau and in the Tyrol region of Austria in 1526. With perhaps a hundred thousand peasants massacred, only the princes benefited from the Peasant's War. Unfortunately for German history, this civil war within the empire failed miserably compared to the comparable seventeenth-century Puritan Revolution in England.

The Twelve Articles, written by a Swabian tanner named Sebastian Lotzer, were the most moderate and representative of peasant demands.[3] Their economic requests were traditional. The religious articles, on the other hand, though moderate, stressed that religious freedom was a means of ending social and economic oppression. In response to the Articles, Luther supported the peasant grievances, but he disapproved of their use of Scripture to support economic or social goals.[4]

Sebastian Lotzer   The Twelve Articles of the
                                      Peasants (1525)[5]

To the Christian Reader Peace and the Grace of God through
Christ.

There are many Antichrists who on account of the assembling of
the peasants, cast scorn upon the gospel, and say: Is this the fruit
of the new teaching, that no one obeys but all everywhere rise in
revolt, and band together to reform, extinguish, indeed kill the
temporal and spiritual authorities. The following articles will answer
these godless and blaspheming fault-finders. They will first of all
remove the reproach from the word of God and secondly give a
Christian excuse for the disobedience or even the revolt of the entire
peasantry. . . . Therefore, Christian reader, read the following articles with care, and then judge. Here follow the articles:

The First Article. First, it is our humble petition and desire, indeed
our will and resolution, that in the future we shall have power and
authority so that the entire community should choose and appoint
a minister, and that we should have the right to depose him should
he conduct himself improperly. The minister thus chosen should
teach us the holy gospel pure and simple, without any human addition, doctrine or ordinance. For to teach us continually the true faith
will lead us to pray God that through His grace His faith may increase within us and be confirmed in us. For if His grace is not
within us, we always remain flesh and blood, which avails nothing;
since the Scripture clearly teaches that only through true faith can
we come to God. Only through His mercy can we become holy. . . .

The Second Article. Since the right tithe is established in the Old
Testament and fulfilled in the New, we are ready and willing to pay
the fair tithe of grain. None the less it should be done properly.
The word of God plainly provides that it should be given to God
and passed on to His own. If it is to be given to a minister, we will
in the future collect the tithe through our church elders, appointed
by the congregation and distribute from it, to the sufficient livelihood
of the minister and his family elected by the entire congregation,
according to the judgment of the whole congregation. The remainder
shall be given to the poor of the place, as the circumstances and
the general opinion demand. . . .

The Third Article. It has been the custom hitherto for men to
hold us as their own property, which is pitiable enough considering
that Christ has redeemed and purchased us without exception, by the

shedding of His precious blood, the lowly as well as the great. Accordingly, it is consistent with Scripture that we should be free and we wish to be so. Not that we want to be absolutely free and under no authority. God does not teach us that we should lead a disorderly life according to the lusts of the flesh, but that we should live by the commandments, love the Lord our God and our neighbor. . . .

The Fourth Article. In the fourth place it has been the custom heretofore that no poor man was allowed to catch venison or wild fowl, or fish in flowing water, which seems to us quite unseemly and unbrotherly, as well as selfish and not according to the word of God. . . . Accordingly, it is our desire if a man holds possession of waters that he should prove from satisfactory documents that his right has been wittingly acquired by purchase. We do not wish to take it from him by force, but his rights should be exercised in a Christian and brotherly fashion. . . .

The Fifth Article. In the fifth place we are aggrieved in the matter of woodcutting, for our noble folk have appropriated all the woods to themselves alone. . . . It should be free to every member of the community to help himself to such firewood as he needs in his home. Also, if a man requires wood for carpenter's purposes he should have it free, but with the approval of a person appointed by the community for that purpose. . . .

The Sixth Article. Our sixth complaint is in regard to the excessive services demanded of us, which increase from day to day. We ask that this matter be properly looked into, so that we shall not continue to be oppressed in this way, and that some gracious consideration be given to us, since our forefathers served only according to the word of God.

The Seventh Article. Seventh, we will not hereafter allow ourselves to be further oppressed by our lords. What the lords possess is to be held according to the agreement between the lord and the peasant. . . .

The Eighth Article. In the eighth place, we are greatly burdened by holdings which cannot support the rent exacted from them. The peasants suffer loss in this way and are ruined. We ask that the lords may appoint persons of honor to inspect these holdings and fix a rent in accordance with justice, so that the peasant shall not work for nothing, since the laborer is worthy of his hire.

The Ninth Article. In the ninth place, we are burdened with the great evil in the constant making of new laws. We are not judged according to the offense but sometimes with great ill will, and sometimes much too leniently. In our opinion we should be judged according to the old written law, so that the case shall be decided according to its merits, and not with favors.

The Tenth Article. In the tenth place we are aggrieved that certain individuals have appropriated meadows and fields which at one time belonged to the community. These we will take again into our own hands unless they were rightfully purchased.

The Eleventh Article. In the eleventh place we will entirely abolish the custom called "Todfall" (heriot), and will no longer endure it, nor allow widows and orphans to be thus shamefully robbed against God's will. . . .

Conclusion. In the twelfth place it is our conclusion and final resolution, that if any one or more of these articles should not be in agreement with the word of God, which we do not think, we will willingly recede from such article when it is proved to be against the word of God by a clear explanation of the Scripture. For this we shall pray God, since He can grant all this and He alone. The peace of Christ abide with us all.

The Article-Letter of the
Black Forest Peasants

Editor's note

Although the numerous peasant demands are remarkable mainly for their moderation, two manifestos were more radical. One is Gaismayr's plan for reform (Document 3). The other is the Article-Letter of the Black Forest peasants. Submitted to the town of Villingen, this document called for the destruction of castles and cloisters and for ostracizing those who refused to join the peasant brotherhood. The contemporary Russian historian M. M. Smirin attempts to prove that Thomas Muentzer instigated these articles with the conspiratiorial goal of eradicating feudalism.[6] Unlike the majority of peasants, these radicals, like Muentzer, refused to compromise with deceitful lords and extended their demands for divine justice beyond the biblical text. It is more likely, however, that Balthasar Hubmaier, an early Anabaptist, helped to compose the Article-Letter, although he was himself not a revolutionary.[7]

The Article-Letter anticipates the emergence of two radical modern movements, in contradiction to each other. On the one hand, violent direct-action methods are described that resemble the use of modern guerilla bands in militarized mass insurrections, often Communist in inspiration. On the other hand, the Article-Letter refers to use of a "worldly ban," which suggests such methods of nonviolent direct action as those used in the successful Indian nationalist movement by Mohandas Gandhi and advocated in the American civil rights movement by Martin Luther King.

In addition, the Article-Letter contains the suggestion that a new society should be established in the Black Forest consisting of peasants and burghers who had absorbed and eliminated the traditional noble and clerical classes. Michael Gaismayr in the Tyrol then made the still more radical proposal that a classless peasant society without towns should result from the revolt of the peasants (see Document 3).

Balthasar Hubmaier (?)   The Article-Letter of the
                             Black Forest Peasants (1525)[8]

Honorable, wise, benevolent lords, friends, and dear neighbors.

Because thus far heavy grievances, against God and all righteousness, have been placed upon the poor common man in town and country, by spiritual and secular lords and authorities, which they have not raised a finger to carry themselves, the result is that the poor common man cannot bear these burdens any longer, if he and his children's children are to avoid becoming beggars.

Therefore this Christian union has the intention and goal, with the help of God, to free themselves, if possible without the use of the sword and spilling of blood, which cannot easily happen without brotherly admonition and unity in all things that have to do with the common Christian good, which are contained in the following articles.

Here then is our friendly petition and brotherly request, that with good will you will join or unite with our Christian union and brotherhood, so that common Christian advantage and brotherly love will again be rebuilt, made fast, and increased. If you do this, the will of God may be accomplished through the fulfillment of His command for brotherly love of the neighbor.

However, if you refuse—which we do not expect from you—we will place you under the worldly ban and recognized power of this letter, and will ask that you remain therein until you refrain from your intention [of not joining], and enter willingly into this Christian union. We do not want to keep this from you, that in good faith we regard you as our dear lords, friends, and neighbors. We ask for a written answer from the council and community, through this messenger. Herewith we commend you unto God.

The worldly ban means the following: that all who are in this Christian union, by their honor and high duty, which they have taken on themselves, against those who refuse to enter into this brotherly union and help further the common good, will have absolutely no fellowship with those who are cut off and are considered dead limbs, neither in eating, drinking, bathing, eating, baking, farming, nor mowing; also, that they exchange neither food, grain, wood, meat, salt, nor anything else, nor may they buy or sell anything to the banned, who must remain in all things as cut-off, dead members, who do not encourage but rather hinder common Christian association and peace.

Also, all markets, forests, meadows, pastures, and water which are not in lawful possession of the banned, shall be prohibited to their use.

Any member of our union who violates the above ban shall be shut out under the same ban and sent to the opposition, with wife and child.

Concerning castles, cloisters, and priestly foundations: from this time on, all of the treason, vexation, and corruption which grows up and flourishes in castles, cloisters, and priestly foundations, shall be placed under the ban.

But where the nobles, monks, or priests shall willingly leave their castles, cloisters, and foundations and shall live in ordinary houses like other newcomers, and wish to enter this Christian union, they shall be received in a friendly way, with their possessions and goods . . . and whatever is their due in God's justice, shall be duly and faithfully given to them.

Concerning those who provide lodging, support, and entertainment for the enemies of this Christian union: they shall be requested in a friendly way to cease such support. If they do not do so, they shall forthwith be declared under the worldly ban.

Editor's note

Though Thomas Muentzer is best known for his connection with the Peasants' War, his leadership there was local and limited, and consequently we have reserved an examination of his revolutionary religious testimonies for Part 2. A more secular and radical revolutionary leader was Michael Gaismayr, a miner's son who became an episcopal secretary and leader of an anti-Hapsburg coalition from the democratic Tyrol.[9] Though influenced by Zwingli's military plans, he opposed Zwingli's moderation for the sake of a proposed constitution for the Tyrol, intended to crush those churchmen, nobles, and townsmen who had betrayed the peasants' revolt of 1525. Nonetheless, Gaismayr displayed a charitable Christian spirit and a desire to remove social evils. Josef Macek, a contemporary Czech historian, maintains that Gaismayr was the only concrete precursor of socialism in the Peasants' War.[10]

Not crushed until 1532, Gaismayr succeeded longer than other peasant leaders in inspiring his free Tyrolese to continue their resistance in order to establish an Alpine peasant state like the earlier Swiss Confederation. He demanded that all "commercial profit" be abolished in this projected classless society. Gaismayr's plan also sought to socialize mines, urban trades, and commerce under a welfare-oriented unitary state. In his hatred of commerce, he remained a medieval man, in spite of his secular and social goals. But Gaismayr's ideals were realized later in a sectarian form when the Anabaptist Hutterites in Moravia eliminated private property and family life and founded continuing communities in which, apart from the leaders, all were equal and all had to do manual labor (see Document 25).[11]

Michael Gaismayr   A Plan of Reform (1526)[12]

1. At the very outset you must pledge your lives and property, not to desert each other but to cooperate at all times; always to act advisedly and to be faithful and obedient to your chosen leaders. You must seek in all things, not your own welfare, but the glory of God and the commonweal, so that the Almighty, as is promised to those who obey Him, may give us His blessing and help. To Him we entrust ourselves entirely because He is incorruptible and betrays no one.

2. All those godless men who persecute the Eternal Word of God, who oppress the poor and who hinder the common welfare, shall be extirpated.

3. The true Christian doctrines founded on the Holy Word of God shall be proclaimed, and you must zealously pledge yourselves to them.

4. All privileges shall be done away with, as they are contrary to the Word of God, and distort the law which declares that no one shall suffer for the misdeeds of others.

5. All city walls, castles, and fortresses shall be demolished. From now on cities shall cease to exist and all shall live in villages. From cities result differences in station in the sense that one deems himself higher and more important than another. From cities come dissension, pride, and disturbances; whereas in the country absolute equality reigns.

6. All pictures, images, and chapels that are not parish churches (which are a horror unto God and entirely un-Christian) shall be totally abolished throughout the land.

7. The Word of God is to be at all times faithfully preached in the empire, and all sophistry and legal trickery shall be uprooted and all books containing such evil writings burned.

8. The judges, as well as the priests in the land, shall be paid only when they are employed in order that their services may be obtained at the least expense.

9. Every year each community shall choose a judge and eight sworn jurors who shall administer the law during that year.

10. Court shall be held every Monday, and all cases shall be brought to an end within two days. The judges, sworn scribes, advocates, court attendants, and messengers shall not accept money from those concerned in the lawsuit, but they shall be paid by the commu-

nity. Every Monday all litigants shall appear before the court, present their cases, and await decision.

11. There shall be only one government in the land, which should be located at Brixen as the most suitable place, because it is in the center of the empire, and contains many monasteries and other places of importance. Hither shall come the officials from all parts of the land, including several representatives from the mines, who shall be chosen for that purpose.

12. Appeals shall be taken immediately to this body and never to Meran, where it is useless to go. The administration at Meran shall be forthwith abolished.

13. At the seat of government shall be established a university wherein the Word of God alone shall be taught. Three learned members of this university, well versed in Holy Scriptures (from which alone the righteousness of God can be taught), shall be appointed members of the government. They shall judge all matters according to the commands of God, as is proper among a Christian people.

Each province shall, after consulting with the others, decide whether the taxes are to be abolished from now on or whether a "free year" shall be established as is ordained in the Bible. In the meanwhile taxes should be collected for public purposes. We must remember that the empire will need money for carrying on war.

It is in the general interest to abolish customs tariffs in the interior but to permit them at the frontiers; this will establish the principle of taxing imports and not exports.

Every man shall pay the tithe according to the Word of God; it shall be spent in the following manner: In each parish there shall be a priest to preach the Scriptures, and he shall be supported from the tithe in a respectable fashion. The rest of the tithe shall be given to the poor; but such regulation shall be made as will do away with the house-to-house begging, so that idle loafers may no longer be permitted to collect charity.

The monasteries and houses of the Teutonic Knights shall be turned into asylums. In some of these only sick people shall be housed; and they must be well cared for with food and medicines. In others old people who can no longer work shall be maintained; and in some, poor uneducated children shall be respectably brought up. The poor who remain at home shall be assisted on the advice of the district judge, since he is best informed. Such people shall be provided for, according to their needs, from the tithe or by charity.

If the tithe be not enough for the support of the priests and the poor, then let each man loyally give charity according to his ability, and any shortage shall be made up from the public treasury. One official shall do nothing else except look after the asylums and the poor. Every judge, each in his own district, shall, by the means of the tithe, charity, and public appeals, be helpful to the poor at their homes. They shall be provided not only with meat and drink, but with clothing and other necessities as well, so that good morals prevail in the land. . . .

No one shall engage in business, and so avoid being contaminated with the sin of usury. Good regulations shall be enacted to prevent scarcity as well as to prohibit overcharging and cheating, so that all things may be sold at an honest and fair price. Let some place in the land be fixed upon (Trent, for example, on account of its central location) where all the manufactured articles shall be made. Silk, cloth, velvet, and shoes shall be produced there under the supervision of an official. Whatever cannot be grown in our country, as spices, shall be imported; shops shall be opened in several appointed places where all sorts of things shall be sold. No profit is to be made, as all things are to be sold at cost. By such means will all deceit and trickery be prevented and all things be bought at their proper value. Money will remain in the country, and this will be for the benefit of the common man. The official and his assistants, charged with the duty of enforcing these regulations, shall be paid fixed salaries. . . .

All smelting houses and mines of tin, silver, copper, and other metals found in the country, which belongs to the nobles or to associations of foreign merchants, such as the Fuggers, Hochstätters, Baumgartners, and others like them, shall be confiscated and given over to public ownership; in all justice, they have forfeited them as they have acquired the mines by unjust and cruel means. The workmen were paid their wages in bad wares and bad money, though in appearance they were given more in amount than their earnings. The prices of spices and other wares rose because of bad currency. All coiners of money who bought silver of these monopolists had to pay their arbitrary prices. This indirectly resulted to the disadvantage of the poor man, who found that the rewards of his labour had decreased. All the merchants through whose hands the bad coins passed demanded still higher prices. As a result the whole world was entangled in this un-Christian usury. In such manner were the princely fortunes made which, in all fairness, should be forfeited.

There shall be a superintendent over all the mines in the country who must be resworn every year. He shall have power to supervise every transaction and shall permit no smelting to be done except by the government. The metals shall be bought when prices are low. The miners shall be paid their wages in cash and not in goods, in order that peace and satisfaction may exist among the workers. If the mines are worked in an orderly and systematic manner there will be enough profit from them to pay the running expenses of the government. If the income is not sufficient for this purpose, a penny tax shall be laid on all to equalize the burden. Every effort should be made, however, to get the most out of the mines. The profits of one mine should be used to open another, because through mining, the country can get the largest income with the least labor.

This is Gaismayr's constitution when he dreams in his chimney corner and imagines himself a prince.

4   A Plan for a Military
          Campaign

Editor's note

Luther's teachings, as interpreted by the peasants, helped to unleash
religious revolt. Yet Luther always opposed social radicalism. Zwingli's
position in Zurich was similar. But Zwingli was able to relate religious
and social radicalism more readily than was Luther.[13] Zwingli is a key
figure in our story. An early humanist, he advocated Erasmian pacifism.
Later he developed his basic Reformation viewpoint, a Pauline-
Augustinian approach to the Bible and theology. In the humanist
tradition, as a citizen and religious leader in Zurich he assumed civic
responsibility and a special prophetic role. For him, realizing the
kingdom of Christ was a legitimate goal in the earthly lives of persons
and communities. Indeed, by 1524 or 1525, he had sketched the
prospects for a great Swiss Protestant political coalition against
Hapsburg Catholic power which was finally realized a century later by
the extraordinary Swedish general Gustavus Adolphus.

Zwingli inspired the Reformed-Calvinist tradition, influenced early
Anabaptism, and contributed important elements to the emerging
Second Reformation position. Zwingli's strategic and tactical military
plan was an establishment counterpart to Gaismayr's premature peasant
constitution, including a link with the Tyrolean rebels. Yet Zwingli fell
on the battlefield in 1531, a year earlier than Gaismayr, a victim of the
Swiss Protestant failure to implement his plan and of the reaction by
the Swiss Catholic cantons to his boldness. Zwingli's patriotic-religious-
social reform, with its incipient Second Reformation characteristics, is
the prototype in the early Reformation of the later Puritan
revolutionaries. In Part 3 we shall examine Zwingli's important
relationship and conflict with the Anabaptists, as the Second
Reformation alternative developed in Switzerland.

Huldreich Zwingli   A Plan for a Military
                                       Campaign (c. 1525)[14]

The author has drawn up this plan for the honor of God and for
the good of the Gospel of Christ, in order that disorder and injustice
may not take over and that the fear of God and innocence may not
be overpowered. . . .

[Part one presents Zwingli's plan for the proper arming of the
Zurich military forces. Then Zwingli considers Zurich's foreign politics of war, directed against the Austrian Hapsburgs. Correspondence
with France and the Duke of Savoy will help mediate between the
two enemies. Zwingli warns that it is not enough for Bern, Glarus,
Basel, Appenzell and Solothurn to be neutral towards Zurich, if
conflict with the Catholic forest cantons threatens. A treaty shall be
drawn up with Graubünden, as with St. Gall, so that a communica-
tions line may extend from Zurich eastward through Etschland, the
valley of the Inn River, and the Tyrol. In this way, freedom from
Austrian control may be secured.]

Graubünden should recruit earnestly and skillfully, in the same
way as in St. Gall. They should announce situations to us where we
would need to help them, and they should inform us in writing about
any anxiety or trouble among members of the confederacy.

Therefore it is good to have the common covenant arranged in an
orderly fashion and printed so that it can be sent to all who are
being recruited through writing or messenger. The Graubündners
should not now be satisfied and only remain neutral. Also this applies
to Bern and others, who thus may not easily be overcome.

Secretly we should also arrange with the Graubündners, that in
the district of the Sarganserland and what lies between us, no one
should be against us. Thus we can reach each other constantly with
people and weapons. And we should suggest to them that they make
secret arrangements with those in the Etschland, the Inn Valley, and
the Tyrol, who are also oppressed.

In certain selected places, we should take over. To all Etschland,
from this hour on, freedom should be given and one regiment of
their own, without the interference of Graubünden, aside from a
yearly tax, so that one may bring help to them if they should need
it, without burdening them. Also, a friendly covenant should be
made with them, to assure them of continuous support.

For the land here discussed, owned by the Emperor, is in Germany, and it is ready to repudiate his rule. . . .

26

Part 2

Conflict with Luther: Zwickau Prophets and Thomas Muentzer

5   A Report Concerning the Zwickau Prophets

Editor's note

While he was an early Lutheran pastor in Zwickau, Thomas Muentzer met and established relations with Nicholas Storch, a weaver and spiritual prophet, and with his associates, Thomas Drechsel and Marcus Stuebner. Their activities led to Muentzer's expulsion from the city in April 1521.[1] Nicholas Hausmann, Muentzer's unsympathetic successor at St. Catherine's Church, wrote to Duke John of Saxony in December 1521, giving the only existing programmatic description of the "Storchian Sect." These Second Reformation Spiritualizers taught a radical biblicism dependent upon direct revelation in visions and dreams. They even rejected infant baptism, since they confidently expected the coming of the millennium within five years, after the ascendancy of the Turk as Antichrist and the annihilation of the godless by the elect.

When the Prophets arrived in Wittenberg, their preaching immobilized Melanchthon, while Carlstadt and Zwilling proceeded to implement radical reforms, including iconoclasm and giving the Lord's Supper in both kinds. Luther's return from exile in March 1522 restored moderation at Wittenberg. He expelled Carlstadt, after eight powerful Invocavit sermons, which declared that evangelical freedom does not mean new legalism.[2] Luther had already found it desirable to go slow on reform, and the Latin mass was temporarily restored. Ever after, Luther put down radicalism at home, suspicious of unsound enthusiasts. He also wrote a relevant treatise against insurrection and rebellion ("Aufruhr und Empoerung") presenting his moderately apolitical dialectic: God is in charge of the world, therefore no Christian insurrection is permitted; on the other hand, the best of Christian deeds are but bold sins, therefore violence for the sake of the neighbor is permitted under authority.[3]

Nicholas Hausmann A Report Concerning the
Zwickau Prophets (1521)[4]

[Quotation from Nicholas Storch]: Those in authority live only in
lust, consume the sweat and blood of their subjects, eat and drink
night and day, hunt, run, and kill. . . . Everyone therefore should
arm himself and attack the priests in their fat nests, beating, killing,
and strangling them, because once the bellwethers are removed, the
sheep are easier to handle. Afterward the land-grabbers and noblemen should be attacked, their property confiscated, and their castles
destroyed. . . .

The external, audible divine word which is preached by the priests
in the daily mass for the living and the dead is sheer tomfoolery
because they [the priests] celebrate it after overloading their bellies
with good food and their heads with fine wine, not to mention their
frolicking at night with "Frau Venus." . . . Like magicians they dress
up in silk and velvet of all colors, make gestures like monkeys when
they take the bread and wine in the sacrament of the altar, and, to
top it off, speak in Latin so that the poor layman does not know at
all whether he is betrayed, sold, or what, and doesn't know what
it is all about. If he [the layman] does not give them [the priests]
his purse, heaven is closed to him. . . .

You can receive the forgiveness of sins without all this nonsense,
in your own quiet home or wherever you are, if you believe in the
revelation of the Spirit. . . .

Don't you believe that God has another word which he will reveal
to you through the Spirit? Why should God be chained to the creature? . . . He is absolutely free. He does what he wills. Thus the
external, audible word of the priests is not the word of God but
their own. . . .

No child should be baptized with water in the church because all
you see in such baptisms is wet water; it is the same as if one would
sprinkle or immerse a dog in it . . . because children have no faith.
But without faith it is impossible to please God. Accordingly, one
should not baptize infants with water, because the water remains
what it is, water.

Editor's note

Under Storch's influence, Thomas Muentzer had broken with Luther's theology. Muentzer now rejected infant baptism (although he never became an Anabaptist or rebaptizer) and taught a spiritualizing Scripture interpretation which moved beyond Luther's emphasis upon justification of the sinner through Christ to insistence upon taking up one's personal cross prior to visitation by the Holy Spirit.[5] Fleeing to Prague from Zwickau, Muentzer attempted to stir up a new Bohemian revolt during his eight-month stay in the old Hussite center.[6] His *Prague Manifesto* appeared in several versions: a short German version (here translated), a longer German version, and related Czech and Latin versions. All still exist in manuscript form.

The *Prague Manifesto* openly advocated wielding the sword against the godless, especially the priests, but also against the learned, following universal proclamation of the Gospel (which Muentzer was doing in Prague). He described his discovery in the church historians Hegisippus and Eusebius of the fall of the church after the death of the apostles. Her restitution would be an apocalyptic event beginning among the Bohemians. Should they fail to heed Muentzer's admonition, they would be handed over to the Antichrist. God would have the Turks slay them within the next year. Then the triumph of the elect would follow.

Since he was more radical than even the left-wing members of the Utraquists, Muentzer's advice went unheeded in Prague. He withdrew, dropping the revolutionary theme for a while. But his distinctive attitude toward religious revolution was already evident, an attitude that combined bitter negativism toward establishment figures, religious and political, with a mystical-apocalyptic religious message which insisted upon active use of violence by the elect against God's enemies. His was a peculiarly volatile manifestation of Second Reformation consciousness.

I, Thomas Muentzer of Stolberg, confess before the whole Church and the whole world, wherever this letter may be displayed, that I can bear witness, with Christ and all the Elect who have known me from my youth up, that I have used my utmost diligence, above all other men, that I might have or attain a higher understanding of holy invincible Christian faith. Yet all the days of my life (God knows, I lie not) I have never been able to get out of any monk or parson the true use of faith, about the profitableness of temptation [Anfechtung] which prepares for faith in the Spirit of the Fear of the Lord, together with the condition that each elect must have the Sevenfold Holy Ghost. I have not learned from any Scholar the true Order of God which he has set in all creatures, not the least word, and that the Whole perfect work is the way to understand the Parts —these are never to be obtained from those who set up to be true Christians, especially from those damned parsons. It is true I have heard from them about the bare word of Scripture, which they have stolen, like thieves and murderers from the Bible, which robbery Jeremiah in chapter 23 calls stealing the Word of God from the mouth of one's neighbor, which they themselves have never once heard from the mouth of God.

Yes, I reckon they are fine preachers, anointed by the Devil to this end. But St. Paul writes to the Corinthians (2d Epis., ch. 3) that the hearts of men are the paper and parchment on which God writes with his fingers his irrevocable Will and Eternal Wisdom, not with ink, and this writing any man can understand if his understanding has been opened. As Jeremiah and Ezekiel say [Ezek. 36:25–27; Jer. 31:33], God writes his law on the third day of Sprinkling, when the understandings of men will be opened, and God has done this from the very Beginning in his Elect, in order that they may not be uncertain, but have an invincible testimony from the Holy Ghost, who gives a sufficient witness to our spirits that we are the children of God. For whoso cannot discern God's spirit in himself, yea, who has not the assurance of this, is not a member of Christ, but of the Devil (Rom. 8). Now the world (led astray through many sects) has long desired exceedingly to know the truth, so that the saying of Jeremiah has come true: the children have asked for bread, but there was nobody to break it to them. But there were many then, as there are now today, who have chucked bread at them, that is the letter of the Word, without breaking it to them.

O mark this, mark it—they have not broken it up for the children. They have not explained the true Spirit of the Fear of the Lord which would have taught them they are irrevocably God's children.

So it comes about that Christians (to defend the truth) are about as competent as knaves, and dare in consequence to jabber in lordly fashion that God does not speak with men any longer, just as though he had now become dumb. And they think it is enough that it should be written down in their books, and be it never so raw, they will spit it out as a stork does with frogs into its nest. They are not like the hen who covers up her young and makes them warm, they do not share out the good nature of the Word of God (which lives nonetheless in all Elect men) in the heart, as a mother gives milk to her child, but they teach them Balaam-wise, so that they keep the poor letter in their mouth, but the heart is a hundred thousand miles off.

On account of such folly, it would be no wonder were God to smite us in pieces for such fool's faith. It is no wonder to me that men of all races reproach us, and none can do otherwise. "Thus and thus it is written." Yes, dear masters, it is superfine work that they have set up in the fowl-house. If a simple person or an unbeliever came among us into the congregation, and we sought to overwhelm him with our silly chatter, he would say, "You are all mad or wicked. What has your Scripture to do with me?" But when we learn the true living Word of God, then perhaps we will win over the unbeliever and judge plainly, when the secrets of his heart are revealed and he will humbly confess that God is in our midst.

See, St. Paul also bears witness to this in I Corinthians 14, where at the same time he says that a preacher must have a revelation, or else he cannot preach the Word. The Devil believes that the Christian faith is true. And, if this be rejected by the children of Antichrist, then they make God mad or wicked, who has said that his Word shall never pass away. But must it not have passed away if God has stopped speaking?

Mark well the Text, if you had something else in mind: Heaven and earth shall pass away but my words shall not pass away [Matt. 24:35]. If that is just written in a Book, and God said it once and then it disappeared into thin air—that cannot then be God's Eternal Word. Then it would be only a creaturely thing, put into our memory from the outside, which is contrary to the True Order and against the rule of holy faith as Jeremiah writes. That is why all the prophets have used this manner of speaking—"Thus saith the Lord!"

They don't say, "Thus did the Lord say," as though it were all over, but they say Now, in this present time.

This insupportable and wicked shaming of Christendom I have taken pitifully to heart through reading with all diligence the Histories of the Fathers. I find that, after the death of the pupils of the Apostles, the immaculate Virgin Church was turned to Whoredom through Adultery (by reason of the Scribes who have always to sit on top) as Hegesippus writes, and after him Eusebius in book 4, chapter 22. Moreover, I find in no Council of the Church that they take seriously the expounded living Order of the undeceivable Word of God, but a lot of kid's stuff. Through God's Inscrutable Will this was allowed, that the work of man might be exposed. But it will never happen, God be praised, that such parsons and Apes should come to constitute the Christian church. Which shall rather be the Elect Friends of the Word of God who learn to prophesy as Paul teaches, that they may truly know how friendly and how heartily God loves to talk with all his Elect. In order to bring this truth to the light of day, I am ready to offer my life, if it be God's will. God will do marvelous things with his Elect, especially in this land. When the New Church begins, this nation shall be a mirror to the whole world. Therefore I appeal to Everyman, to come to the defence of God's Word. And also that I may make visibly plain among you in the Spirit of Elijah those who have taught you to sacrifice to the Idol Baal. If you will not do this, then God will let you be beaten by the Turk in the coming Year. I know truly what I am saying, that it is so. Therefore I will suffer those things which Jeremiah had to suffer. Take this to heart, dear Bohemians. I demand an account of you, not only such as Peter teaches but as God himself demands. I will give account to you also, and, if I do not in fact possess the knowledge of which I boast so openly, then am I a child of temporal and eternal death. I can give no higher pledge. Christ be with you.

Given at Prague in 1521
on All Saint's Day

A Sermon before the Princes on Daniel Two

Editor's note

Back in a German pastorate at Allstedt by 1523, Muentzer made use of a better opportunity to put his beliefs into practice. He introduced a striking German liturgy, and he began denouncing Luther in print for failure to take the Gospel seriously. He also combined his mystical-apocalyptic faith with an effort to form a league or covenant of the elect, which would establish a theocratic society. When Duke John, the Saxon elector's brother, came to hear Muentzer preach at Allstedt, Muentzer boldly presented himself as a new Daniel, inviting the Saxon princes to advance his revolutionary program in which the godless would be slain by the elect and an egalitarian society would be inaugurated by God himself. As in the *Prague Manifesto*, Muentzer's sermon applied the millenarian views of Daniel to future events, attempting to show how the fallen church would be succeeded by a latter-day church more glorious than that of the Apostles.

Instead of anticipating the fifth monarchy, Muentzer taught that the fifth monarchy was then present as the fallen established church. But it would soon pass away if the princes would make use of their predestined role, joining the other covenanted people in punishing the godless representatives of the fifth monarchy ruled by the Antichrist.[8] Muentzer now was thinking that Allstedt might become the center of radical reform, replacing Wittenberg. He saw the prophecy of Joel confirmed in the outpouring of the Spirit within himself and others, and he believed that his eschatological dream of equality of possessions was being realized by the covenant of miners and magistrates.

Luther saw Muentzer, in part at least correctly, as an advocate of a medieval doctrine in which subjective religious experience predominated. He warned the Saxon princes in a sharp letter of the dangers of disastrous revolution in Muentzer's plans. After hesitating, Duke John and his son John Frederick, who was more favorable to radicalism, finally repudiated Muentzer. Expelled from Allstedt, Muentzer attempted to form a peasant league of the elect, and found the opportunity he was looking for in the unrest which was unleashing the Peasants' War.

A Sermon before the Princes
on Daniel Chapter Two
(1524)[9]

. . . Whoever wishes, by reason of his fleshly judgment, to be utterly
hostile about visions [and dreams] without any experience of them,
rejecting them all, or [again, whoever] wishes to take them all in
without any distinction . . . will have a poor run of it and will hurl
himself against the Holy Spirit. For God speaks clearly, like this
text of Daniel, about the transformation of the world. He will prepare it in the Last Days in order that His name may be rightly
praised. He will free it of its shame, and will pour out His Holy
Spirit over all flesh, and our sons and daughters shall prophesy and
shall have dreams and visions. For if Christendom is not to become
apostolic (Acts 2:16) in the way anticipated in Joel, why should
one preach at all? To what purpose then the Bible with its visions?

It is true, and I know it to be true, that the Spirit of God is
revealing to many elect, pious persons a decisive, inevitable, imminent reformation [accompanied] by great anguish, and it must be
carried out to completion. Defend oneself against it as one may, the
prophecy of Daniel remains unweakened, even if no one believes it,
as also Paul says to the Romans (3:3). This passage of Daniel is
thus as clear as the sun, and the process of ending the fifth monarchy
of the world is in full swing. . . .

O beloved lords, how handsomely the Lord will go smashing
among the old pots with His rod of iron (Ps. 2:9). Therefore, you
much beloved and esteemed princes, learn your judgments directly
from the mouth of God and do not let yourselves be misled by your
hypocritical parsons nor be restrained by false consideration and
indulgence. For the Stone [made] without hands, cut from the mountain [which will crush the fifth kingdom], has become great. The
poor laity [of the towns] and the peasants see it much more clearly
than you. Yea, God be praised, it has become so great [that] already,
if other lords or neighbors should wish to persecute you for the
gospel's sake, they would be driven back by their own people! . . .

The pitiable corruption of holy Christendom has become so great
that at the present time no tongue can tell it all. Therefore a new
Daniel must arise and interpret for you your vision and this
[prophet], as Moses teaches (Deut. 20:2), must go in front of the
army. He must reconcile the anger of the princes and the enraged
people. . . .

Now if you want to be true governors, you must begin government at the roots, and, as Christ commanded, drive his enemies from the elect. For you are the means to this end. . . . Christ says it sufficiently (Matt. 7:19, John 15:2, 6): Every tree that bringeth not forth good fruit is rooted out and cast into the fire. . . . For the godless person has no right to live when he is in the way of the pious. In Exodus 22:18 God says: Thou shalt not suffer evildoers to live. Saint Paul also means this where he says of the sword of rulers that it is bestowed upon them for the retribution of the wicked as protection for the pious (Rom. 13:4). God is your protection and will teach you to fight against his foes (Ps. 18:34). He will make your hands skilled in fighting and will also sustain you. But you will have to suffer for that reason a great cross and temptation in order that the fear of God may be declared upon you. . . .

Look at Psalms 44:5 and I Chronicles 14:11. There you will find the solution in this way. They did not conquer the land by the sword but rather through the power of God. But the sword was the means, as eating and drinking is for us a means of living. In just this way the sword is necessary to wipe out the godless (Rom. 13:4). That this might now take place, however, in an orderly and proper fashion, our cherished fathers, the princes, should do it, who with us confess Christ. If, however, they do not do it, the sword will be taken from them (Dan. 7:26–27). . . . Otherwise the Christian church cannot come back again to its origin. The weeds must be plucked out of the vineyard of God in the time of harvest. Then the beautiful red wheat will acquire substantial rootage and come up properly (Matt. 13:24–30). The angels, however, who sharpen their sickles for this purpose are the serious servants of God who execute the wrath of the divine wisdom (Mal. 3:1–6). . . .

Editor's note

Late in 1524, Luther wrote his first tract on theological radicalism, *A Letter to the Saxon Princes*.[10] He maintained that rulers must not inhibit proclamation of the gospel, but that they may interfere when civil insurrection is preached. Muentzer replied with his most polemical defense. Yet even here, Muentzer treated social revolution as secondary to his primary theological concern. He wished to restore the earnestness of the law among Christians, leading in turn to the gathering of the elect.

Commenting on Luke 1, Muentzer opposed his Spirit-possessed faith to the merely historical faith of the Wittenbergers. The Bible confirms rather than is the source of faith, Muentzer affirmed. Each soul must first be crushed with doubt and suffering before faith becomes real. But Muentzer did not condone social inequities as conducive to spirituality. Leaving medieval concepts of poverty behind at this point, Muentzer demanded community of possessions in order to meet human material needs and to deliver the saints from preoccupation with worldly goods.[11] Muentzer's means for carrying out his revolutionary purpose was the covenant of the elect, which was conceived not along the lines of conspiratorial cadres so much as in continuity with Jeremiah's prediction (31:31) that God's eternal covenant with his people would soon be fulfilled in a new covenant of spiritual inwardness.[12] Therefore princes as well as the common people could be included in its ranks. The crucial measure of covenant loyalty for Muentzer was obedience to the divine will.

Having fled from Mühlhausen because of difficulties put in his way there, Muentzer was able to persuade John Hut to print his *Defense* in Nuernberg. He had little success preaching among the peasants near the Swiss border. But upon his return to Mühlhausen, Muentzer seized the leadership of the rebelling Thuringian peasants, as his *Defense* anticipates. Whether or not social revolution was secondary to Muentzer, the peasants' revolt in Thuringia provided him with a fateful opportunity to put his covenant ideas into effect among the poor.

Thomas Muentzer Highly Provoked Defense
[against Luther] (1524)[13]

Highly provoked defense and answer against the spiritless, soft-living flesh at Wittenberg, which has befouled pitiable Christianity in perverted fashion by its theft of Holy Scripture.

Thomas Muentzer from Alstedt

All praise, honor, dignity, titles and glory belong to Thee alone, Thou eternal Son of God (Phil. 2). Thy Holy Spirit has always appeared, on account of the scribes, those graceless lions, as the worst of all devils (John 8).

Thus it is no great surprise that the most ambitious scribe of all, Doctor Liar, becomes more and more a fool. Without mortifying his name and comfort, he covers himself with Thy Holy Scripture, using it in a deceiving manner, being in nothing less interested than to have dealings with Thee (Isa. 58). . . .

The Jews continually wanted to bring slander and downfall upon Christ, even as Luther now tries to do to me. He chides me emphatically and tells me of the mercy of the Son of God and of his dear friends to whom I preached the sternness of the Law. I pointed out that it is not suspended because of the ungodly transgressors (even though they are rulers) and that it should be administered with all seriousness, as Paul instructed his disciple Timothy, and through him all ministers of souls (I Tim. 1), to preach to the people. He says clearly that all those shall be afflicted who fight and strive against sound doctrine. This no one can deny. Paul passes the same judgment against the lustful transgressor (I Cor. 5). I have printed this as I preached it before the Saxon Rulers, without deception, showing them the sword in the Scriptures that they should use it in order that no insurrection might develop. In short: transgression must be punished; neither the great nor the small may escape from it (Numbers 15).

But then Cousin Steplightly, that tame fellow, comes along and claims that I want to stir up insurrection. This he supposedly read in my letter to the miners. He mentions one, but omits the most incisive part. I stated clearly before the Rulers that the entire congregation is in possession of the sword and the key of loosing. Quoting from Daniel 7, Revelation 6, Romans 8, and I Kings 8, I said that the princes are not lords, but servants of the sword. They should not do as they pleased (Deut. 17), but should do right. According

to ancient and honorable custom the people must be present if someone is to be tried and judged correctly according to the Law of God
(Num. 15). Why? If the magistrate misjudges, then the Christians
present will repudiate and not tolerate it, for God demands an account of innocent blood (Ps. 78 [79]). It is the greatest monstrosity
on earth that no one will take care of the needy. As is described in
Job 41, the mighty do as they please.

The poor Flatterer wants to cover himself with a spurious mercy
of Christ, greatly contrary to the word of Paul in I Timothy 1. In
his booklet on commerce he says that princes should punish thieves
and robbers without hesitation. But he is silent about the origin of
all thievery. He is a herald who wants to earn thanks through the
shedding of the people's blood for the sake of worldly goods. This
God assuredly has not told him. The ground of usury, theft, and
robbery is our lords and princes, who claim all creatures as their
own. All must be theirs—the fish in the water, the birds in the air,
the harvest of the earth (Isa. 5). They proclaim the so-called command of God among the poor, saying "God commanded that you
shall not steal." But this does not help them, since they suppress all
men, pinch and flay the poor farmer, the artisan, and all the living
(Mic. 3). If someone steals the smallest thing, he must hang. And
Doctor Liar says "Amen!" Since the princes do not want to get rid
of the cause of insurrection it is their own fault that the poor man
becomes their enemy. How, under these conditions, could things
ever be changed? If I say this, I am rebellious. So let it be. . . .

The blameless Son of God appropriately compared the ambitious
scribes with the devil, giving us in the Gospel a means to judge,
namely his spotless Law (Ps. 18 [19]). They [the Scribes] longed to
kill him, for they said, "Unless we restrain him, all the people will
believe in him and adhere to him. Behold, they already run after
him in great crowds. If we allow him to carry out his cause we will
have lost, and then we shall be poor people" (John 11). Then came
Caiaphas, Doctor Liar, and gave good advice to his princes. He took
good care of the matter and said that he feared for his countrymen
near Alstedt. But the truth, as everybody in the country can testify,
is that the poor people longed so eagerly for truth that the streets
were crowded with people from different places who had come to
hear the service of Scriptural singing and preaching at Alstedt.
Luther could not have done it at Wittenberg even had he broken
his back. This one sees well in his German Mass. He was quite

ambitious and concerned about it that he first of all talked his prince
into not letting my church order appear in print. When nobody paid
attention to the Pope of Wittenberg, he thought: "Let us be patient,
I shall take care of the matter that I break the pilgrimage into
pieces." This ungodly fellow is shrewd-headed in pondering such
things (Ps. 35 [36]). His intentions were, as you see, to promote
his teaching through the hatred of the laity against the clergy. Had
he possessed the right love to rebuke, he would not have put himself
in place of the Pope. Neither would he have flattered the princes, as
is clearly written (Ps. 9 [10]). He interpreted this very Psalm to
apply not only to the Pope but also to himself. He wants to make
bailiffs of St. Peter and St. Paul, in order to defend his executioners.

But Doctor Liar is a simple man when he writes that I should not
be prevented from preaching or that they should watch that the
spirit at Alstedt keeps its fists quiet. Let us see, dear brethren in
Christ, if he is a learned man. Of course, he is learned. In two or
three years the world will have opportunity to see the terrible,
insidious grief he has brought. But in writing in this manner he
wants to wash his hands in innocence, so that no one might notice
how he persecutes truth. He claims that his preaching is the Word
of God because it evokes so much persecution. I am astounded how
this shameless monk can claim to be terribly persecuted—sitting in
front of his glass of wine and enjoying his whore's feast. He can do
none other then be a scribe (John 10). We shall not do anything to
you because of your good works, but because of your blasphemy we
shall stone you to death. Thus they spoke to Christ, even as this
fellow speaks to me: Not on account of your preaching, but your
rebellion you must be expelled.

Beloved brethren. It is not a bad affair going on at the present,
particularly since you have no judgment in the matter. You assume
that if you stop supporting the parsons everything is in order. But
you do not realize that you are now a hundred times one thousand
worse off than before. From now on you will be bombarded with a
new logic which is said to be the Word of God. But you have the
command of Christ (Matt. 7). Study it by heart and no one will
deceive you, whatever he writes or says. You must attend carefully
to Paul's admonition to the Corinthians (II Cor. 11): See that your
minds are not corrupted from the simplicity of Christ. The scribes
have interpreted this simplicity with the full treasure of divine wisdom (Col. 2), greatly contrary to Genesis 3, where God warned

Adam with a single commandment of future grief, that he be not led astray by the creaturely lust, but have his pleasure in God alone, as is written: Delight thyself in God.

Doctor Liar wants to advance a strong argument against me, by pointing out the simplicity of his teaching and the accomplishment of his penetrating thought. Yet in the last analysis he does not care for preaching, for, he says, there must be sects. He asks the prince not to stop my preaching. I had hoped that he would discuss with me and give me hearing before the world, while affirming that he would depend only on the Word. Now he changes and tries to utilize the princes. This was a shrewd scheme, lest anyone say: Well, now they themselves persecute the gospel; they should let me preach and not prohibit it. Nonetheless I should keep my hand still and not put anything into print. Indeed, quite smartly conceived, saying like the Jews: "We do not persecute you for your good works, but for your blasphemy." . . .

He would deal with everything through the Word, but then does not want to use the Word for the justification or condemnation of my case. All he wants to do is to present an evil case against me among the mighty so that no one persecutes my teaching because it is rebellious. Whoever wants a clear judgment must not love rebellion, but must not be opposed to justified insurrection either. He must pursue a reasonable middle way, or lest he would love or hate my teaching too much, according to his own convenience, which is not my intention.

It would be more appropriate for me to instruct the poor folk with good doctrine than to get involved with this blasphemous monk who wants to be a new Christ, who with his blood brought much good for Christendom. Besides there was the gain of a fine new thing: priests may get married! . . .

Be ashamed, you archscoundrel, that in servile fashion you want to be in favor of an erring world wishing to justify all mankind (Luke 9). You know well whom to rebuke. The poor monks and priests and merchants cannot defend themselves; therefore you can easily slander them. But no one is to judge the godless rulers, even if they trample on Christ with their feet.

To please the peasants, you write that the princes will perish through the Word of God. You say in your commentary on the latest imperial mandate that the princes shall be pushed from their thrones. You prefer them, nonetheless, to merchants. You should pull your princes by their noses, for they have deserved it more than the others. Have they lowered their tribute and extortion? Although you have scolded the princes, you still cheer them up, you new pope, giving them monasteries and churches. They are well pleased with you. I warn you that the peasant may strike loose. You always speak of faith and you write that I fight against you under your shield and protection. Well, one can see my sincerity and your foolishness, for I have been under your shield and protection as a sheep among wolves (Matt. 10). Did you not have greater power over me there than elsewhere? Could you not anticipate what would yet come of this? I was in your territory in order that you should not have any excuse. You say: under our shield and protection. O, how do you reveal yourself! I take it that you consider yourself a ruler. Why do you boast of such shield and protection? In all my letters I never sought his [the ruler's] protection. I did not want him to fight his own people over the goatstable and Mary's image at Malderbach.[14] Thus he wanted to intrude in town and country, not aware that the poor people had to live in danger day and night for the sake of the gospel. Do you suppose that the country does not know to guard and defend itself? May God have mercy on Christendom if she does not have Him as guardian who created her (Ps. 110 [111]).

You say that I was expelled and have wandered about for three years, and that I lament of much suffering. What about this? With your pen you have given me a bad and deceitful name among many good people. This I can easily prove. With your blasphemous mouth you have publicly called me a devil. Thus you treat all your opponents. Like a raven you can do nothing but shout your name. You and that uncooked Laurentius of Nordhausen know well what has been given to evildoers to kill me.[15] You are no murderous or rebellious spirit, but you do incite and chase like a hellhound. Duke George will invade Prince Frederick's territory and thereby do away with general peace—and yet you cause no insurrection. You are a ground serpent which gambols over rocks (Prov. 30). . . .

You deny the true Word, and present to the world only outward appearance. You turn into an archdevil by making God a cause of evil. This you do on the basis of a passage in Isaiah, against all reasoning. Is this not the most terrible punishment of God over you? You are blind, yet you want to be the leader of the blind in the world, making God responsible that you are a poor sinner and a poisonous worm with your excreted meekness. This is a result of your fanatic reasoning which you got from your Augustine. Truly it is blasphemous to despise men impudently concerning free will. . . .

If Doctor Liar had permitted me to preach, or defeated me before the people, or had allowed his princes to judge me when I was present at Weimar, at the time when they questioned me at his request, I should not have brought up this matter. At last it was decided that the prince would leave it to the severe Judge of the Last Day to decide the matter. He did not want to resist the tyrants who for the sake of the gospel were his obligation. It would be a fine thing if it were turned over to the court, for the peasants would be in favor. It would be a fine thing if everything were relegated to the last judgment. Then the peasants would have reason for doing right. They say: I let the judge decide. But the rod of the godless is used in the meantime.

When I returned from the hearing at Weimar, I intended to preach the solemn Word of God. But then came my councilmen and wanted to turn me over to the worst enemies of the Gospel. When I learned this, I could stay no longer. I wiped their dust from my shoes for I saw with open eyes that they paid more attention to their oaths and duties than to the Word of God. They resolved to serve two masters, one against the other. This despite the fact that on their side most obviously stood God, who, having saved them from the clutches of the bear and lion, would have also saved them from the hands of Goliath (I Sam. 17), even though this Goliath trusted in his armor and sword. David will teach them. Saul also began well, but David after a long delay, had to carry it out. For your dear friends David is a symbol of you, O Christ; you will diligently protect them throughout eternity. Amen.

In the year 1524

O Doctor Liar, you deceptive fox; with lies you made sad the heart of the just whom God did not sadden. You have strengthened the power of the ungodly evildoers so that they remain on their old paths. You shall be like a captured fox. The people shall be freed and God alone shall be Lord.

Editor's note

Muentzer was a prophet, not an organizer or a general like Cromwell.
Manfred Bensing, a contemporary East German historian, depicts
Muentzer as a Lenin-like figure with a maximal, a minimal, and a
realistic-tactical program similar to the worldly ban of the Article-
Letter.[16] But Bensing also sees Muentzer as a theologian who interpreted
the defeat of the peasants (unfortunately, from Bensing's perspective)
as a divine judgment upon their own egotism. The failure was real, and
it was tragic. Discovered under bedcovers, Muentzer, the revolutionary
leader, made the customary confession and recantation which torture
delivers.

Although his crime was sedition rather than heresy, the execution of
Muentzer anticipated the harsh reintroduction of the anti-Donatist laws
of Justinian against Anabaptism at the April 1529 Imperial Diet of
Speyer. Following that date, First Reformation leaders and princes (with
the exception of Philip of Hesse and, more ambiguously, Luther) joined
Catholics in executing Anabaptists with fire and sword.[17] The Anabaptists
for a century or more faced arrest, examination, prosecution, imprisonment, and possible torture and execution. Claus-Peter Clasen has been
able to enumerate only 845 Anabaptists known to have been executed
between 1525 and 1618. He concludes that Anabaptism had a large
following only during the first five years, and that from then on an
average of three thousand people joined the movement every ten years,
making it a minor episode among a population of several million in
southern and central Germany, Switzerland, and Austria.[18] Clasen
omitted North Germany and the Netherlands.

Yet the torture and execution of Second Reformation leaders like
Muentzer, Hubmaier, and the Muenster prophets have made a permanent
impression upon the consciousness of western European churchmen.
Decapitated, his head placed upon a stake, Muentzer and his violent
effort to set up an earthly kingdom of the elect still exerted attraction.
We shall see his ideas appear again in this story. Indeed, he is the
ambivalent hero of Protestant theocracy, and the Anabaptists also felt
his influence.

Confession of Thomas Muentzer, alleged pastor at Allstedt, apprehended among the rebellious peasants at Frankenhausen, given on Shrove Tuesday, after Cantate, 1525 [May 16, 1525]. . . .

3. In Klettgau and Hegau near Basel, Muentzer had announced some articles, how one should rule according to the Gospel, and added some further articles. They would have taken him in there, but he said thank you, no. He did not start the rebellion there—it already existed. Oecolampadius and Hugowaldus had been in the same place and preached. Muentzer himself preached there about unbelieving rulers and people, and that judgment must occur because of that. The letters which he received from them at that time were saved for him by Muentzer's wife in Mühlhausen.

4. He said that the castles are too fully laden and also oversupplied with servants, and there are a great many hardships put on the people.

5. He said that a prince should be allowed to ride with only eight horses, a count with four horses, and a nobleman with two horses, and not more. . . .

12. The house of Apels von Ebeleben was plundered and damaged by the brethren from Mühlhausen. It was a troublesome house. They found articles there which they looked into. But Muentzer was not acquainted with it. Partially, they were the Twelve Articles of the Black Forest peasants and others . . . [sentence incomplete].

13. The Council of Mühlhausen did not want to join the covenant, but let the ordinary people enter it.

14. Nicholas Storch and Marcus Stuebner from Zwickau had met with Luther at Wittenberg, in a little room, where Muentzer had also been. Luther let it be known that he was against them, and punched the Allstedt spirit in the nose; but Muentzer had not personally been there at that time. . . .

Spoken under torture:

6. He started the uprising in order that all Christendom should be made equal and that the princes and lords, who did not wish to stand up for the Gospel, should be driven out and killed. . . .

8. The article was directed as follows: all things are common, and should be distributed to each according to his need, as necessity arises. Any prince, count, or lord who refused to do this, after first being earnestly informed, should be beheaded or hanged. . . .

Thomas Muentzer   Recantation (May 17, 1525)

The following articles were stated uncoerced and well thought through by Thomas Muentzer, in the presence of the Noble Lord Philipp, Count of Solms, etc., Master Gebhardt, Count and Lord of Mansfeld. . . . He asked that he be reminded of them in case he should forget, so that he could tell them with his own mouth to everyone just before his death.

First of all, he had opposed governmental authority and preached too lightly concerning it. Thus his listeners and he . . . had entered into wicked and wanton insurrection, rebellion, and disobedience. He asked, for the sake of God, that they should not be offended thereby. He wanted especially to live obediently under the government ordained and ordered by God, and asked that they forgive his trespasses.

Secondly, he had also preached rebelliously and seductively some views, folly, and errors concerning the blessed sacrament of the holy body of Christ much against the order of the universal Christian Church. He now would in peace and concord keep everything which this same Christian Church has always believed and still does believe. He would die as a true and reconciled member of this Church, asking it to witness such before God and the world, to pray to God for him, and to forgive him in brotherly manner.

Finally, it would be his request that his recent letter be sent to those of Mühlhausen and that his wife and child might receive all his belongings.

Part 3   **Conflict
with Zwingli:
Swiss and
South German
Anabaptists**

Editor's note

In terms of chronological development and of importance, the First Reformation innovations of Huldreich Zwingli in Zurich, Switzerland, were second only to those of Martin Luther in Wittenberg, Germany. We have referred previously to the importance of Zwingli's patriotic-religious-social reform in connection with alternative proposals made by direct participants in the Peasants' War (Document 4). Zwingli's theological and practical significance as the originator of the Reformed tradition (the chief competitor to the Lutheran tradition among First Reformation founders) was profound, although John Calvin's influence was even greater on the Protestant world, from his later and internationally more strategic Reformed stronghold in Geneva.

Having dismantled much of medieval religion in his pioneering civic reformation at Zurich during the first disputation of January 1523, Zwingli began to draw back slightly when image-breaking occured among his radical followers. The magistrates sponsored a second disputation in October at Zurich for discussion of images and the mass. Under the influence of Zwingli and his Protestant friends, agreement was again reached that images should be removed and the mass replaced by a memorial Lord's Supper. But for both theological and tactical reasons, Zwingli insisted that the state was competent to delay the demands of Scripture for the sake of conciliating Catholic conservatives.

Zwingli's advanced followers—the patrician Conrad Grebel, the iconoclast Simon Stumpf, the humanist martyr-to-be Felix Mantz, and the well-known pastor Balthasar Hubmaier—now objected openly for the first time that the scriptural norm was being subordinated to traditional notions of a Christian society. From Zwingli's own biased testimony, written a year later,[1] we gather that in 1523 the radicals had not yet clarified their position regarding the use of violence in reform. Zwingli accused Stumpf of advising him that the priests should first be slain (à la Thomas Muentzer). Then Zwingli had turned down the radical proposal that a separate Protestant church be formed which would eventually enable the majority to dominate the city council. The radicals

still seemed to anticipate the victory of Protestantism through political
coercion. Only after a further rift appeared at the second disputation
and Zwingli refused to give the radicals free reign, did rebaptism occur
as an issue among the emerging Second Reformation radicals, along
with programmatic suggestions for radical separation and nonviolent
resistance. The germ of a free church—separationist Christianity, in
accord with New Testament standards—had come alive.

                    The Second Zurich Disputation
                    (October 1523)[2]

. . . Burgomaster: "In the name of God! Now that the discussion on
this article [on the Mass] has been concluded, my lords will be
happy to agree to it."

[The question was accordingly put to the company, with everybody in agreement. Therefore he bade everybody return as previously
instructed to the city hall at twelve the next day. . . .]

[At this point Conrad Grebel stood up and expressed his belief
that, since the priests were present, they should be instructed how
they were to observe the Mass henceforth. For it would serve no
purpose if nothing were accomplished in altering the Mass. Much
had been said about the Mass, but none wished to permit this abomination to God to continue. Even worse abuses were present in the
Mass, which ought to be discussed.]

Zwingli: "My lords will decide the appropriate manner in which
the Mass is to be practiced in the future."

Simon Stumpf: "Master Ulrich! You do not have the power to
reserve judgment to my lords, for judgment has already been given:
The Spirit of God decides. If my lords were to arrive at some decision contrary to the judgment of God, I would implore Christ for
the guidance of his spirit and would teach and act in opposition."

Zwingli: "That is true. I would also preach and act in opposition
if they were to make some contrary decision. I have not reserved
judgment to them. They should not pass judgment on the word of
God—not only they, but the whole world as well should not do so.
This assembly has not been convened for the purpose of passing
judgment, but of gaining understanding and discovering from Scripture whether or not the Mass is a sacrifice. Accordingly, they shall
give advice on the most convenient means of establishing without
disturbance the proper manner [of practicing the Mass].

[. . . So much for the second day.]

[Discussion of the third and last day. . . .]

Burgomaster: "Esteemed, gracious lords, presiding officers. You may now in the name of God resume the discussion of the Mass. . . ."

Conrad Grebel: "Dear brothers in Christ, our Savior. Because the Mass is not a sacrifice, as is declared and proclaimed out of Holy Scripture, so there are still other abuses, which the devil has brought forth, about which we must consent to speak; for, my lords, your mandate speaks about all abuses of the Mass. Therefore, I wish that those would open the matter further who are better able to speak about how we can seek diligently the divine will—since I am a poor speaker and have a bad memory."

[Then Dr. Balthasar Hubmaier spoke at length.] . . . He said also that he had not been so pleased for a whole year as when he had heard that here they were going to discuss the abuses of the Mass, of which there are still many more, as Conrad Grebel has shown.

Ulrich Zwingli: "Conrad Grebel has requested us to take up the abuses, to which I say: Everything not instituted by Christ, which has been added in the course of time—this is truly an abuse. Since, however, one cannot abolish such additions all at once, it is necessary to combat them by preaching the word of God persistently and firmly! . . . "

Conrad Grebel: There were still other abuses besides these. Namely, he would like to know whether the bread had to be leavened or unleavened, for it seemed to him that since Christ had used leavened bread he had wanted the saints to likewise.

Zwingli: "It cannot be established which kind of bread was used. The question is not an important one. Every congregation can decide for itself the kind of bread it wishes to use, leavened or unleavened."

Grebel: "It is well to recall that the word in the text is 'panis' [bread] and should not be taken to mean 'sinwel' [wafer]."

Zwingli: "And to require bread in the form of wafers would not be proper. Christ certainly meant that one could take the usual kind of bread without thereby commiting a sin."

Grebel: "Hence *everything* is left to the congregation."

Zwingli: "Yes, everything not clearly expressed by the word of God is left to the congregation, insofar as the clear intent is not altered. With respect to leavened or unleavened bread, congregational usage alone decides, for the question has little importance! . . .

Grebel: "It is also an abuse when the priest places the bread in our mouths, as if we had no hands, indeed as if it were more proper for the priest than for us to touch the body of Christ."

Zwingli: "This is not at all important. We do not have clear scriptural evidence here. For this reason we have had deacons or servers who have administered the bread."

Grebel protested vigorously that everyone should take the bread himself.

Someone in the room said: "Since we are all weak, it is necessary for someone to hold out the bread and put it in our mouths."

Zwingli: "We do not know from the word of God whether Christ placed his body in the hands of the disciples or not. . . . Therefore it can be left to each congregation to decide for itself." . . .

Following the acquiescence of Conrad Grebel, the spokesman for Küssnacht by Lake Zurich, Conrad Schmid, rose and with great seriousness delivered the following speech: "The two articles under discussion—namely, that one should neither make, have, nor honor images and that the Mass is not a sacrifice—have been so clearly explained, and supported so convincingly with Holy Writ by Master Ulrich and Master Leo, that they cannot be refuted. Yet some people are so precipitous as to believe that we should also take action on the articles and effect changes immediately. In my view, it would not be advisable to abolish things of this nature so hastily, because people are for the most part so involved everywhere in Christian abuses that they would more easily permit abolition of the Mass, almost of Christ himself, than they would of intercession by the saints through their images. . . ."

Editor's note

Following the second Zurich disputation, Grebel and his associates proposed that Zwingli should appeal for an election so that a new "Christian" council could be constituted: "a special group of people and kind of church was to be raised up, . . . having all things in common."[3] Here was the democratic Swiss counterpart to Muentzer's appeal to the princes. Zwingli rejected the appeal. Grebel then developed a new program of withdrawal from the peoples' church. His letter to Muentzer is a programmatic statement of a Christian fellowship based upon voluntary membership, independent of the state. It was Zwinglian in its biblical method, but already Grebel and his friends called for withdrawal from the state, secular law, and war. Here was the first Protestant free-church document. It also evidenced delay—adult baptism was still a proposal. But the zeal of the Swiss Brethren to "go forward with the word and establish a Christian church with the help of Christ and his rule" already indicated what sort of missioners the Anabaptists would be, with their church structures quite free from the limited parish system inherited from ancient Rome. After Anabaptism was begun and they were exiled from Zurich, the Swiss Brethren quickly set up new congregations from Berne and Basel to St. Gall and Appenzell in Switzerland, and in Strassburg, the cities of Swabia, and on into Austria and Moravia. The Second Reformation was about to revolutionize the old structures of the church.

Conrad Grebel et al.   A Letter to Thomas Muentzer
                                            (1524)[4]

Dear Brother Thomas:

    For God's sake do not marvel that we address thee without title and request thee like a brother to communicate with us by writing, and that we have ventured, unasked and unknown to thee, to open communications between us. God's Son, Jesus Christ, who offers Himself as the one master and head of all who would be saved, and bids us be brethren by the one common word given to all brethren and believers, has moved us and compelled us to make friendship and brotherhood and to bring the following points to thy attention. Thy writing of two tracts on fictitious faith has further prompted us. Therefore we ask that thou wilt take it kindly for the sake of Christ our Savior. If God wills, it shall serve and work to our good. Amen.

Just as our forebears fell away from the true God and from the one true, common, divine word, from the divine institutions, from Christian love and life, and lived without God's law and gospel in human, useless, un-Christian customs and ceremonies, and expected to attain salvation therein, yet fell far short of it, as the evangelical preachers have declared, and to some extent are still declaring, so today too every man wants to be saved by superficial faith, without fruits of faith, without baptism of trial and probation, without love and hope, without right Christian practices, and wants to persist in all the old manner of personal vices, and in the common ritualistic and anti-Christian customs of baptism and of the Lord's Supper, in disrespect for the divine word and in respect for the word of the pope and of the antipapal preachers, which yet is not equal to the divine word nor in harmony with it. In respecting persons and in manifold seduction there is grosser and more pernicious error now than ever has been since the beginning of the world. In the same error we too lingered as long as we heard and read only the evangelical preachers who are to blame for all this, in punishment for our sins. But after we took Scripture in hand too, and consulted it on many points, we have been instructed somewhat and have discovered the great and harmful error of the shepherds, of ours too, namely, that we do not daily beseech God earnestly with constant groaning to be brought out of this destruction of all godly life and out of human abominations, to attain to the true faith and divine practice. The cause of all this is false forbearance, the hiding of the divine word, and the mixing of it with the human. Aye, we say it harms all and frustrates all things divine. There is no need of specifying and reciting.

While we were marking and deploring these facts, thy book against false faith and baptism was brought to us, and we were more fully informed and confirmed, and it rejoiced us wonderfully that we found one who was of the same Christian mind with us and dared to show the evangelical preachers their lack, how that in all the chief points they falsely forbear and act and set their own opinions, and even those of Antichrist, above God and against God, as befits not the ambassadors of God to act and preach. Therefore we beg and admonish thee as a brother by the name, the power, the word, the spirit, and the salvation, which has come to all Christians through Jesus Christ our Master and Savior, that thou wilt take earnest heed to preach only the divine word without fear, to set up and guard only divine institutions, to esteem as good and right only what may be found in pure and clear Scripture, to reject, hate, and curse all devices, words, customs, and opinions of men, including thy own.

(1) We understand and have seen that thou hast translated the Mass into German and hast introduced new German hymns. That cannot be for the good, since we find nothing taught in the New Testament about singing, no example of it. Paul scolds the learned among the Corinthians more than he praises them, because they mumbled in meeting as if they sang, just as the Jews and the Italians chant their words song-fashion. (2) Since singing in Latin grew up without divine instruction and apostolic example and custom, without producing good or edifying, it will still less edify in German and will create a faith of outward appearance only. (3) Paul very clearly forbids singing in Ephesians 5:19 and Colossians 3:16, since he says and teaches that they are to speak to one another and teach one another with psalms and spiritual songs, and if anyone would sing, he should sing and give thanks in his heart. (4) Whatever we are not taught by clear passages or examples must be regarded as forbidden, just as if it were written: "This do not; sing not." (5) Christ in the Old and especially in the New Testament bids his messengers simply to proclaim the word; Paul too says that the word of Christ profits us, not the song. Whoever sings poorly gets vexation by it; whoever can sing well gets conceit. (6) We must not follow our notions; we must add nothing to the word and take nothing from it. (7) If thou wilt abolish the Mass, it cannot be accomplished with German chants, which is thy suggestion perhaps, or comes from Luther. (8) It must be rooted up by the word and command of Christ. (9) For it is not planted by God. (10) The Supper of fellowship Christ did institute and plant. (11) The words found in Matthew 26, Mark 14, Luke 22, and I Corinthians 11, alone are to be used, no more, no less. (12) The server, a member of the congregation, should pronounce them from one of the evangelists or from Paul.

(13) They are the words of the instituted meal of fellowship, not words of consecration. (14) Ordinary bread ought to be used, without idols and additions. (15) For [the latter] creates an external reverence and veneration of the bread, and a turning away from the inward. An ordinary drinking vessel too ought to be used. (16) This would do away with the adoration and bring true understanding and appreciation of the Supper, since the bread is nought but bread. In faith, it is the body of Christ and the incorporation with Christ and the brethren. But one must eat and drink in the Spirit and love, as John shows in chapter 6 and the other passages, Paul in I Corinthians 10 and 11, and as is clearly learned in Acts 2. (17) Although it is simply bread, yet if faith and brotherly love precede it, it is to be received with joy, since, when it is used in the church, it is to show us that we are truly one bread and one body, and that we are and wish to be true brethren with one another, etc. (18) But if one is found who will not live the brotherly life, he eats unto condemnation, since he eats it without discerning, like any other meal, and dishonors love, which is the inner bond, and the bread, which is the outer bond. (19) For also it does not call to his mind Christ's body and blood, the covenant of the cross, nor that he should be willing to live and suffer for the sake of Christ and the brethren, of the head and the members. (20) Also it ought not to be administered by thee. That was the beginning of the Mass that only a few would partake, for the Supper is an expression of fellowship, not a Mass and sacrament. Therefore none is to receive it alone, neither on his deathbed nor otherwise. Neither is the bread to be locked away, etc., for the use of a single person, since no one should take for himself alone the bread of those in unity, unless he is not one with himself—which no one is, etc. (21) Neither is it to be used in "temples" according to all Scripture and example, since that creates a false reverence. (22) It should be used much and often. (23) It should not be used without the rule of Christ in Matthew 18:15–18, otherwise it is not the Lord's Supper, for without that rule every man will run after the externals. The inner matter, love, is passed by, if brethren and false brethren approach or eat it [together]. (24) If ever thou desirest to serve it, we should wish that it would be done without priestly garment and vestment of the Mass, without singing, without addition. (25) As for the time, we know that Christ gave it to the apostles at supper and that the Corinthians had the same usage. We fix no definite time with us, etc.

Let this suffice, since thou art much better instructed about the
Lord's Supper, and we only state things as we understand them. If
we are not in the right, teach us better. And do thou drop singing
and the Mass, and act in all things only according to the word, and
bring forth and establish by the word the usages of the apostles.
If that cannot be done, it would be better to leave all things in Latin
and unaltered and mediated [by a priest]. If the right cannot be
established, do not then administer according to thy *own* or the
priestly usage of Antichrist. And at least teach how it ought to be,
as Christ does in John 6, and teaches how we must eat and drink
His flesh and blood, and takes no heed of backsliding and anti-
Christian caution, of which the most learned and foremost evangelical preachers have made a veritable idol and propagated it in all the
world. It is much better that a few be rightly taught through the
word of God, believing and walking aright in virtues and practices,
than that many believe falsely and deceitfully through adulterated
doctrine. Though we admonish and beseech thee, we hope that thou
wilt do it of thy own accord; and we admonish the more willingly,
because thou hast so kindly listened to our brother and confessed
that thou too hast yielded too much, and because thou and Carlstadt
are esteemed by us the purest proclaimers and preachers of the
purest word of God. And if ye two rebuke, and justly, those who
mingle the words and customs of men with those of God, ye must
by rights cut yourselves loose and be completely purged of popery,
benefices, and all new and ancient customs, and of your own and
ancient notions. If your benefices, as with us, are supported by interest and tithes, which are both true usury, and it is not the whole
congregation which supports you, we beg that ye free yourselves of
your benefices. Ye know well how a shepherd should be sustained. . . .

Go forward with the word and establish a Christian church with
the help of Christ and His rule, as we find it instituted in Matthew
18:15–18 and applied in the epistles. Use determination and common prayer and decision according to faith and love, without compulsion or command. Then God will help thee and thy little sheep
to all sincerity, and the singing and the tablets will cease. There is
more than enough of wisdom and counsel in the Scripture, how all
classes and all men may be taught, governed, instructed, and turned
to piety. Whoever will not amend and believe, but resists the word
and action of God and thus persists, such a man, after Christ and
His word and rule have been declared to him and he has been

admonished in the presence of the three witnesses and the church, such a man, we say, taught by God's word, shall not be killed, but regarded as a heathen and publican and let alone.

Moreover, the gospel and its adherents are not to be protected by the sword, nor are thus to protect themselves, which, as we learn from our brother, is thy opinion and practice. True Christian believers are sheep among wolves, sheep for the slaughter; they must be baptized in anguish and affliction, tribulation, persecution, suffering, and death; they must be tried with fire, and must reach the fatherland of eternal rest, not by killing their bodily, but by mortifying their spiritual, enemies. Neither do they use worldly sword or war, since all killing has ceased with them—unless, indeed, we would still be of the old law. And even there [in the Old Testament], so far as we recall, war was a misfortune after they had once conquered the Promised Land. No more of this.

On the matter of baptism thy book pleases us well, and we desire to be further instructed by thee. We understand that even an adult is not to be baptized without Christ's rule of binding and loosing. The Scripture describes baptism for us, thus, that it signifies that, by faith and the blood of Christ, sins have been washed away for him who is baptized, changes his mind, and believes before and after; that it signifies that a man is dead and ought to be dead to sin and walks in newness of life and spirit, and that he shall certainly be saved if, according to this meaning, by inner baptism he lives his faith; so that the water does not confirm or increase faith, as the scholars at Wittenberg say, and [does not] give very great comfort [nor] is it the final refuge on the deathbed. Also baptism does not save, as Augustine, Tertullian, Theophylact, and Cyprian have taught, dishonoring faith and the suffering of Christ in the case of the old and adult, and dishonoring the suffering of Christ in the case of the unbaptized infants. We hold (according to the following passages: Gen. 8:21; Deut. 1:39, 30:6, 31:13; and I Cor. 14:20; Wisd. of Sol. 12:19; I Pet. 2:2; Rom. 1, 2, 7, 10 [allusions uncertain]; Matt. 18:1–6, 19:13–15; Mark 9:33–47, 10:13–16; Luke 18:15–17; etc.) that all children who have not yet come to the discernment of the knowledge of good and evil, and have not yet eaten of the tree of knowledge, that they are surely saved by the suffering of Christ, the new Adam, who has restored their vitiated life, because they would have been subject to death and condemnation only if Christ had not suffered; but they're not yet grown up to the infirmity of our broken nature—unless, indeed, it can be proved that Christ did not suffer for children. But as to the objection that faith is demanded of all who are to be saved, we exclude children from this and hold that they are saved without faith, and we do not believe from the above passages [that children must be baptized], and we conclude from the description of baptism and from the accounts of it (according to which no child was baptized), also from the above passages (which alone apply to the question of children, and all other scriptures do not refer to children), that infant baptism is a senseless, blasphemous abomination, contrary to all Scripture, contrary even to the papacy; since we find, from Cyprian and Augustine, that for many years after apostolic times believers and unbelievers were baptized together for six hundred years, etc. Since thou knowest this ten times better and hast published thy protests against infant baptism, we hope that thou art not acting against the eternal work, wisdom, and commandment of God, according to which only believers are to be baptized, and are not baptizing children.

Editor's note

The question of baptizing adults now became crucial for the radicals
and others in Zurich. Fathers—Grebel among them—had not brought
their newborn children to be baptized. If repentance for sins was to
precede baptism, the whole state church system would crumble. Grebel
and his friends wished to discuss the issues with Zwingli, hoping that he
and the council might adopt believers' baptism as a scriptural necessity.
The radicals combined biblical literalism with an emphasis upon spiritual
experience and conversion. Two unsuccessful private discussions were
held with Zwingli. Since his way to the council through Zwingli remained
blocked, Felix Mantz, son of a Zurich priest and well trained in Hebrew,
then addressed a written protest and defense to the magistrates, arguing
that infant baptism was unbiblical. Zwingli's written proof for infant
baptism, which followed, played down the importance of baptism, and
admitted that six other groups of agitators in Zurich troubled him more.[5]
In spite of his desire for unity, Zwingli refused to permit baptism of
adults. The next move was up to the radicals.

Felix Mantz   A Protest and Defense
                                      (1524 or 1525)[6]

Wise, farsighted, graceful, dear gentlemen and brethren. You know
well that some are teaching that Holy Scripture demands that a
newborn child must be baptized, while others believe that infant
baptism is bad, false, and was originated by the Antichrist and the
Pope. Among the latter, I have been accused of encouraging disorder, an utterly untruthful charge. I have never taken part in sedition and have never talked or spoken in any way anything which
would lead to it, as all those with whom I have ever had anything
to do will testify of me. Hence such a charge is unjust to me. . . .

[Mantz goes on to expound his position on baptism, believing that it will be easy to settle the question if only everyone will stand fast on the principle which Zurich professes to follow, namely the sole authority of Scripture in matters of faith.]

. . . One can clearly see how the apostles understood the command of Christ as above related from Matthew [28:19], namely, that as they went forth they should teach all nations that to Christ is given all power in heaven and in earth, and that forgiveness of sins in His name should be given to everyone who believing on His name should do righteous works from a changed heart. After the receiving of this teaching and the descent of the Holy Spirit which, by speaking in tongues, was evidenced to those who had heard the word of Peter [Acts 10:40], they were thereafter poured over with water [baptized] meaning that just as they were cleaned within by the coming of the Holy Spirit so they also were poured over with water externally to signify the inner cleansing and dying to sin.

As evidence that this is the meaning of baptism we read in Acts 22 that Ananias spoke these words to Paul: "The God of our fathers hath appointed thee to know his will, and to see the Righteous One, and to hear a voice from his mouth. For thou shalt be a witness for him unto all men of what thou hast seen and heard. And now why tarriest thou? arise, and be baptized, and wash away thy sins, calling on his name." From these words we clearly see what baptism is and when it shall be practiced, namely upon one who having been converted through God's word and having changed his heart now henceforth desires to live in newness of life, as Paul clearly shows in Romans 6, dead to the old life, circumcised in his heart, having died to sins with Christ, having been buried with Him in baptism and arisen with Him again in newness of life, etc. To apply such things as have just been related to children is without any, and against all Scripture. . . .

We are certain, Master Ulrich, that you also understand this interpretation of baptism, better than we, but we do not know why you aren't open. We do know certainly that if the Word of God be allowed to speak of itself freely and singly, no one will be able to withstand it, . . . if only freedom be given and the truth be treated with trust. . . . I most earnestly entreat you, do not stain your hands with innocent blood, supposing that you are serving God should you kill or exile persons. . . .

Editor's note

On January 17, 1525, the Zurich council summoned Zwingli and his
opponents for a disputation at the city hall concerning baptism. Scripture
was to be the judge. But the form of invitation indicated that the council
had already designated the opponents of infant baptism as the errant
ones. Heinrich Bullinger, Zwingli's successor, recalled the events later,
from the same perspective held by Zwingli and the council.[7] The results
were predictable: the Grebel group was crushed. The council ordered all
children to be baptized within eight days of birth. Disobedient persons
would be banished. Two days later the council prohibited assemblies of
the dissidents. Grebel and Mantz were forbidden to speak. Reublin,
Brötli, Haetzer, and Castelberger were banished, since they were not
citizens of Zurich. Zwingli had shown that he could be no less firm
toward radicals than Luther had been.

Heinrich Bullinger   A History of the Reformation
                              (recalling 1525)[8]

A colloquy or disputation was called by the council for January 17,
1525, to be held in the city hall before councillors and Zurich citizens as well as scholars. At that time Mantz, Grebel, and also
Reublin were present to argue their case that children could not
believe and did not understand the meaning of baptism. Baptism
should be administered to believers to whom the Gospel had been
preached who understood it, and who therefore desired baptism,
wanting to kill the old Adam and live a new life. Of this children
knew nothing; therefore, baptism did not belong to them. They
quoted passages from the Gospels and the Acts of the Apostles and
showed that the Apostles did not baptize children, but only mature
and understanding people. Thus should it be done today. Since there

had been no proper baptism, infant baptism was not valid and everyone should be baptized again.

Zwingli responded with the reasoning which he subsequently published in a pamphlet dedicated to the people of St. Gall entitled *Concerning Baptism, Rebaptism, and Infant Baptism*.[9] The Anabaptists could neither refute his arguments nor maintain their own. . . . After the disputation the Anabaptists were earnestly admonished by the council to desist from their position and be quiet, since they could find no support in the Word of God.

This, however, did not impress them. They said that they had to obey God rather than men. Restlessness and discord increased considerably. . . . Therefore, on March 20 a second disputation was held with them and their followers, of whom several had been arrested. In this second disputation they cited no more scriptural quotations than they had in the first. A lively discussion was held with them. Afterwards, the council talked earnestly with them and admonished them to retract their views, since such detrimental separation and division would not be tolerated any more. Several Anabaptists were kept in prison; others were banished from the region. This, however, resulted in nothing more than they continued in their ways. . . .

The Anabaptists also insisted that though a disputation had been held they had never received a real opportunity to present their case and Zwingli would not let anyone talk freely. Restlessness and danger increased more and more. Therefore, the honorable city council of Zurich was prompted to call a colloquy which was to be especially free and open. Everyone was to say freely what could be supported with sacred Scripture. On the day of the disputation many Anabaptists from other places, such as St. Gall, were present. The doctor from Waldshut, an Anabaptist [Hubmaier], was expected, but did not come. Thus, Grebel and Mantz together with their associates represented the case.

Against them stood Master Huldreich Zwingli, Master Leo Jud, and Caspar Grossman. The propositions to be debated were the following: The children of Christians are no less the children of God than their parents, as was the case in the Old Testament. If they are the children of God, who will prevent them from receiving water baptism? Circumcision was to the men of old the same sign which baptism is to us. Inasmuch as circumcision was given to children, baptism shall likewise be given to children. Rebaptism finds no support, example, or proof in the Word of God. Those who are

rebaptized therefore crucify Christ anew—either because of stub-
bornness or innovation. . . .

After the colloquy, Grebel, Mantz, and other Anabaptist patriarchs were cited before the council and admonished to desist from
their views which had publicly been found to be false. Since these
quarrelsome heads did not agree, they were kept in the tower. Soon,
however, they were discharged and informed that if they continued
their separatism they would be most severely punished.

Editor's note

The birth of the Anabaptist movement occurred on the evening of
January 21, 1525, in Zollikon near Zurich.[10] A former priest (Blaurock)
received baptism upon confession of sin from the hand of a former
playboy (Grebel) in the home of a Hebrew scholar (Mantz). Blaurock
then baptized the others. The later account by Braitmichel, a Hutterite
chronicler of Moravia, preserved the excitement of the participants, who
felt that by defying impure Christendom they had restored the church
of Christ and, in the midst of opposition, had obeyed Scripture and
Christian conscience. There the sober nature of the Swiss Christian
revolution became evident.

The initial introduction of believers' baptism stressed more the adult's
need for repentance than it did his capacity for belief. Rather than being
continuators of the worn-out sacrament of (infant) baptism, Grebel
and his associates were preachers of repentance who brought their
hearers to a felt consciousness of sin and their need for forgiveness.
Believers then were baptized, "in the union of God with a good
conscience" (I Pet. 3:21), which also brought them into the covenant of
the church and pledged them to serve God in all faithfulness, even
witnessing to the ends of the earth (the Great Commission, Matt.
28:19–20). Radical ferment at Zurich thus was instituted in accord with
traditional, scriptural norms, with little external emotion. But the Zurich
Anabaptists had begun a new phase of ecclesiastical and social history.

Caspar Braitmichel   The Beginnings of the
                                        Anabaptist Movement
                                        (c. 1565)[11]

. . . Because God wished to have his own people, separated from all
peoples, he willed for this purpose to bring in the right true morning
star of his truth to shine in fullness in the final age of this world,
especially in the German nation and lands, the same to strike home
with his Word and to reveal the ground of divine truth. In order
that his holy work might be made known and revealed before everyman, there developed first in Switzerland an extraordinary awaken-
ing and preparation by God as follows:

It came to pass that Ulrich Zwingli and Conrad Grebel, one of
the aristocracy, and Felix Mantz—all three much experienced and
men learned in the German, Latin, Greek, and also the Hebrew,
languages—came together and began to talk through matters of
belief among themselves and recognized that infant baptism is un-
necessary and recognized further that it is in fact no baptism. Two,
however, Conrad and Felix, recognized in the Lord and believed
that one must and should be correctly baptized according to the
Christian ordinance and institution of the Lord, since Christ himself
says that whoever *believes* and is baptized will be saved. Ulrich
Zwingli, who shuddered before Christ's cross, shame, and persecution, did not wish this and asserted that an uprising would break
out. The other two, however, Conrad and Felix, declared that God's
clear commandment and institution could not for that reason be
allowed to lapse.

At this point it came to pass that a person from Chur came to
them, namely a cleric named George of the House of Jacob, commonly called "Bluecoat" [Blaurock] because one time when they
were having a discussion of matters of belief in a meeting this George
Cajacob presented his view also. Then someone asked who it was
who had just spoken. Thereupon someone answered: The person
in the blue coat spoke. Thus thereafter he got the name of Blaurock.
. . . This George came, moreover, with the unusual zeal which he
had, a straightforward, simple parson. As such he was held by
everyone. But in matters of faith and in divine zeal, which had been
given him out of God's grace, he acted wonderfully and valiantly
in the cause of truth. He first came to Zwingli and discussed matters
of belief with him at length, but accomplished nothing. Then he was
told that there were other men more zealous than Zwingli. These

men he inquired for diligently and found them, namely, Conrad
Grebel and Felix Mantz. With them he spoke and talked through
matters of faith. They came to one mind in these things, and in the
pure fear of God they recognized that a person must learn from the
divine Word and preaching a true faith which manifests itself in love,
and receive the true Christian baptism on the basis of the recognized
and confessed faith, in the union with God of a good conscience,
[prepared] henceforth to serve God in a holy Christian life with all
godliness, also to be steadfast to the end in tribulation.

And it came to pass that they were together until fear began to
come over them; yea, they were pressed in their hearts. Thereupon,
they began to bow their knees to the Most High God in heaven and
called upon him as the Knower of hearts, [and] implored him to
enable them to do his divine will and to manifest his mercy toward
them. For flesh and blood and human forwardness did not drive
them, since they well knew what they would have to bear and suffer
on account of it. After the prayer, George Cajacob arose and asked
Conrad to baptize him, for the sake of God, with the true Christian
baptism upon his faith and knowledge. And when he knelt down
with that request and desire, Conrad baptized him, since at that time
there was no ordained deacon to perform such work. After that was
done the others similarly desired George to baptize them, which he
also did upon their request. Thus they together gave themselves to
the name of the Lord in the high fear of God. Each confirmed the
other in the service of the gospel, and they began to teach and keep
the faith. Therewith began the separation from the world and its
evil works.

Soon thereafter several others made their way to them—for example, Balthasar Hubmaier of Friedberg, Louis Haetzer, and still
others, men well instructed in the German, Latin, Greek and Hebrew
languages, very well versed in Scripture, some preachers and other
persons, who were soon to have testified with their blood.

The above-mentioned Felix Mantz they drowned at Zurich because of this true belief and true baptism, who thus witnessed stead-
fastly with his body and life to this truth. .

. . . Thus did [the movement] spread through persecution and
much tribulation. The church increased daily, and the Lord's people
grew in numbers. This the enemy of the divine truth could not endure. He used Zwingli as an instrument, who thereupon began to
write diligently and to preach from the pulpit that the baptism of
believers and adults was not right and should not be tolerated—

contrary to his own confession which he had previously written and taught, namely that infant baptism cannot be demonstrated or proved with a single clear word from God. But now, since he wished rather to please men than God, he contended against the true Christian baptism. He also stirred up the magistracy to act on imperial authorization and behead as Anabaptists those who had properly given themselves to God and with a good understanding had made covenant of a good conscience with God.

Finally it reached the point that over twenty men, widows, pregnant wives, and maidens were cast miserably into dark towers, sentenced never again to see either sun or moon as long as they lived, to end their days on bread and water, and thus in the dark towers to remain together, the living and the dead, until none remained alive—there to die, to stink, and to rot. Some among them did not eat a mouthful of bread in three days, just so that others might have to eat.

Soon also there was issued a stern mandate at the instigation of Zwingli that if any more people in the canton of Zurich should be rebaptized, they should immediately, without further trial, hearing, or sentence, be cast into the water and drowned. Herein one sees which spirit's child Zwingli was, and those of his party still are.

However, since the work fostered by God cannot be changed and God's counsel lies in the power of no man, the aforementioned men went forth, through divine prompting, to proclaim and preach the evangelical word and the ground of truth. George Cajacob or Blaurock went into the county of Tyrol. In the meantime Balthasar Hubmaier came to Nicholsburg in Moravia, [and] began to teach and preach. The people, however, accepted the teaching and many people were baptized in a short time.

15

The Schleitheim Confession
of Faith

Editor's note

The Swiss Brethren movement was abortive as a revolution.[12] It lacked important revolutionary preconditions, such as an unstable establishment adversary or lack of cooperation between Zwingli and the council, which might have strengthened the Second Reformation position. In fact, the external military threat of the Catholic cantons was evidently more important to the Zurichers (at least to Zwingli) than was the conflict aroused by opposition Reformation teaching. Moreover, the Second Reformation party was not united in its program, nor did it seem to be clear as to goals and procedures. As a result, the Zwinglians effectively crushed Anabaptist leadership. Mantz was publicly drowned in 1527; Grebel had already died of the plague in 1526; Hubmaier had been imprisoned and tortured in 1525; others were expelled.

To be sure, the Anabaptists at Waldshut under Hubmaier were successful in the whole community, even linking up with the local Peasants' War and showing signs of enlisting mass revolutionary loyalty (see Document 16). But under the leadership of Michael Sattler, a South German, the radical apolitical tendencies of Grebel were vigorously developed in confrontation with less separatist Anabaptists such as John Denck in Strassburg, where Sattler may also have encountered the millennial views of Melchior Hofmann.[13]

Amid sharp persecution, Sattler turned away from what he regarded as the demonic forms of Christian government, Zwinglian and Catholic alike. At Schleitheim on the Swiss-German border, he drew up a statement demanding complete separation between Christians and the world, including in his definition of a Christian a refusal to use physical force. Instead of distinguishing between Gospel and Law, as did Luther, Sattler separated them. Stopped short of anarchy by St. Paul (and repudiating antinomian excesses by St. Gall Anabaptists), Sattler's articles were based on the New Testament, interpreted Christocentrically in a legalistic and moralistic way. No longer could a Christian be a magistrate, participate in government, or have anything to do with the evil world. Later becoming definitive for Mennonite teaching, the *Seven Articles*

were revolutionary in their alienation from government in a clearer and
more extreme way than Grebel's teachings had been. True to his
doctrine, Sattler was arrested by Hapsburg authorities in Rottenburg, and
there was tried, tortured, and burned after a celebrated trial in 1527.

Michael Sattler   The Schleitheim Confession
                                     of Faith [Seven Articles]
                                     (1527)[14]

Dear brethren and sisters, we who have been assembled in the Lord
at Schleitheim on the Border, make known in points and articles to
all who love God that as concerns us we are of one mind to abide
in the Lord as God's obedient children, [His] sons and daughters,
we who have been and shall be separated from the world in everything, [and] completely at peace. To God alone be praise and glory
without the contradiction of any brethren. In this we have perceived
the oneness of the Spirit of our Father and of our common Christ
with us. For the Lord is the Lord of peace and not of quarreling,
as Paul points out. That you may understand in what articles this
has been formulated you should observe and note [the following].

A very great offense has been introduced by certain false brethren
among us, so that some have turned aside from the faith, in the way
they intend to practice and observe the freedom of the Spirit and of
Christ. But such have missed the truth and to their condemnation
are given over to the lasciviousness and self-indulgence of the flesh.
They think faith and love may do and permit everything and nothing
will harm them nor condemn them, since they are believers. . . .

But you are not that way. For they that are Christ's have crucified
the flesh with its passions and lusts. You understand me well and
[know] the brethren whom we mean. Separate yourselves from them,
for they are perverted. Petition the Lord that they may have the
knowledge which leads to repentance, and [pray] for us that we may
have constancy to persevere in the way which we have espoused,
for the honor of God and of Christ, his Son, Amen.

The articles which we discussed and on which we were of one
mind are these: (1) Baptism; (2) The Ban (Excommunication);
(3) Breaking of Bread; (4) Separation from the Abomination; (5)
Pastors in the Church; (6) The Sword; and (7) The Oath.

First. Observe concerning baptism: Baptism shall be given to all
those who have learned repentance and amendment of life, and who
believe truly that their sins are taken away by Christ, and to all

those who walk in the resurrection of Jesus Christ, and wish to be buried with him in death, so that they may be resurrected with him, and to all those who with this significance request it [baptism] of us and demand it for themselves. . . .

Second. We are agreed as follows on the ban: The ban shall be employed with all those who have given themselves to the Lord, to walk in his commandments, and with all those who are baptized into the one body of Christ and who are called brethren or sisters, and yet who slip sometimes and fall into error and sin, being inadvertently overtaken. . . .

Third. In the breaking of bread we are of one mind and are agreed [as follows]: All those who wish to break one bread in remembrance of the broken body of Christ, and all who wish to drink of one drink as a remembrance of the shed blood of Christ, shall be united beforehand by baptism in one body of Christ which is the Church of God and whose head is Christ. . . .

Therefore it is and must be [thus]: Whoever has not been called by one God to one faith, to one baptism, to one Spirit, to one body, with all the children of God's Church, cannot be made [into] one bread with them, as indeed must be done if one is truly to break bread according to the command of Christ.

Fourth. We are agreed [as follows] on separation: A separation shall be made from the evil and from the wickedness which the devil planted in the world; in this manner, simply that we shall not have fellowship with them [the wicked] and not run with them in the multitude of their abominations. This is the way it is: Since all who do not walk in the obedience of faith, and have not united themselves with God so that they wish to do his will, are a great abomination before God, it is not possible for anything to grow or issue from them except abominable things. For truly all creatures are in but two classes, good and bad, believing and unbelieving, darkness and light, the world and those who [have come] out of the world, God's temple and idols, Christ and Belial; and none can have part with the other.

To us then the command of the Lord is clear when he calls upon us to be separate from the evil and thus he will be our God and we shall be his sons and daughters. . . .

Fifth. We are agreed as follows on pastors in the Church of God: The pastor in the Church of God shall, as Paul has prescribed, be one who out-and-out has a good report of those who are outside the faith. This office shall be to read, to admonish and teach, to warn, to discipline, to ban in the Church, to lead out in prayer for the advancement of all the brethren and sisters, to lift up the bread when it is to be broken, and in all things to see to the care of the body of Christ, in order that it may be built up and developed, and the mouth of the slanderer be stopped. . . .

Sixth. We are agreed as follows concerning the sword: The sword is ordained of God outside the perfection of Christ. It punishes and puts to death the wicked, and guards and protects the good. In the Law the sword was ordained for the punishment of the wicked and for their death, and the same [sword] is [now] ordained to be used by the worldly magistrates.

In the perfection of Christ, however, only the ban is used for a warning and for the excommunication of the one who has sinned, without putting the flesh to death—simply the warning and the command to sin no more.

Now it will be asked by many who do not recognize [this as] the will of Christ for us, whether a Christian may or should employ the sword against the wicked for the defense and protection of the good, or for the sake of love.

Our reply is unanimously as follows: Christ teaches and commands us to learn of Him, for He is meek and lowly in heart and so shall we find rest to our souls. Also Christ says to the heathenish woman who was taken in adultery, not that one should stone her according to the law of His Father (and yet He says, As the Father has commanded me, thus I do), but in mercy and forgiveness and warning, to sin no more. Such [an attitude] we also ought to take completely according to the rule of the ban.

Secondly, it will be asked concerning the sword, whether a Christian shall pass sentence in worldly dispute and strife such as unbelievers have with one another. This is our united answer: Christ did not wish to decide or pass judgment between brother and brother in the case of the inheritance, but refused to do so. Therefore we should do likewise.

Thirdly, it will be asked concerning the sword, Shall one be a magistrate if one should be chosen as such? The answer is as follows: They wished to make Christ king, but He fled and did not view it as the arrangement of His Father. Thus shall we do as He did, and follow Him, and so shall we not walk in darkness. . . .

Finally it will be observed that it is not appropriate for a Christian to serve as a magistrate because of these points: The government magistracy is according to the flesh, but the Christians' is

according to the Spirit; their house and dwelling remain in this world,
but the Christians' are in heaven; their citizenship is in this world,
but the Christians' citizenship is in heaven; the weapon of their conflict and war are carnal and against the flesh only, but the Christians'
weapons are spiritual, against the fortification of the devil. . . .

Seventh. We are agreed as follows concerning the oath: The oath
is a confirmation among those who are quarreling or making promises. In the Law it is commanded to be performed in God's name,
but only in truth, not falsely. Christ, who teaches the perfection of
the Law, prohibits all swearing to his [followers], whether true or
false—neither by heaven, nor by the earth, nor by Jerusalem, nor
by our head—and that for the reason which he shortly thereafter
gives, for you are not able to make one hair white or black. So you
see it is for this reason that all swearing is forbidden: we cannot
fulfill that which we promise when we swear, for we cannot change
[even] the very least thing on us. . . .

Dear brethren and sisters in the Lord: These are the articles of
certain brethren who had heretofore been in error and who had
failed to agree in the true understanding, so that many weaker consciences were perplexed, causing the name of God to be greatly
slandered. Therefore there has been a great need for us to become
of one mind in the Lord, which has come to pass. To God be praise
and glory! . . .

Keep watch on all who do not walk according to the simplicity
of the divine truth which is stated in this letter from [the decisions
of] our meeting, so that everyone among us will be governed by the
rule of the ban and henceforth the entry of false brethren and sisters
among us may be prevented.

Eliminate from you that which is evil and the Lord will be your
God and you will be his sons and daughters. . . .

Editor's note

Hubmaier, a learned pastor of Waldshut, was the established scholar won by the Swiss Anabaptists.[15] His active political stance remained that of Zwingli, with his notion that power is best legitimized through Christian government, and its corollary that subjects may remove tyrants if it can be done without public chaos. Hubmaier failed to rally Swiss and peasant support against the Hapsburgs, and fled to Nicholsburg, Moravia, after he had been repudiated by Zwingli for Anabaptism. In the meantime, Hubmaier's convert at Augsburg, John Denck, and Denck's convert, John Hut, spread Muentzer-like Anabaptism throughout South Germany. Hut especially continued Muentzer's apocalyptic hopes without open violence. Having successfully brought Anabaptism to a town (Waldshut) and to a lordship (Nicholsburg), Hubmaier maintained his own position in the latter against nonresistant Anabaptist refugees who had flocked to the lordship he had won. He also attempted to resist Anabaptist radicals who were hoping for apocalyptic vengeance. Thus Hubmaier's Nicholsburg writing on government sounds like a refutation of the Schleitheim article on the sword.

Having developed beyond his unsavory pre-Protestant stage of anti-Jewish pogroms at Regensburg, Hubmaier was further discredited by his own execution at Vienna by the Hapsburgs in 1528. He had been more than usually successful in establishing legitimate Second Reformation enclaves through the use of politics. Yet Lord Lichtenstein had been unable to protect him at Nicholsburg. The combined accusation of earlier sedition at Waldshut and Anabaptist heresy overcame support for him among the magistrates. The nonresistant Anabaptists blamed Hubmaier's failure on his willingness to make use of politics. When 1528 passed without Christ's coming, Hut's chiliastic hopes failed also, with the result that former advocates of Muentzer's naked sword also abandoned hopes for Hut's sheathed sword along with Hubmaier's political activism, and most Anabaptists became *Staebler* (men of the staff), having put away the sword entirely. Separatist traditions thus prevailed

among the Moravian Hutterites as they had earlier done among the
Swiss Brethren, and as they were later to do among Mennonites, in
reaction against the disaster at Muenster.

Balthasar Hubmaier   On the Sword (1527)[16]

"The kings of this world," says Christ, "lord it, and those in authority are called 'Gracious lords.' But you not so."—Luke 22:
25–26.

What great a maxim you make there, and especially of the words
"But you not so," I cannot satisfactorily tell. But I take pity on you
as before. For you have not well seen either the preceding or the
following words, for if you did you would understand them right
and we should soon come to agreement. Well, then we will begin
this passage three lines farther back, and the meaning will then
appear plain. Thus reads the text: "There arose a contention among
the disciples, which of them should be ruler," who should have the
authority in external and carnal things, since the secular authority
is over flesh and body and over temporal things, but not over the
the soul. To him according to the divine order the sword is entrusted, not that he may fight, war, strive, and tyrannize with it, but
to defend the wise, protect the widow, maintain the pious, and to
tolerate all who are distressed or persecuted by force. This is the
duty of the magistrate, as God himself many times in the Scripture
declares it, which may not take place without blood and killing,
wherefore God had hung the sword at his side, and not a fox's tail.

The Last Passage a Sanction of
Magistracy among Christians

Let every man be subject to the magistrate and power, for there is
no power apart from God. But the power everywhere is ordained by
God, so that he who sets himself against the power strives against
the ordinance of God. But he who strives will receive condemnation
of himself. For the rulers do not make the good work fear but the
evil. Wilt thou not fear? then do good, so shalt thou have praise
from the same. But if thou doest evil, then fear, for authority bears
not the sword in vain. He is God's servant, a judge for punishment
over him that does evil. So you are obliged to submit, not alone
because of the punishment, but because of conscience; wherefore you

must also give tribute, for they are God's servants who provide such protection [Rom. 13:1–6]. This passage alone, dear brothers, is enough to sanction the magistracy against all the gates of hell. . . .

But the magistrate will punish the wicked, as he is bound to do by his own soul's salvation; and if he is not able to do this alone, when he summons his subjects by bell or gun, by letter or any other way, they are bound by their soul's salvation also to stand by their prince and help him, so that according to the will of God the wicked may be slain and uprooted.

Nevertheless, the subjects should carefully test the spirit of their ruler, whether he is not incited by haughtiness, pride, intoxication, envy, hatred, or his own profit, rather than by love of the common weal and the peace of society. When that is the case, he does not bear the sword according to the ordinance of God. But if you know that the ruler is punishing the evil only so that the pious may remain in peace and uninjured, then help, counsel, stand by him, as often and as stoutly as you are able; thus you fulfill the ordinance of God and do his work, and not a work of men.

But if a ruler should be childish or foolish, yea, even entirely unfit to rule, one may with reason then escape from him and choose another, since on account of a wicked ruler God has often punished a whole land. But if it may not well be done, reasonably and peaceably and without great shame and rebellion, he should be suffered as one whom God has given us in his anger, and wills (since we are worthy of no better) thus to chastise us for our sins.

He then who will not aid the magistrate to seek out the widows and orphans and other oppressed, and to punish the outragers and ravishers of the land, contends against the ordinance of God and will come to the judgment, since he acts contrary to the command and ordinance of God, who wills that the pious should be protected and the wicked punished. . . . Where are they then that say, "A Christian may not bear the sword"? If a Christian may not be a servant of God, if he may not obey the command of God without sin, then were God not good. He has made an ordinance which a Christian may not fulfill without sin—that is blasphemy!

Accordingly, I counsel you with true love, brothers, turn back, take heed to yourselves. You have stumbled badly, and under a cloak of spirituality and humility have devised much mischief against God and brotherly love. All affairs remain more peaceful where one sees a Christian ruler and his subjects agree in a manly, brotherly, and Christian fashion, and many a tyrant would cease his striving and urging against God and all reason, and sheathe his sword according to the command of God. Yet if God wills that we should suffer, his will cannot be hindered by our protection.

To sum up: no one can deny that to protect the pious and punish the wicked is the strict command of God, which stands to the judgment day. . . . In the second place: the text clearly points out that each of the disciples desired the pre-eminence, and they were quarreling which among them should be greatest. Jesus could not see such a quarrel. It belongs to no Christian, out of lust for authority, to contend to be a ruler, but much rather to flee from it. . . . He exalts himself above none, but takes well to heart the word of Christ that the foremost shall be as a servant. . . .

So, dear brothers, make no patchwork of the Scripture, but putting the foregoing and following words together in one entire judgment, you will then come to a complete understanding of the Scriptures, and you will see how the text does not forbid the magistracy to the Christian, but teaches one not to quarrel, war, and fight for it, nor conquer land and people with the sword and force. That is against God. Also we should not greatly desire to be saluted as Lords, like secular kings, princes, and lords. For the magistracy is not lordship and knighthood, but service according to the ordinance of God. . . .

Part 4

The Kingdom of Muenster: North German and Dutch Anabaptists

Editor's note

Anabaptism was carried to North Germany and the Netherlands by a
Swabian furrier and lay preacher, Melchior Hofmann, who repudiated
his Lutheran faith in Strassburg for Anabaptism.[1] Hofmann's own
fellowship resulted, separate from other Anabaptist groups led by Kautz,
Reublin, Marpeck, and Denck. Moving on to introduce the Protestant
and Anabaptist faith in East Friesland, Hofmann proclaimed the new
Ordinance of God, based on Christ's commission for the reborn to enter
the church through the covenant of baptism.

Hofmann used marital imagery to interpret the urgency and discipline
of that covenant, which was also a recurrent epiphany of Christ.
Persecution followed for his converts. The basis for Hofmann's chiliasm
was confidence that the Bible taught that man's fallen history was about
to be consummated in a new age. Concluding that Christ would come
in 1533, Hofmann hurried to be imprisoned in Strassburg, so that the
Lord might come after a half-year. Though his political views remained
quietistically Lutheran, Hofmann's speculations set the stage for the
excitement which culminated in the Muenster Kingdom.

Hofmann had as great an influence upon Northwest German and
Dutch Second Reformation thinking as did Pilgram Marpeck upon Swiss
or Upper German Anabaptists. His belief in the heavenly flesh of Christ
and in vigorous apocalyptic mission runs through several peaceful and
revolutionary sects in the North, including the more violent Muensterites
and Batenburgers, the spiritualizing Davidjorites, and the Obbenite-
Mennonites among proponents of nonviolent resistance.[2] Although he
was more a catalyst than a cause of Muenster, Hofmann's teaching
helped produce the closest approach of Anabaptism to a revolutionary
mass movement.

Melchior Hofmann   The Ordinance of God
                                      (1530)[3]

In the first place, the Lord Jesus Christ proclaims to his apostles and disciples that he has received from his Heavenly Father all power, might, strength, spirit, mind, and will and promises that he [will] be a king, prince, and captain both in heaven and on earth, and that his rule extends over all, whatever it may be called. . . .

Thus is the Son of Man—a savior of his people and the anointed peacemaker for all believers, a reconciler, advocate, and high priest, yea, the "mouth" of the spiritual Moses and eternal Heavenly Father—[ever] sending forth his friends, servants, and apostolic emissaries in order to assemble for him his Bride out of the bonds of darkness, out of the realm and all the power of the devil and Satan, out of all that belongs to this world—into the Kingdom of God and of the Lord Jesus Christ. And the King of Kings shuts no one out [of the Kingdom]. . . .

All those who hear this and do not stop up their ears but rather attend with alertness [will] inherit their salvation and [will] not despise it. Thus it is the duty of every qualified apostle that they go forth from the mouth of the Most High God—which mouth the Lord Christ Jesus is, and the true apostles the mouth of the anointed Savior—in order to teach all peoples and to proclaim to them the friendly message and to bring the kiss rich in joys from the mouth of the Bridegroom, yea, this holy gospel of the crucified Christ Jesus, the Word of eternal life, who has paid for all misdeeds. And he has been established by his Father as a lord over all the creatures of God, both in heaven and on earth. . . .

It is further the order and command or law of the Lord for his apostolic emissaries, according to which they have also in fact instructed, called, and admonished the people, requiring and urging through the gospel and the Word of God that they also who have surrendered themselves to the Lord should lead themselves out of the realm of Satan and from the kingdom of darkness and from this world and that they should purify themselves and lead themselves into the spiritual wilderness and also wed and bind themselves to the Lord Jesus Christ, publicly, through that true sign of the Covenant, the water bath and baptism.

They have also taught and been taught and received all knowledge of Jesus Christ and wish to have him for Lord, King, and Bridegroom, and bind themselves to him and betroth themselves to him through the covenant of baptism and also give themselves over to him dead and crucified and hence are at all times subject, in utter zeal, to his will and pleasure. That is then such a true and certain covenant as takes place when a bride with complete, voluntary, and loving surrender and with a truly free, well-considered betrothal, yields herself in abandon and presents herself as a freewill offering to her lord and bridegroom. . . .

Now in this final age the true apostolic emissaries of the Lord Jesus Christ will gather the elect flock and call it through the gospel and lead the Bride of the Lord into the spiritual wilderness, betroth, and covenant her through baptism to the Lord. . . . For in the New Covenant, the Third Day, that third lunar festival, that is, the spiritual Feast of Tabernacles, will be in the spiritual wilderness; and the last appearance of all that is lunar (II Esd. 5:4).[4]

Such a figurative meaning the Lord Christ Jesus intends [when] he goes before his flock at the head to be a model. He comes to John the Baptist at the Jordan, covenants and betroths, yea, offers himself, his whole self, to his Heavenly Father, to whom he lets himself also through John the Baptist be baptized and betrothed and covenanted through the water bath, during [which time he is] detached from his own will, and, through God's covenant, absorbed into the will of the exalted Father, [and prepared] to live eternally unto him. . . .

In just such a manner *all* children of God and brothers of the Lord Jesus Christ should imitate him and also covenant and betroth themselves to the Lord Jesus Christ, under the covenant of God, and give themselves over to him in truth, as a freewill offering, just as he has given himself over to him, his Heavenly Father. . . .

To such a victory all the promises of God tend, namely: that to all such victors the true Kingdom of God is given here and now as their inheritance; that the same enter into the Holy [of Holies] and come to the Sabbath and the true rest completely naked and re-signed to enter the bed of the Bridegroom where the righteous [re-]birth takes place and where one is instructed by God and the Word. And the soul is completely wedded by the grace of God. There the old Adam is put off completely, the individual quite naked, is rid of all. . . . These are then made pious and have the cleansing through the blood of Christ Jesus, and in such there is nothing more that is blameworthy to be found, as has already been said. . . .

Such aforesaid promises, such an ordinance—this is the content of that high covenant of God and of the Lord Jesus Christ. It is the sign of the covenant of God, instituted solely for the old, the mature, and the rational, who can receive, assimilate, and understand the teaching and the preaching of the Lord, and not for the immature, uncomprehending, and unreasonable, who cannot receive, learn, or understand the teaching of the apostolic emissaries: such are immature children; such also are bells which toll for the dead, and churches, and altars, and all other such abominations. . . .

Accordingly, all human notions are sternly forbidden by the Lord, and infant baptism is absolutely not from God but rather is practiced, out of willfulness, by anti-Christians and the satanic crown, in opposition to God and all his commandment, will, and desire. Verily, it is an eternal abomination to him. . . .

When now the bride of the Lord Jesus Christ has given herself over to the Bridegroom in baptism, which is the sign of the covenant, and has betrothed herself and yielded herself to him of her own free will and has thus in very truth accepted him and taken him unto herself, thereupon the Bridegroom and exalted Lord Christ Jesus comes and by his hand—the apostolic emissaries are the hand—takes bread (just as a bridegroom takes a ring or a piece of gold) and gives himself to his bride with the bread (just as the bridegroom gives himself to his bride with the ring) and takes also the chalice with the wine and gives to his bride with the same his true bodily blood, so that just as the bride eats a physical bread in her mouth and drinks the wine, so also through belief in the Lord Jesus Christ she has physically received and eaten the noble Bridegroom with his blood in such a way that the Bridegroom and the outpouring of his blood is [one] with hers—and the broken and crucified Christ Jesus. She is in him and, again, he is in her, and they together are thus one body, one flesh, one spirit, and one passion, as bridegroom and bride. . . .

But to the satiated, courtly, rich, and murderous spirits his simple word will become as blood and poison and even death, yea, a table, whereat they are strangled and hanged and receive eternal damnation. . . . Therefore it has been held [in respect to] the ban from the time of the apostles that they who would live according to the will of Satan (as Saint Paul in Gal. 5:19–21 on the first fruits clearly indicated), after three warnings [Matt. 18:15–18] were ejected from Christ Jesus and his Kingdom and delivered over into the Kingdom of Satan and the devil. But insofar as the same turned back in their hearts and gave themselves over to improvement of their wicked way of life, they were again accepted by the congregation through the servants of God and received again into the congregation of the body of Christ Jesus and into the fellowship of his blood. O how well it went when such an ordinance was maintained in the true fear of God!

With all such true apostolic servants and their following the anointed Savior has promised that he wishes to be all the days until the end of this transient world, that is to say: he with his word, Spirit, mind, will, and well-being in her; and she with her spirit, feeling, and all her heart in him. . . . For God the Merciful Father has sent by his power into the world, into flesh, his own eternal Word who has become himself flesh and corporal, in form like unto another man, without sin, and he became a physically visible Word before his death, and also after his resurrection. As such he remains unto eternity. He did not take flesh upon himself but became himself flesh and corporal, in order that he might himself give salvation and pay for the sin of the whole world by means of his guiltless suffering, dying, and the pouring out of his blood. . . .

Therefore . . . do not quarrel and struggle much over words and take a piece somewhere out of God's Word and hold fast to it stubbornly and without understanding. Do not excoriate as lies all other words which are against it and thus abuse and make the apostles and the prophets along with the Holy Spirit of God into liars. For all words of God are of equal weight, also just and free, to him who acquires the right understanding of God and the Key of David.[5] The cloven claws and horns [only] the true apostolic heralds can bear, because [to explicate] the Scripture is not a matter for everybody—to unravel all such involved snarls and cables, to untie such knots—but only for those to whom God has given [the power]. . . .

Let us—all of us who fear God in truth—earnestly pray to God that we may be saved through Christ Jesus from having to think beyond what is the will, the truth, and the command of the Lord to the end that we hold not to our own opinion and to the leaven of the Pharisees and to the manner of the doctors of Scripture, but rather regard it and flee from it as eternal death and follow only after the true understanding of Christ Jesus in order thus to be taught by God himself in our hearts and conscience. Thereto may God help us, the gracious, merciful Father, through Christ Jesus, our Savior and eternal Redeemer. Amen.

Editor's note

In 1531, a 1525 anticlerical movement of the guilds of the city of
Muenster in North Germany against their Catholic bishop embraced
Lutheranism under an eloquent pastor, Bernhard Rothmann.[6] A Wassen-
berg preacher, Henry Roll, then introduced Anabaptist views to
Rothmann. Late in 1533, Rothmann published a confession in which he
advocated believers' baptism and a symbolic view of the Lord's Supper,
which opened Muenster's gates to still more radical chiliasts. Now
Muenster succeeded Hofmann's Strassburg as the new Jerusalem. In
January 1534 two Dutch envoys of John Matthys began rebaptizing in
Muenster, and John of Leiden arrived shortly thereafter.[7] The two
foreign prophets quickly dominated the city, which was then besieged by
the bishop and Protestant forces.

Rothmann was spokesman for the prophets. His first confession of
1534 guided other Anabaptists to Muenster and brought over mercenary
troops when copies were thrown into the camp of the enemy. Rothmann
showed in the last chapter that peaceful Anabaptism in Muenster became
militant only when threatened from outside, and that many Muenster
citizens joined the Anabaptists in defending their city against the bishop.
He also noted that politically supervised communism had been introduced because of military needs but also in an effort to restore the
communal life of the early church (Acts 2:44). In addition, Rothmann
justified the introduction of polygamy, which made sense because of the
few males left within the besieged city.[8] Rothmann explained to the
saints that polygamy was in accordance with the practice of the Old
Testament patriarchs. Communism and plural marriage had been
appointed by God, Rothmann preached, in the New Israel at Muenster.
The introduction of polygamy and John of Leiden's theocratic rule
completed the shift at Muenster from New Testament restoration to a
militant Old Testament messianism.

Bernhard Rothmann   A Confession of Faith and
                             Life of the Church of Christ
                             of Muenster (1534)[9]

Matthew 10, Luke 12. Whoever confesses me before men, him will
I confess before my Heavenly Father.

. . . Concerning Faith

We confess and believe that there is one God and that he rewards
those who seek after him (Heb. 11:6). . . .

We believe also in Jesus Christ, the Son of the living God, who
became man for us poor sinners and died on the cross for our sins
and those of the world, in order that we, freed from sin, might become pure and unspotted in all of our deeds, as it becomes our
calling. . . .

We believe in the Holy Spirit, the master of truth and comforter
of the heavy-laden. Those who remain in Christ are assured through
this Spirit that they will be free and comforted, and that their faith
is the true one.

. . . Concerning Faith in
Christ Jesus

We hold to and believe also in Christ. We confess that Christ Jesus,
crucified under Pontius Pilate, is the true, living Son of God, who
though similar to the Father in glory, lowered and humbled himself,
taking on the form of a servant, and became like humanity, obedient
to the Father unto death, even the death of the cross (Phil. 2); thus
he died and was buried, and rose from the dead on the third day,
and empowered his Kingdom; he then ascended into Heaven, exalted
there over all existence, and is seated at the right hand of the
almighty Father, from where we all are awaiting him, with love and
longing, in readiness for his coming Day, when his enemies will be
laughed at and put under his feet, for he will judge both the living
and the dead.

... Concerning Two Articles of
Faith in Christ, in Which We
Differ from Catholics and
Lutherans

First, Catholics, Lutherans, and others say that Christ was conceived by Mary and took on flesh from Mary's body. We cannot
believe that.[10] . . . John 1 says, "the Word is become flesh," not
Mary's seed. . . . We believe that there is only one Christ, not originating from Mary's flesh and blood, but, as the article of faith
contains, who is conceived by the Holy Spirit, born from Mary the
Virgin. . . . Our savior Christ, the living Son of God, became man
and died in the likeness of sinful flesh, but he did not become sinful
flesh (Rom. 8). . . .

Second, we do not like what the Catholics and Lutherans teach
concerning Christ's works, the fruit of faith.[11] The papists make
little use of faith and also of the good works of Christ, for they are
busy in works which are arranged by their idol, the Antichrist from
Rome, and his tonsured monks, as all know well. But the Lutherans
emphasize faith too much and think little about good works. The
fruit of the true Gospel cannot be found among them, but rather the
opposite, namely, sexual laxity, drunkenness, and gluttony, and
whatever belongs to a fleshly life. . . .

We know and confess, as the Scripture says, that we by nature are
children of wrath, and that no one may be justified before God
except through faith in Christ Jesus (Rom. 3), for he is the only
Mediator who can bring us to salvation (Tim. 5). . . .

For if you look properly into Scripture, you will easily find that
it is not alone faith in Christ which is necessary, but also that we
must become modeled after Christ, so that we follow his footsteps
in all obedience, that we do everything that God has commanded,
and that we refrain from all unrighteousness. . . . Thus, with Scripture, we hold to the necessity of faith and of good works also. . . .

Concerning Baptism

Concerning baptism, we hold to what the Scripture teaches, namely,
that baptism is the covenant of a good conscience with God
(I Pet. 3), and further, the other part, that we are forgiven in
Christ, which means the death of the flesh and all our good works.[12]
And therefore, where no good work is, no one but those who believe
truly may be baptized. Up to now, they are all pushed into water,

which you can do to cats and dogs. But there is no baptism, and
there should be no baptism except belief. As Christ also says (Matt.
16), "Whoever believes and is baptized will be saved." There you
see the two commands of Christ for blessedness. First, he emphasizes faith, through which, out of pure grace, we receive forgiveness
of sins and in the power of the blood of Christ win free access to
the Father. Second, he emphasizes baptism, which cleanses from sin
those who are unbelievers, ties them to God and makes them
obedient, having died to the world, and living according to his will.
For this purpose baptism in Christ is ordained, and one shall use it
in the way the whole Scripture witnesses: Romans 6, Galatians 3,
I Peter 3, Acts 3, 8, 10, 16, 22. . . .

Concerning Life

Since the just shall live by faith, those who want to be made blessed
in Christ must not live according to the flesh, but walk in the Spirit
(Rom. 8). . . . Also, it is written, almighty God, be praise and
thanks forever, that we should live in the fear of God, and also
together lovingly, so that no one among us is too dear to another
one. For we have community of love with each other, as is proper
and as the Scripture says, and also as the Christian article of belief
says, so that with David we can say (Ps. 133:1), "See, how blessed
it is when brothers live together."

And, oh, would to God that the whole world would be converted
to God in their hearts, and would live in a community of love, or at
least that those who bear the name of Christ would take and keep
his commands in their hearts: then much treachery and blood judgment would cease. We witness, before the eyes of God, that we
would rather die the death before we would do or allow, willingly
or knowingly, what is against the Word of God.

Concerning Marriage

Marriage, we say and hold with Scripture, is a binding and obliging
of man and woman in the Lord (Matt. 19, I Cor. 7, Gen. 3).
Marriage is an image of Christ and his church (Eph. 5). Whoever
comes together outside of the Lord has no marriage. . . . The
marriage of unbelievers is sin and impure, and is no marriage before
God. . . . Marriage should be honored by all men; God will judge
fornicators and adulterers. Because marriage is an honorable and

glorious state, no one should enter it lightly, but with pure and true hearts, seeking only the honor and will of God. . . .

We hear, among other evil tidings about us, that in a platonic or nicolaitan fashion, we have wives in common among us and make no distinctions between blood relationships. But this like other statements is fully slanderous and lying. We know that Christ said, "You shall not commit adultery, but I say unto you, whoever looks at a woman lustfully has already committed adultery in his heart." Were such a one to be found among us, we would not permit such circumstances, but would put him under the ban and give his flesh over to the devil. Likewise, regarding grades of relationship, we hold according to the Scriptures (Lev. 18).

The True Causes of Our Present Quarrels

In this city we have busied ourselves to free God's Word from babylonian and papist captivity. After that, the same bishop and his followers sought to push and tear us away from living in God's honor. But we remained steadfast through God's grace. . . . Since they could not succeed in spite of terrible pressure against us, they made a sealed treaty with us that we should no longer be coerced in matters of faith. . . . They did not keep their treaty, for they imprisoned and killed one of our brothers because of his belief.

The godless papists on Wednesday before Martini [November 5, 1533] sought to expel the preachers from the city with weapons, indeed to cut off their noses and ears and to hang them up between two dogs.[13] But God intervened for his little flock and gracefully prevented such a tyrannical and bloody undertaking. Again, it was agreed that they should leave us in peace in matters of faith, and not interfere with us.

Finally that event occurred, from which this war mostly originates. On Monday before Fastnacht [February 9, 1534], the papists, wearing weapons under their clothing, agreeing with the bishop and the canons, sought to take the city by force and deal with us as they wished.[14] In order to prevent this, we then assembled our forces in the marketplace. The godless [probably Lutherans] set up fortifications in the Uberwasser [Church]. Since they were there, and we stood in the marketplace, praying to God who alone helps and protects us, they then opened two doors and let in the bishop's representatives and many people, in order to drive us out. They also

marked themselves and all of the homes of the godless with wreaths
of straw: all who were not so marked, were to be taken away and
plundered. Wasn't that a treacherous deed? But the Almighty pitied
us in our innocence, and with visible wonders, slew our enemies and
drove them out. Since they couldn't reach their goal, because God
wouldn't permit it, they left with their people.

Thus they have begun our present war. Only God knows what the
end will be. We place ourselves under his protection, without fear
for what man will do to us. . . . Yes, they say, we have driven them
out on Friday, February 27, and did not send after them what belonged to them.[15] Yes, it is true. For think, if justice had been done
them, what would they have deserved! We have always previously
let them take their belongings, but not this time, since we are besieged. It was enough that we let them go, for they were openly
God's and our enemy, and we knew that they would try to do
everything evil they could against us.

So it has happened with us, and thus rebellion occurred. In spite
of the devil and the whole world, we did nothing except according
to God's Word and will, and upon this faith were baptized. The
children of men always know how to color things after their own
desires. But may God help truth, and now to Him we commit ourselves and those who fear Him (I John 2:4). Printed in Muenster.

**Thirteen Statements of the
Order of Life and A Code
for Public Behavior**

Editor's note

Following Matthys's death in a sortie against the enemy, John of Leiden
established the rule of the second King David in Zion, moving beyond
New Testament community of goods and previous eschatological
expectation to a realized messianism. The Muenster kingdom now
claimed universal dominion. A Muensterite apostle, like the earlier
Thomas Muentzer, now proclaimed that King John would rule the whole
world and slay all other rulers. The King's seal symbolized that the world
and both authorities, spiritual and secular, belonged to the new David
(a golden apple pierced by two golden swords). Its slogan was "One king
established over all" and "One God, one faith, one baptism."[16] The
former council was replaced by Twelve Elders of the Tribes of Israel.
Although God's laws were now inscribed in the hearts of the elect,
thirteen statements of the order of life spelled them out with frequent
threats of death.

A similar code was issued for public behavior, even listing job
assignments. Ideological and practical communism was enforced in the
city under siege. John of Leiden's executioner, Knipperdolling, even
proposed a slogan: "One God, one pot, one egg, and one kitchen."[17] The
restoration of Zion was completed when polygamy was reintroduced with
a show of male chauvinism and Old Testament rhetoric. A sociological
study of property holding by Rammstedt shows, however, that the ruling
system remained the same in Muenster—only the ruler had changed.[18]

The Twelve Elders of
Muenster

Thirteen Statements of the
Order of [Private] Life
(mid-1534)[19]

Although all of us in this holy church of Muenster, in whose hearts the law and the will of God are inscribed by the finger of God . . . should readily fulfill them, we, twelve elders of the nation, shall nevertheless summarize them briefly in a list in order that the new state may be protected so that each one may see what to do and what not to do. . . .

The Scripture directs that those who are disobedient and unrepentant regarding several sins shall be punished with the sword:

1. Whoever curses God and his holy Name or his Word shall be killed (Lev. 24).

2. No one shall curse governmental authority (Ex. 22, Deut. 17), on pain of death.

3. Whoever does not honor or obey his parents (Ex. 20, 21) shall die.

4. Servants must obey their masters, and masters be fair to their servants (Eph. 6).

5. Both parties who commit adultery shall die (Ex. 20, Lev. 20, Matt. 5).

6. Those who commit rape, incest, and other unclean sexual sins should die (Ex. 22, Lev. 20). . . .

7. Avarice is the root of all evil (I Tim. 6).

8. Concerning robbery, you shall not steal (Ex. 20, Deut. 27): Cursed be he who narrows his neighbor's boundary.

9. Concerning fraud and overcharging (I Thess. 4): The Lord will judge this.

10. Concerning lying and defamation (Wisd. [of Sol.] 1): A lying mouth destroys a soul.

11. Concerning disgraceful speech and idle words (Matt. 12): Men must account for every idle word they speak, on the Day of Judgment.

12. Concerning strife, disputes, anger, and envy (Gal. 5, I John 4): Whoever hates his brother is a murderer.

13. Concerning slander, murmuring, and insurrection among God's people (Lev. 19): There shall be no slanderer or flatterer among the people.

. . . Whoever disobeys these commandments and does not truly repent, shall be rooted out of the people of God, with ban and sword, through the divinely ordained governmental authority.

The Twelve Elders of   A Code for Public Behavior
Muenster   (mid-1534)[20]

The elders of the congregation of Christ in the holy city of Muenster, called and ordained by the grace of the most high and almighty God, desire that the following duties and articles be faithfully and firmly observed by every Israelite and member of the house of God.

1. What the Holy Scriptures command or prohibit is to be kept by every Israelite at the pain of punishment.

2. Everybody is to be industrious in his vocation and fear God and his ordained government. Government authority does not carry the sword in vain, but it is the avenger of evildoers.

3. Every elder is to have a servant as assistant to carry out his orders.

4. Five elders are to supervise the day and night watches, personally inspecting them, lest the negligence of the watch lead the city into danger. . . .

6. Every day from seven to nine o'clock in the morning and from two to four o'clock in the afternoon, six elders are to sit in the market at the appointed place and settle all differences with their decisions.

7. What the elders in common deliberation in this new Israel have found to be good is to be proclaimed and announced by the prophet John of Leiden as faithful servant of the Most High and the holy government to the congregation of Christ and the entire congregation of Israel.

8. Lest among the sincere and unblemished Israelites open transgression against the Word of God be tolerated, and in order that the evildoer and transgressor, if apprehended at an obvious transgression, meet his just punishment, the swordbearer, Bernhard Knipperdoling, will punish him according to his deed. . . .

9. In order to keep the proper order concerning the administration of good, the food-masters are every day to prepare dishes of the kind as was hitherto customary for the brothers and sisters. These are to sit modestly and moderately at separate tables. They must not demand anything apart from what is served to them. . . .

10. Those having guard duty during the day are to eat only
after the others have left, so that the necessary watches are not
neglected. . . .

29. When a stranger who does not adhere to our religion, be it
brother, countryman, or relative, comes to this our holy city, he is
to be referred to the swordbearer, Knipperdoling, so that he can talk
with him. This is not to be done by anyone else.

30. A baptized Christian is not to converse with any arriving
person or pagan stranger and is not to eat with him, lest there arise
the suspicion of treacherous consultation. . . .

33. If, according to God's will, someone is killed by the enemy
or departs otherwise in the Lord, noone is to take his belongings,
such as weapons, clothes, etc. They are to be brought to the swordbearer Knipperdoling, who in turn will pass them on to the elders,
who will then give them to the lawful heirs.

Editor's note

Rothmann's second apologetic booklet revealed the conservative nature
of usual revolutionary ideology. His chiliasm was strongly primitivistic.
Franklin H. Littell has shown the revolutionary effects which resulted
from the blending of the radical hope for the restoration of all things
with the expectation of the restitution of the apostolic church.[21] For
Rothmann the restitution was not a class struggle nor an overthrow of
existing order. Rather, opposition forces at all citizen levels were strug-
gling to restore ideal Christian conditions. Christ was about to return,
and he had already established his kingdom at Muenster. Both community
of goods and polygamy were supported from that religious perspective,
which was at the same time social and communal. Rothmann's apology
is persuasive, demonstrating the strength of its appeal to the embattled
citizens. Indeed, there is evidence that if John of Leiden had attacked the
bishop's army in August 1534 instead of proclaiming himself king, he
might have broken the siege. But it is questionable whether a more
secular ideology would have had an appeal comparable to that of
Rothmann's formidable restitution theology.

Bernhard Rothmann   A Restitution . . . of Christian
Teaching, Faith, and Life . . .
through the Church of Christ
at Muenster (October 1534)[22]

From the history of the people of God we learn that God brings about a restitution after each fall. In Christ a state of well-being had begun and he had restored what had fallen. But it did not last. The higher Jesus Christ has raised mankind, the deeper they have fallen. The papacy brought about the last, dreadful fall, after which the eternal restoration of all things, begun in Christ, shall follow in majesty. . . .

God the Almighty rightly began the restitution, when he awakened Martin Luther. When Luther, however, would not further God's grace, but remained lying in his own pride and filth, then the Antichrist became evident, and the true Gospel began to appear. But the fullness of truth was magnificently introduced in Melchior Hofmann, John Matthys, and here in our brother, John of Leiden. Thus the Kingdom of Christ has begun in Muenster. What has been restored by God in the New Zion will now be shown, point by point.

1. God has again restored the Scripture through us. He has abundantly made his will known to us. And as we earnestly put into practice what we understand, God teaches us further every day.

2. The Muensterites hold to the true understanding of Scripture. . . . Old Testament and New Testament are one. As there is one God, so there is one Scripture. Its purpose is that we know God and his Son, and that we be made perfect for all good works. Everything is portrayed previously in the Old Testament, before it is dealt with in the New Testament. Much more, everything which we await in the New Testament, has been openly anticipated in the Old Testament.

3. God has restored to us the true knowledge of the coming of Christ in the flesh and of his Incarnation. . . . The eternal Word became flesh in Christ, but He did not receive his flesh from Mary's seed. . . .

4. At Muenster, the true knowledge of salvation and satisfaction has been restored. Christ died, not to save the elect, but that all people of the whole world might be saved, without exception. . . .

5. Here true Christian doctrine is restored. "Repent and believe the Gospel. Refrain from evil and do Good." When a man repents and believes in the Gospel, then he is baptized and becomes a member of the holy congregation. From then on, he must follow as a

brother and heir of Christ, in obedience, righteousness, and holiness. If he remains faithful, he will be saved.

6. Baptism is here restored. The Antichrist began child-washing, and made an idol out of water, with his magic. True baptism belongs only to those who understand and believe in Christ.

7. Through God's grace, the true church has been restored to Muenster. For 1,400 years, the truth has been falsified and repressed. . . . The true, holy church cannot be found either among Catholics or Evangelicals. The latter would have better remained papists, than to have taught half-truths, for a half-truth is no truth. . . .

8. We uphold God's commands and good works. The Catholics regard their scheming hypocrisies as true good works, while the Evangelicals emphasize faith too much and misunderstand when they openly say that good works do not help toward salvation. In sum, God wishes obedience and fulfillment of his purpose. The true Christian believes rightly in Christ, and walks uprightly in all His commands.

9. God has restored at Muenster a sound understanding of free will. God has given free will to mankind, so that man might choose good or evil.

10. The living communion of saints has been restored, which provides the basis for community of goods among us. For not only have we put all our belongings into a common pool under the care of decons, and live from it according to our needs: we praise God through Christ with one heart and mind and are eager to help one another with every kind of service. And accordingly everything which has served the purposes of self seeking and private property, such as buying and selling, working for money, taking interest and practising usury—even at the expense of unbelievers—or eating and drinking the sweat of the poor (that is, making one's own people and fellow-creatures work so that one can grow fat) and indeed everything which offends against love—all such things are abolished amongst us by the power of love and community. We know that such sacrifices are pleasing to the Lord. And indeed no Christian or saint can satisfy God if he does not live in such community or at least desire with all his heart to live in it.

11. We have again been given a sound understanding of the Lord's Supper. . . . The Antichrist teaches that he can make a god out of bread. . . . Rather, the Lord's Supper is a remembrance of the Lord. . . . We gather in an appropriate place, after searching our hearts to test whether we are worthy to participate, so that we might,

with true faith, make known the death of the Lord and, in true love for another, break bread with each other. . . .

12. God has restored the true practice of holy matrimony amongst us. Marriage is the union of man and wife—"one" has now been removed—for the honor of God and to fulfill his will, so that children might be brought up in the fear of God. . . .

Freedom in marriage for the man consists in the possibility for him to have more than one wife. . . . This was true of the biblical fathers until the time of the Apostles, nor has polygamy been forbidden by God. What God has provided for, and has been honorably practiced by the holy friends of God, cannot now be forbidden or called shameful.

But the husband should assume his lordship over the wife with manly feeling, and keep his marriage pure. Too often wives are the lords, leading their husbands like bears, and all the world is in adultery, impurity, and whoredom. Nowadays, too many women seem to wear the trousers. The husband is the head of the wife, and as the husband is obedient to Christ, so also should the wife be obedient to her husband, without murmuring and contradiction. . . .

13. Previously, there has been no true understanding of the glory of the Kingdom of Christ on earth. This has been interpreted as referring to the Last Day and to the Kingdom of Heaven. We know, however, that this Kingdom must be fulfilled during our generation, and that the scriptural reference to the Kingdom of Christ must be awaited here on earth. . . .

With his well-armed servants, Christ will defeat the devil and all unrighteousness, and then He will enter into his Kingdom, in full justice and peace. . . . In sum, the people of Christ must inherit the earth. The prophets and the psalmist, together with Christ's parables and the Apocalypse, undeniably give proof of this. . . .

14. Almighty God has renewed the government among us, according to his Word. Previous governments have been so depraved that they have been against God. Now He has raised up a living and mighty Kingdom and Seat of David, in which, through the sword of righteousness, the Kingdom is purified among us and spread out from here, so that a true and peaceful Solomon may enter and possess it. . . .

Human speech is too limited, and the time is too short to tell of all the wonders which the righteous in Muenster have experienced, and still do experience daily. The covenant-comrades outside the city can only come and see what has come to pass. . . .

Editor's note

Rothmann's third apologetic booklet on revenge completed his ideological development. Now he argued, like Muentzer, that there was no point in waiting for God to slay the godless from heaven. Rather, the covenanted elect must root out the godless, before the end comes. The leading Muenster theologian had moved at last beyond Hofmann's peaceful chiliasm. Actually, Matthys's fatal sortie in April (à la Gideon) and Hille Fiekes's Judith-like attack on the bishop anticipated Rothmann's arguments. But his hopes were in vain, though his booklet encouraged frantic efforts by Dutch Anabaptists. The end came for the Muenster kingdom in June 1535. Rothmann's fate is uncertain. John of Leiden, Knipperdolling, and Krechting were flayed alive and their bodies hung in iron cages on the church tower, where the cages remain. Thus the wrath of Christendom descended upon the Kingdom of Muenster.

Bernhard Rothmann   Concerning Revenge
                                 (December 1534)[23]

Psalms 149:1, 6–9.

Concerning the present and the impending wrath of God on the babylonian tyranny, through the glory of all his saints: a report to all brethren scattered here and there.

That the babylonian captivity and godless tyranny will not only be judged but requited doubly, we hold to be so clear and evident on the basis of the whole Old and New Testament Scriptures that it is not necessary to write about it, above all to the brethren, concerning whom we know that they together await these events, knowing that they are certain, just as the brethren wait eagerly for the time when God has completed his activity. This we wish to remain certain of, and to affirm single-mindedly, that the time of wrath is here, and in what way it shall occur. . . .

Concerning the Time of Wrath

The wisdom-writer says: "Everything has its time" and "God judges all things in due season" [Eccles. 3:1, 17]. Just as there is a time of fall and devastation, so there also is a time of wrath and of the restitution of all things, as Acts 3:21 teaches. . . .

Having diligently searched for the time and prayed about it, we have reached the following conclusion, on the basis of Holy Scripture, through God's grace. It is always the time to do God's will, in order that the devil and his kingdom may be opposed and overcome. But God foresaw how long his servants would have to suffer, so that when the suffering of his saints was fulfilled, righteousness might prevail and unrighteousness be condemned and rooted out over the entire world. . . .

Now God has risen in his wrath against his enemies. Whoever wishes to be God's servant, must arm himself in the same way and manner. That time is now here. The day of wrath has begun meaningfully in our midst, and will spread over the entire world. . . .

The imprisonment of fallen Christendom is twenty times longer than the babylonian captivity, just as the sin of Christians was greater than that of the fleshly Israel. The babylonian captivity lasted seventy years, and twenty times seventy makes fourteen hundred. One truly finds that the number of years of this terrible captivity has run its course. Thus we believe, and you must confess it, that the time is already here. . . .

Some of you are still waiting, saying that God himself will come from heaven with his angels to bring revenge against the godless. No, dear brothers. He will come, that is true, but the revenge must be executed first by the servants of God. . . . Thus we, who are covenanted with the Lord, must be His instruments to root out the godless on the day which the Lord has prepared. . . . As Malachi 4:3 says: "Ye shall tread down the wicked; for they shall be ashes under the soles of your feet, in the day that I make, says the Lord of Hosts."

How the Wrath Shall Occur

. . . We must think over the prophecy of Jeremiah correctly (Jer. 8–9; 18–24). Not only should you perceive from it that God's wrath will take place in the last days, but also that it is now at hand, and how the wrath shall occur, namely, that innocent Abel shall use

Cain's murderous weapons against Cain, so that the godless shall fall into the grave.

God promises that he will awaken David for his people. For David prepared with wrath and battle a kingdom of peace for Solomon, and assembled whatever was necessary for the magnificent Temple of God. Then peaceful Solomon came, ruled all of Israel with power and glory, and rebuilt God's Temple with great wisdom. Now also, before the true Solomon, Christ, comes in full power and glory (I Cor. 15:51–58), he has promised to awaken a new David from his people. . . .

Our duke and prince [John of Leiden] has appeared and has already been established upon the throne of David, as formerly the prophet said, "A king, who rules over all" (Ezek. 11:22). God has awakened the promised David, armed together with his people, for revenge and punishment on Babylon. You have now heard what will happen, what rich reward awaits us, and how gloriously we shall be crowned, if only we fight bravely. Whether we live or die, we know that we cannot be lost (II Tim. 2:5; II Cor. 6:9).

God, the Lord of Hosts, who has planned these events from the beginning of the world, and told them through his prophets, may he awaken your heart with the strength of his Spirit and arm you and his whole Israel for the battle, as he pleases, for the sake of his praise and the growing triumph of his Kingdom.

Part 5

The Peaceable Kingdom: Mennonite and Hutterite Reaction

Editor's note

After Muenster fell, apocalptic crusading was discredited among
Anabaptists, while other churchmen saw Anabaptists only as fanatics.
Obbe Philips and especially Menno Simons then reasserted the original
Melchiorite teachings, but without chiliasm and in a stable congregational
form. The more deeply disillusioned Philips defected, however, from
his own movement.[1] Like that of other Spiritualizers unrepresented in
this collection (Carlstadt, Sebastian Franck, Caspar Schwenckfeld), his
radicalism consisted in reducing the church to spiritual inwardness.
Philips saw Hofmann as lacking authority in his spiritual claims, and he
was not about to be fooled again. His account of the Muenster tragedy is
an unmatched spiritual revelation, which displeased the Mennonites,
who owed their baptismal beginnings to Philips.

Obbe Philips lacked organizational boldness. But like most Anabaptists, his conscience was clear, and he spoke the unvarnished truth.
Philips showed remarkable consistency in repudiating fanaticism, in spite
of oversensitive doubts about his own apostolate (he had been ordained
by a disciple of John Matthys) and his lack of confidence in the mission
of those he had ordained (his brother Dietrich, David Joris, and Menno
Simons). Like Menno Simons, Obbe Philips had been moved by the
execution of the first Dutch Anabaptist martyr in 1531. Filled with hope
for the restitution of the apostolic church after he was rebaptized, Philips
continued to restrain the Amsterdam Melchiorites from Muenster
excesses. His unusual toleration of religious dissent places him in the
small group of noble Spiritualizers, far removed in spirit from
bloodthirsty revolutionary fanaticism.

In the first place, we must with all understanding concede and confess that the first church of Christ and the apostles was destroyed
and ruined in early times by Antichrist. . . . All who with us are
called Evangelical know that the whole of the papacy is a Sodom,
a Babylon, an Egypt . . . the work or service of Antichrist. . . .

Thus have we altogether let go all such offices and commissions
and have not wished to re-establish the same, seeking only how each
one might fear, serve, and honor his God and best pursue the way
to service before God in righteous love, peace, and humility.

As these very devout hearts have resolved that they shall serve
God in all such quiet simplicity after the manner of the Fathers and
Patriarchs, . . . and followed without preacher, teacher, or any external assembly, so have some men not been content to serve God
in the simplicity of the Spirit, . . . but have wished to have visible
gods which they could hear, touch, and feel and thus proposed that
there must be established a congregation, assembly, ordination, office, and order, as though no one could be saved unless he stood in
such a congregation or order.

And this was in time revealed, as it was in Israel, which could
no longer exist without a king. Then would they establish a kingdom
the same as the heathen, . . . and thereby angered God no little. . . .
Thus in time this holiness was deceptive and the fieriness became
apparent in some who could no longer contain themselves in such
simplicity; and they presented themselves as teachers and envoys of
God, professing to have been compelled in their hearts by God to
baptize, preach, and teach, and establish a new church, since the
ancient church had perished.

Among these were Doctor Balthasar Hubmaier, Melchior Rinck,
John Hut, John Denck, Louis Haetzer, and Thomas Muentzer. . . .
Among these Melchior Hofmann stood out. He came from upper
Germany to Emden to baptize around three hundred persons publicly in the church in Emden, both burgher and peasant, lord and
servant. . . . This Melchior was a very fiery and zealous man, a very
smooth-tongued speaker who was celebrated for his very great calling and commission, and wrote heatedly against Luther and Zwingli
concerning baptism and other articles. And he interpreted the whole
Apocalypse, in which everyone can hear of what remarkable and
wonderful things are found therein. . . .

This Melchior did not remain longer at Emden but set up as teacher John Trijpmaker, who was well disposed in his eyes and who was a preacher at Emden. Whereupon, Melchior left him; and departed for Strassburg when his zeal drove him hastily on to heed the prophecy of an old man of East Frisia who had prophesied of him that he would freely spread his ministry over the whole earth with the help of his ministers and supporters.

Thus, through the mediation of this prophecy, Melchior removed to Strassburg and there began to preach and to teach here and there in the houses of the burghers. Then to be brief, the authorities sent their servants to take him prisoner. When Melchior saw that he was going to prison, he thanked God that the hour had come and threw his hat from his head and took a knife and cut off his hose at the ankle, threw his shoes away, and extended his hand with the fingers to heaven and swore by the living God who lives there from eternity to eternity that he would take no food and enjoy no drink other than bread and water until the time that he could point out with his hand and outstretched fingers the One who had sent him. And with this he went willingly, cheerfully, and well comforted to prison. . . . During this time the preachers of Emden rose up and condemned all those who were disposed to imitate Melchior in his manner of preaching and calumniating baptism so severely that great dissension and insurrection daily broke out among the burghers; and the preachers resolutely got the upper hand.

Thus it happened that John Trijpmaker, whom Melchior had ordained as a teacher, fled to Amsterdam, taught and baptized there and in other places those whom he found willing and ready. This he did until he was taken prisoner, as were six or seven others, and taken to The Hague to be condemned and put to death. This was, in short, the commencement of the first commission and became the beginning of the movement. . . .

Now when John Trijpmaker was dead, there was no longer anyone who dared to take over or assume the office of apostleship, although there were many who were readily baptized, for baptism came rapidly into vogue among many plain and simple souls. At the same time Melchior had written from prison that baptism should be suspended for two years. Only teaching and admonishing in quiet [were permitted] as with the Temple of Zerubbabel, Ezra, and Haggai. . . .

While Melchior was in prison and John Trijpmaker was dead and no one dared to take up or assume the office of apostleship, there

rose up a prophet in Strassburg named Leonard Joosten, to whom
Melchior was as much devoted as to Elijah, Isaiah, Jeremiah, or one
of the other prophets. . . . Shortly thereafter there also rose up two
prophetesses in Strassburg, the one called Ursula, wife of Leonard
Joosten, the other Barbara. . . . One of the prophetesses prophesied
—and that through a vision—that Melchior was Elijah. . . . Some
among them held that Doctor Caspar Schwenckfeld should be considered Enoch. At that time it was also prophesied that Strassburg
would be the New Jerusalem, and after Melchior was in prison for
a half year, according to the prophecy of the old man in East Frisia,
he would leave Strassburg with 144,000 true preachers, apostles,
and emissaries of God, with powers, signs, and miracles, and with
all such strength of the Spirit that no one could resist them. Thereafter Elijah and Enoch would stand upon the earth as two torches
and olive trees. No one might harm or hinder them; and they would
be dressed in sacks. . . .

Now when these teachings and consolations with all the fantasies,
dreams, revelations, and visions daily occurred among the brethren,
there was no little joy and expectation among us, hoping all would
be true and fulfilled. . . . Before the half year of Melchior's prophesied imprisonment came to an end there arose a baker of Haarlem
named John Matthys, who had an elderly wife whom he deserted,
and he took with him a brewer's daughter who was a very pretty
slip of a girl and had great knowledge of the gospel. . . . He carried
her secretly with him to Amsterdam and brought her to a clandestine
place. When he came there, he professed to have been greatly driven
by the Spirit and [told] how God had revealed great things to him
which he could tell to no one, [and] that he was the other witness,
Enoch.

Now when the friends or brethren heard of this, they became ap-
prehensive and know not what they should best do. For Melchior,
whom they regarded as Elijah, had written that they should follow
Zerubbabel and Haggai in building the "Temple": they should refrain
from baptizing for two years. They had also heard that Cornelius
Polterman was Enoch. When John Matthys learned of this, he carried on with much emotion and terrifying alarm, and with great and
desperate curses cast all into hell and to the devils to eternity who
would not hear his voice and who would not recognize and accept
him as the true Enoch. . . . After much negotiation they attached
themselves to John Matthys and became obedient.

John Matthys as Enoch and an envoy of God (for so he professed to be) introduced them into the office of apostle and sent them out in pairs as true apostles and emissaries of Christ. Some, such as Gerard Boekbinder and John of Leiden, departed for Muenster. Thereafter, through his corrupt activities, John of Leiden became king of Muenster, all of which Gerard Boekbinder later told me in Amsterdam in the presence of Jacob van Campen and several others. . . .

During these events there came to us in Leeuwarden in Frisia two of these commissioned apostles, namely, Bartholomew Boekbinder and Dietrich Kuyper. When some of us gathered together with the others, about fourteen or fifteen persons, both men and women, they proposed and proclaimed to us peace and patience with some words and instructions, and therewith they began to reveal the beginning of their apostleship and the compulsion of the Spirit, and how John Matthys had come to them with such signs, miracles, and agitation of the Spirit that words failed them to describe it enough to us, and they said we should not doubt but that they were no less sent forth with power and miracle than the apostles at Pentecost. Those same words I have reflected on a hundred times. They also comforted us and said we need have no anxiety nor fear as we had long had because of the great tyranny since no Christian blood would be shed on earth, but in a short time God would rid the earth of all shedders of blood and all tyrants and the godless—which at that time did not please me too well in my heart and mind although I did not dare to contradict this because it was then the time that none dared to say much in opposition. . . .

Thus did we on that day almost all permit ourselves to be baptized. The following day, when they were ready to go on, they summoned us along with John Scheerder, at the suggestion of other brethren, and with the laying on of hands laid upon us the office of preaching, [commissioning us] to baptize, teach, and stand before the congregation, etc. . . . and after they had done these things with us, they immediately went forth the same day.

Eight days later came Peter Houtzagher with the same commission, and baptized Dietrich Philips and several others at the time when I was outside the town in the countryside to preach, so that I did not speak with this Peter. But they told me all about it and that there were many of the Zwinglians there who contradicted him so that he did not accomplish much there. After a day or two he de-

parted again for Amsterdam, and as soon as this Peter Houtzagher
was outside Leeuwarden, all prophecy and spiritual braggadocio
ceased. . . . In the meantime Scheerder, my companion, and I set
out again for Leeuwarden on a Sunday and when we arrived at the
town gates around midday, there stood the gatekeeper, who was
about to close the portals. He spoke to us as he saw us approaching
and said that if we wanted to get in, we must enter quickly. When
we heard this we were much alarmed and we asked what the trouble
was. He said: There are Anabaptists in the town who will all be
taken prisoners. Then we became even more frightened and thought
of the prophecies. Nevertheless, we had not reckoned on this and
we gathered up courage and went into the town in the bright midday.
In entering the house I found my wife much distressed, and she
told me of the business about Peter Houtzagher, that some had
strongly spoken out against his word and commission, which resulted
in a great clamor and persecution, begging me to get out of the way
to some other house until it was dark (for it was winter, between
Christmas and Candlemas).

These three men, dear friends, who boasted to us of such commission and apostolic offices and told us that no more blood would be
shed on earth, themselves shortly thereafter through the driving of
the Spirit, walked through Amsterdam [March 23, 1534]. One cried
out: The new city is given to the children of God. Another called:
Repent ye, repent ye and do penance. The third cried: Woe, woe to
all the godless.

Now, as they were captured in the midst of these outcries, they
and some fifteen or sixteen other teachers and brethren were taken
as insurrectionists and Anabaptists to Haarlem, where they were
all condemned and tortured to death. Some were smothered and
put on a pike; then the others were beheaded and set on a wheel.
This I myself thereafter saw and stood among the executed with
some brethren who had traveled with me because I was curious to
know which in the heap those three were who had baptized us and
had proclaimed such calling and promise to us. But we could not
identify them, so frightfully were they changed by the fire and smoke,
and those on the wheels we could not recognize either, nor tell one
from the other. See, dear friends, so did it come to pass with the
first commission among us and such was the reliability of their
prophecies. . . .

After this some others arose who were made teachers by the previous ones mentioned and who had been ordained by John Matthys
—such as Jacob van Campen, a teacher of Amsterdam, Damas of

Hoorn, Leonard Boekbinder, Cornelius from the Brielle, Nicholas
of Alkmaar, Maynard of Delft, and many others, with all of whom
I have spoken and dealt much with—and such strange instruction
was heard among them! One corrupted marriage. The second taught
nothing but parables. The third would pardon no one nor recognize
him as brother who fell into apostasy after baptism and herewith
referred to the willful and knowing sin unto death. The fourth would
have the baptism of John before the baptism of Christ, etc. Others
stood firmly by visions, dreams, and prophecies. Some also were of
the opinion that when the brethren and teachers were put to death,
they would immediately be resurrected and would rule on earth with
Christ a thousand years, and all that they left behind them would
be restored to them a hundredfold. . . . Some had spoken with God,
others with angels—until they got a new trek under way to Muenster.
During this business, those at Muenster accepted the teaching and
commission of the emissaries of John Matthys, namely, Gerard
Boekbinder and John of Leiden; and in time, with the message and
their apostolic role, they took Muenster with the sword and by force.

In this business, the most prominent in Muenster were John
Matthys and John of Leiden, who later became king of Muenster,
also Bernard Rothmann. If one were to describe the beginning and
end of all those events and how it all transpired, one would have to
write a book about it—of the books, writings, and letters they daily
sent to us, of the great signs, wondrous visions, and revelations they
had daily—since such highly celebrated prophets and prophecies
came so quickly to an end and misrepresented themselves. One may
perceive of what spirit they were the children and by what spirit
they were led and driven. Thus we leave this and look further to how
they represented themselves to us in order that we may clarify a
little the trek to Muenster.

This lively interchange with Muenster took place rapidly through
letters and through diverse teachers from Holland who professed
that Muenster and not Strassburg was the New Jerusalem. For Melchior was forgotten with his prophets and prophetesses, with his
apostleship of 144,000 true apostles of Christ out of Strassburg,
with his Elijah role, and all his boasting. . . . This Melchior, who
was to have been Elijah, was soon scorned and forgotten by the
brethren, as already described, when they had Enoch in the Netherlands.

Just as John Matthys was truly Enoch with the true commission
and apostolic office, so he also came to his end and received his
reward according to his works. Melchior died in prison and did not

come out again as the prophets and prophetesses had predicted, and all his intentions with all his following toppled to the ground and came to nothing more. John Matthys, as an apostle and Enoch, was beaten before the gates of Muenster in a skirmish or hostile encounter, for he daily strode there in his armor and with his musket like a wild man out of his senses. He was so fierce and bloodthirsty that he brought various people to their deaths; yea, and he was so violent that even his enemies for their part were terrified of him, and when finally in a tumult they became too powerful for him, they were so incensed that they did not just kill him like other people but hacked and chopped him into little pieces, so that his brethren had to carry him in a basket when the tumult was over. . . .

Thus it continued with muskets, pikes, harquebuses, and halberds. Thus would they fight and no longer suffer. They would put on the armor of David; they would deal out to the godless double their tyranny according to the Scripture. Muenster and not Strassburg was then Jerusalem. Amsterdam was given to the children of God. There one insurrection followed another [notably May 10, 1535]. There the godless would meet their end and be punished. But all that came to nothing. . . .

God knows that Dietrich and I could never find it in our hearts that such onslaughts were right; we taught firmly against this, but it did us no good, for most of the folks were inclined to this . . . Were it not for the love I felt for the simple hearts who were daily misled by the false brethren, I would long ago have left them and departed from all my acquaintances with some of these innocent hearts. . . . I am still miserable of heart today that I advanced anyone to such an office while I was so shamefully and miserably deceived that I did not stop forthwith, but permitted myself to bring poor souls to this —that I through the importuning of the brethren commissioned to the office [apostleship] Dietrich Philips in Amsterdam, David Joris in Delft, and Menno Simons in Groningen.

It is this which is utter grief to my heart and which I will lament before my God as long as I live, before all my companions, as often as I think of them. At the time that I took leave of those brethren I had warned Menno and Dietrich and declared my commission unlawful and that I was therein deceived. I wished from my heart that they had not touched or assumed such an office. I wanted to free my soul in a confession of this before God, acknowledging my guilt and deception. . . . And when I still think of the resigned suffering which occurred among the brethren in Amsterdam, in the Old

Cloister [in Bolsward],[3] in Hazerswoude, in Appingedam, in the
Sandt [in Groningen], and above all at Muenster, my soul is troubled
and terrified before it. I shall be silent about all the false commissions, . . . revelations, . . . and unspeakable spiritual pride which
immediately from the first hour stole in among the brethren. For
those baptized one day cried on the morrow about all the godless,
that they must be rooted out. And actually, as soon as anyone was
baptized, he was at once a pious Christian and slandered all people
and admitted no one on earth to be good but himself and his fellow
brethren. . . . And who can express the great wrangling and dissension among the congregations, of debating and arguing about the
Tabernacle of Moses, the cloven claw, about the commission, the
armor of David, about the thousand-year Kingdom of Christ on
earth, about the incarnation, baptism, belief, Supper, the promised
David, second marriage, free will, predestination, the conscious sin
unto death. . . . Thus it is that a reasonable, impartial Christian may
truly say that it is no Christian congregation but a desolate abomination. . . . Thus was the beginning of the commission and apostolic
office of Elijah and Enoch continued by the teachers and its end
revealed and sufficiently exhibited. . . .

23

My Conversion, Call, and
Testimony

Editor's note

Menno Simons, a former Catholic priest, emerged after Muenster as the
organizational leader of Anabaptists in the North.[4] Repudiating the
violence of Muenster, in which his brother was involved, Menno
experienced conversion from moral shallowness to separate uprightness,
and from what he regarded as doctrinal error (Potestant, Catholic, and
Muensterite) to sound faith. Menno's account of his conversion shows
the clear position he reached and his ordering ability. Eventually the
Mennonites returned to the earlier apolitical principles of the Swiss
Schleitheim Confession. In spite of his rigorous separatism, Menno's
rejection of war did not at first reject Christian rulership. Active himself,
Menno tried to balance doctrine and life, God and man, in his semi-
perfectionist communities. Growing openness toward culture, culminating
in Rembrandt, was one of his legacies to Dutch Mennonitism. His name
became permanently associated, however, with the separate form of
continuing Anabaptism. Going underground to join the Anabaptist
movement in its second generation, Menno's life was hard, and his effort
to stabilize and structure the post-Muenster Anabaptist church involved
him in severe innerchurchly conflicts, of which the most notable was his
reluctant assent to a rigid policy of excommunication (the "ban"),
including forced separation of married couples by the church if one
partner were faithless. This rigid policy of the ban, sponsored by Leonard
Bouwens, Menno's most rigorous associate,[5] resulted in the first permanent Mennonite schism of 1557, which pitted the liberal Waterlanders or
Doopsgezinden (baptism-favorers), who continued Menno's slight
accommodationism among Dutch Mennonites, against the dominant
separatism of Swiss-German Mennonitism.

It happened in the year 1524, the twenty-eighth of my life, that I assumed the duties of a priest in my paternal village called Pinjum. Two others of about my age also officiated in the same functions. The one was my pastor, fairly well educated. The other was below me. Both had read the Scriptures a little, but I had never touched them, for I feared if I should read them, I would be misled. Behold, such an ignorant preacher was I for nearly two years.

In the year following it occurred to me, as often as I handled the bread and wine in the mass, that they were not the flesh and blood of the Lord. I thought that the devil was suggesting this so that he might separate me from my faith. I confessed it often, sighed, and prayed; yet I could not come clear of the ideas.

The two young men mentioned earlier and I spent our time emptily in playing [cards] together, drinking, and in diversions as, alas, is the fashion and usage of such useless people. And when we touched upon the Scriptures I could not speak a word with them without being scoffed at, for I did not know what I was driving at, so concealed was the Word of God from my eyes.

Finally, I got the idea to examine the New Testament diligently. I had not gone very far when I discovered that we were deceived, and my conscience, troubled on account of the aforementioned bread, was quickly relieved, even without any instructions. I was in so far helped by Luther, however, that human injunctions cannot bind into eternal death. . . .

Afterwards it happened, before I had ever heard of the existence of brethren, that a God-fearing, pious hero named Sicke Snijder was beheaded at Leeuwarden for being rebaptized. It sounded very strange to me to hear of a second baptism. I examined the Scriptures diligently and pondered them earnestly, but could find no report of infant baptism.

After I had noticed this I discussed it with my pastor and after much talk he had to admit that there was no basis for infant baptism in Scripture. Still I dared not trust my own understanding, but consulted several ancient authors. They taught me that children are by baptism cleansed from their original sin. I compared this idea with the Scriptures and found that it did violence to the blood of Christ.

Afterwards I consulted Luther. For I sought for the basis of baptism. He taught me that children were to be baptized on account of their own faith. I perceived that this also was not in accordance with the Word of God.

Thirdly I consulted Bucer. He taught that infants are to be baptized so that they might be the more carefully nurtured in the way of the Lord. I perceived that this doctrine was also without foundation.

Fourthly I consulted Bullinger. He pointed to the covenant and to circumcision. This I found likewise to be incapable of scriptural proof.

When I noticed from all these that writers varied so greatly among themselves, each following his own wisdom, then I realized that we were deceived in regard to infant baptism. . . .

Although I had now acquired considerable knowledge of the Scriptures, yet I wasted that knowledge through the lusts of my youth in an impure, sensual, unprofitable life, and sought nothing but gain, ease, favor of men, splendor, name, and fame, as all generally do who sail that ship.

And so, my reader, I obtained a view of baptism and the Lord's Supper through the illumination of the Holy Ghost, through much reading and pondering of the Scriptures, and by the gracious favor and gift of God. . . .

Next in order the sect of Muenster made its appearance, by whom many pious hearts in our quarter were deceived. My soul was much troubled, for I perceived that though they were zealous they erred in doctrine. I did what I could to oppose them by preaching and exhortations, as much as in me was. I conferred twice with one of their leaders, once in private and once in public, but my admonitions did not help, because I myself did that which I knew was not right.

The report spread that I could silence these persons beautifully. Everybody defended himself by a reference to me, no matter who. I saw plainly that I was the stay and defense of the impenitent, who all leaned on me. This gave me no little qualm of conscience. I sighed and prayed: Lord, help me, lest I become responsible for other men's sins. My soul was troubled and I reflected upon the outcome, that if I should gain the whole world and live a thousand years, and at last have to endure the wrath of God, what would I have gained?

Afterwards the poor straying sheep who wandered as sheep without a proper shepherd, after many cruel edicts, garrottings, and slaughters, assembled at a place near my place of residence called

Oude Klooster. And, alas! through the ungodly doctrines of Muenster, and in opposition to the Spirit, Word, and example of Christ,
they drew the sword to defend themselves, the sword which the Lord
commanded Peter to put up in its sheath.

After this had transpired the blood of these people, although
misled, fell so hot on my heart that I could not stand it, nor find
rest in my soul. I reflected upon my unclean, carnal life, also the
hypocritical doctrine and idolatry which I still practiced daily in
appearance of godliness, but without relish. I saw that these zealous
children, although in error, willingly gave their lives and their estates
for their doctrine and faith. And I was one of those who had disclosed to some of them the abominations of the papal system. But
I myself continued in my comfortable life and acknowledged abominations simply in order that I might enjoy physical comfort and
escape the cross of Christ.

Pondering these things my conscience tormented me so that I
could no longer endure it. I thought to myself . . . if I through bodily
fear do not lay bare the foundations of the truth, nor use all my
powers to direct the wandering flock who would gladly do their duty
if they knew it, to the true pastures of Christ—oh, how shall their
shed blood, shed in the midst of transgressions, rise against me at
the judgment of the Almighty and pronounce sentence against my
poor, miserable soul! . . .

I began in the name of the Lord to preach publicly from the
pulpit the word of true repentance, to point the people to the narrow
path, and in the power of the Scripture openly to reprove all sin
and wickedness, all idolatry and false worship, and to present the
true worship; also the true baptism and the Lord's Supper, according
to the doctrine of Christ, to the extent that I had at that time received from God the grace.

I also faithfully warned everyone against the abominations of
Muenster, condemning king, polygamy, kingdom, sword, etc. After
about nine months or so, the gracious Lord granted me his fatherly
spirit, help, and hand. Then I, without constraint, of a sudden,
renounced all my worldly reputation, name, and fame, my unchris-
tian abominations, my masses, infant baptism, and my easy life, and
I willingly submitted to distress and poverty under the heavy cross
of Christ. In my weakness I feared God; I sought out the pious, and
though they were few in number I found some who were zealous
and maintained the truth. I dealt with the erring, and through the

help and power of God with his Word, reclaimed them from the snares of damnation and gained them to Christ. The hardened and rebellious I left to the Lord.

And so you see, my reader, in this way the merciful Lord through the liberal goodness of his abounding grace took notice of me, a poor sinner, stirred in my heart at the outset, produced in me a new mind, humbled me in his fear, taught me to know myself in part, turned me from the way of death and graciously called me into the narrow pathway of life and the communion of his saints. . . .

It happened about one year after this while I was secretly exercising myself in the Word of God by reading and writing that some six, seven, or eight persons came to me who were of one heart and one soul with me, beyond reproach as far as man can judge in doctrine and life, separated from the world after the witness of Scripture and under the cross, men who sincerely abhorred not only the sect of Muenster, but the cursed abominations of all other worldly sects. . . . They urged me to put to good use the talents which I, though unworthy, had received from the Lord.

At last, after much prayer, before the Lord and his church I gave these conditions: that we should pray earnestly to the Lord for a season. Then if it should be pleasing to his holy will that I could or should labor to his praise, he would give me such a mind and heart as would say to me with Paul, Woe is me, if I preach not the Gospel. And if not, that he might employ means so that nothing would come of it. . . .

In this way, my reader, I was not called by the Muensterites nor any other seditious sect as it is falsely reported concerning me, but I have been called, though unworthy, to this office by the people who had subjected themselves to Christ and his Word, led a penitent life in the fear of God, served their neighbors in love, bore the cross, sought the welfare and the weal of all men, loved righteousness and truth, and abhorred wickedness and unrighteousness. And so I, a miserable sinner, was enlightened of the Lord, was converted to a new mind, fled from Babel, entered into Jerusalem, and finally, though unworthy, was called to His high and heavy service. . . .

He who purchased me with the blood of his love . . . knows that I seek not wealth, nor possessions, . . . but only the praise of the Lord, my salvation, and the salvation of many souls. Because of this, I with my poor, weak wife and children have for eighteen years endured excessive anxiety, oppression, affliction, misery, and persecution. . . . Yes, when the preachers repose on easy beds and soft

pillows, we generally have to hide ourselves in out-of-the-way cor-
ners. When they at weddings and baptismal banquets revel with pipe,
trumpet, and lute, we have to be on our guard when a dog barks
for fear the arresting officer has arrived. When they are greeted as
doctors, lords, and teachers by everyone, we have to hear that we
are Anabaptists, bootleg preachers, deceivers, and heretics, and be
saluted in the devil's name. In short while they are gloriously
rewarded for their services with large incomes and good times, our
recompense and portion must be fire, sword, and death. . . . He that
feareth God let him read and judge.

Editor's note

Having left "Babylon" (the Roman Catholic Church) after the fall of
Muenster, Menno Simons responded favorably to the eschatological
views of the radical prophets, without ever believing their exaggerated
claims for themselves or engaging in chiliastic speculations. Menno took
seriously the Pauline teaching about the "new creature" in Christ. The
new believer could have an "obedient flesh" derived from Christ's
heavenly flesh. Since Christ alone was the promised David, Menno taught
an Erasmus-like nonresistant pacifism for the Christian, as opposed to
war, the device of Antichrist. He consistently repudiated accusations that
he had ever advocated Muensterite sedition or communism.

Yet Menno, advancing in his last years to rejection of capital punishment as well as war, did not completely deny the possibility that a
Christian might wield the sword of justice. He wavered between withdrawing from and transforming the world. Menno ardently defended
religious liberty because the new creature in Christ must be free from
external coercion. At the same time, he insisted that faith must issue in
obedience, including the scriptural ordinances of baptism, the supper, and
the ban. In the decade following his death, Menno's followers crystal-
lized his teaching into more radical apoliticism than he himself had
exemplified. The rigid conservatism of the Mennonites replaced the more
radical dialectic of Menno.

Menno Simons   A Reply to False Accusations
(1552)[7]

I. In the first place, they complain and accuse us of being Muensterites, and warn all people to beware of us and take an example from those of Muenster.

Answer. We do not like to reprove and judge those who are already reproved and judged of God and man; yet since we are assailed so fiercely with this matter and without basis in truth, therefore we would say this much in defense of all of us—that we consider the doctrine and practice of those of Muenster in regard to king, sword, rebellion, retaliation, vengeance, polygamy, and the visible kingdom of Christ on earth a new Judaism and a seductive error, doctrine, and abomination, far removed from the Spirit, Word, and example of Christ. Behold, in Christ Jesus, we lie not.

Besides, I can fearlessly challenge anybody that none under heaven can truthfully show that I ever agreed with the Muensterites in regard to these points. From the beginning until the present moment I have opposed them diligently and earnestly, both privately and publicly, with mouth and pen, for over seventeen years, ever since according to my ability I confessed the Word of the Lord and knew and sought His holy name. [Menno's very first booklet, directed against John of Leiden, appeared in the spring of 1535. Hence this present reply is of the year 1552.]

I also according to my small talent have faithfully warned everybody against their errors and abomination, just as I would want other people to do for my soul. And, in passing, I have pointed and returned several of them to the true way by the grace, assistance, and power of the Lord.

I have never seen Muenster nor have I ever been in their fellowship. And I trust that by the grace of God, I shall never eat nor drink with such if there should be any left, even as the Scripture teaches me, unless they sincerely acknowledge their abomination, and truly repent, and follow the truth and the Gospel in a genuine way.

Behold, kind reader, this is my understanding and opinion of the Muensterites, and it also is the opinion of all those who are known and accepted of us as brethren and sisters, that is, those who on account of the false doctrine, unclean pedobaptism, and Supper of the preachers, are visited with such a flood of misery, oppression, and anxiety, and who assert and testify unto death their pure doctrine of baptism and Supper, with a humble confession and a pious, blameless life.

But all those who repudiate the cross of Christ, as did the Muensterites, and turn their backs upon the Word of the Lord; who go back to their worldly love, howbeit with a pious exterior; who agree with the false religion again and fellowship with it, walk in pomp, pride, and drunkenness, walk again on the broad road, even though they may be baptized—these we do not know nor accept as brethren and fellows, inasmuch as they do not abide in the Word of the Lord. . . .

II. In the second place, they say that we will not obey the magistracy.

Answer. The writings which we have published during several years past prove clearly that this accusation against us is untrue and false. We publicly and unequivocally confess that the office of a magistrate is ordained of God, even as we have always confessed, since according to our small talent we have served the Word of the Lord. And moreover, in the meantime, we have obeyed them when not contrary to the Word of God. We intend to do so all our lives. For we are not so stupid as not to know what the Lord's Word commands in this respect. Taxes and tolls we pay as Christ has taught and himself practiced. We pray for the imperial majesty, kings, lords, princes, and all in authority. We honor and obey them (I Tim. 2:2; Rom. 13:1). And yet they cry that we will not obey the magistrates, in order that they may disturb the hearts of those that have authority and excite them to all unmercifulness, wrath, and bitterness against us, and that by their continual agitation the bloody sword may be used against us without mercy and never be sheathed, as may be seen. . . .

III. In the third place, they say that we are seditionists and that we would take cities and countries if we had the power.

Answer. This prophecy is false and will ever remain so; and by the grace of God, time and experience will prove that those who thus prophesy according to the Word of Moses are not of God. Faithful reader, understand what I write.

The Scriptures teach that there are two opposing princes and two opposing kingdoms: the one is the Prince of peace; the other the prince of strife. Each of these princes had his particular kingdom and as the prince is so is also the Kingdom. The Prince of peace is Christ Jesus; His kingdom is the kingdom of peace, which is His church; His messengers are the messengers of peace; His Word is

the word of peace; His body is the body of peace; His children are
the seed of peace; and His inheritance and reward are the inheritance of peace. In short, with this King, and in his kingdom and
reign, it is nothing but peace. Everything that is seen, heard, and
done is peace.

We have heard the word of peace, namely, the consoling Gospel
of peace from the mouth of His messengers of peace. We, by His
grace, have believed and accepted it in peace and have committed
ourselves to the only, eternal, and true Prince of peace, Christ Jesus,
in His Kingdom of peace and under His reign, and are thus by the
gift of His Holy Spirit, by means of faith, incorporated into His
body. And henceforth we look with all the children of His peace for
the promised inheritance and reward of peace.

Such exceeding grace of God has appeared unto us poor, miserable sinners that we who were formerly no people at all and who
knew of no peace are now called to be such a glorious people of
God, a church, kingdom, inheritance, body, and possession of peace.
Therefore we desire not to break this peace, but by His great power
by which He has called us to this peace and portion, to walk in this
grace and peace, unchangeably and unwaveringly unto death.

Peter was commanded to sheathe his sword. All Christians are
commanded to love their enemies; to do good unto those who abuse
and persecute them; to give the mantle when the cloak is taken, the
other cheek when one is struck. Tell me, how can a Christian defend
scripturally retaliation, rebellion, war, striking, slaying, torturing,
stealing, robbing and plundering and burning cities, and conquering
countries?

The great Lord who has created you and us, who has placed our
hearts within us knows, and He only knows that our hearts and
hands are clear of all sedition and murderous mutiny. By His grace
we will ever remain clear. For we truly confess that all rebellion is
of the flesh and of the devil. . . .

IV. In the fourth place, some of them charge that we have our
property in common.

Answer. This charge is false and without truth. We do not teach
and practice community of goods. But we teach and maintain by
the Word of the Lord that all truly believing Christians are members
of one body and are baptized by one Spirit into one body (I Cor.
12:13); they are partakers of one bread (I Cor. 10:18); they have
one Lord and one God (Eph. 4:5, 6).

Inasmuch as then they are one, therefore it is Christian and reasonable that they piously love one another, and that the one member be solicitous for the welfare of the other, for this both the Scripture and nature teach. The whole Scripture speaks of mercifulness and love, and it is the only sign whereby a true Christian may be known. As the Lord says, By this shall all men know that you are my disciples (that is, that ye are Christians), if ye love one another (John 13:35). . . .

Concerning Community of Goods

Editor's note

Besides the Mennonites (from whom a radical split, the Amish, occurred in Switzerland about 1690), the second continuing group of Anabaptists were the Hutterites. Before Muenster, Jakob Hutter (a hatter) began a communal type of Anabaptism among refugees to the Tyrol (1533).[8] Hutter was martyred after two years. But the Hutterites, whose one hundred Bruderhofs (farm colonies) numbered 25,000 persons in Moravia and Slovakia during their most flourishing period, 1560 to 1590, still preserve Christian communism today, numbering about 10,000 members in 120 colonies in the United States and Canada. The second Hutterite founder, Peter Riedemann, wrote his confession of faith for Philip of Hesse, who had imprisoned him in the 1540s.[9] Its brief section on community of goods is included here. The Hutterites based their complete sharing of goods upon the Bible.[10] Their motives were brotherly love, Gelassenheit (a mystical term meaning complete yielding to God's will), and obedience to divine commandments. During their long struggles, the Hutterites often found that the Turks treated their communities more fairly than did the Christians. Although the Hutterites did not impose their system of community of goods by force, as did Thomas Muentzer and the Muensterites, they achieved the most radical and successful social revolution in sixteenth-century Germany. Few communities in history have for so long a time curbed the influences of private property and family life in a viable religious community.

Now, since all the saints have fellowship in holy things, that is in
God, who also hath given to them all things in His Son Christ
Jesus—which gift none should have for himself, but each for the
other; as Christ also hath nought for Himself, but hath everything
for us, even so all the members of His body have nought for themselves, but for the whole body, for all the members. . . .

Now, since all God's gifts—not only spiritual, but also material
things—are given to man, not that he should have them for himself
or alone but with all his fellows, therefore the communion of saints
itself must show itself not only in spiritual but also in temporal
things; that as Paul saith, one might not have abundance and
another suffer want, but that there may be equality. . . .

Furthermore, one seeth in all things created, which testify to us
still today, that God from the beginning ordained nought private for
man, but all things to be common. But through wrong taking, since
man took what he should not and forsook what he should take, he
drew such things to himself and made them his property, and so
grew and became hardened therein. Through such wrong taking and
collecting of created things he hath been led so far from God that he
hath even forgotten the Creator, and hath even raised up and
honored as God the created things which had been put under and
made subject to him. And such is still the case if one steppeth out
of God's order and forsaketh the same.

Now, however, as hath been said, created things which are too
high for man to draw within his grasp and collect, such as the sun
with the whole course of the heavens, day, air, and suchlike, show
that not they alone, but all other created things are likewise made
common to man. That they have thus remained and are not possessed by man is due to their being too high for him to bring under
his power, otherwise—so evil had he become through wrong taking
—he would have drawn them to himself as well as the rest and
made them his property.

That this is so, however, and that the rest is just as little made by
God for man's private possession, is shown in that man must forsake all other created things as well as this when he dies, and can
carry nothing with him to use as his own. For which reason Christ
also called temporal all things foreign to man's essential nature, and

saith, "If ye are not faithful in what is not your own, who will
entrust to you what is your own?"

Now, because what is temporal doth not belong to us, but is
foreign to our true nature, the law commandeth that none covet
strange possessions, that is, set his heart upon and cleave to what
is temporal and alien. Therefore whosoever will cleave to Christ
and follow Him must forsake such taking of created things and
property, as He Himself also saith, "Whosoever forsaketh not all
that he hath cannot be my disciple." . . . Now, he who thus becometh free from created things can then grasp what is true and
divine; and when he graspeth it, and it becometh his treasure, he
turneth his heart toward it, emptieth himself of all else and taketh
nought as his, and regardeth it no longer as his but as of all God's
children. Therefore we say that as all the saints have community in
spiritual gifts, still much more should they show this in material
things, and not ascribe the same to and covet them for themselves,
for they are not their own; but regard them as of all God's children,
that they may thereby show that they are partakers in the community
of Christ and are renewed into God's likeness. . . .

For this reason the Holy Spirit also at the beginning of the church
began such community right gloriously again, so that none said that
aught of the things that he possessed was his own, but they had all
things in common; and it is his will that this might still be kept, as
Paul saith, "Let none seek his own profit but the profit of another,"
or, "Let none seek what benefiteth himself but what benefiteth
many." Where this is not the case it is a blemish upon the church
which ought verily to be corrected. If one should say, it was so
nowhere except in Jerusalem, therefore it is now not necessary, we
say, Even if it were nowhere but in Jerusalem, it followeth not that
it ought not to be so now. For neither apostles nor churches were
lacking, but rather the opportunity, manner, and time.

Therefore this should be no cause for us to hesitate, but rather
should it move us to more and better zeal and diligence, for the
Lord now giveth us both time and cause so to do. That there was no
lack of either apostles or churches is shown by the zeal of both. For
the apostles have pointed the people thereto with all diligence and
most faithfully prescribed true surrender, as all their epistles still
prove today.

And the people obeyed with zeal, as Paul beareth witness—especially of those of Macedonia—saying, "I tell you of the grace that

is given to the churches in Macedonia. For their joy was the most rapturous since they had been tried by much affliction, and their poverty, though it was indeed deep, overflowed as riches in all simplicity. For I bear witness that with all their powers, yea, and beyond their power, they were themselves willing, and besought us earnestly with much admonition to receive the benefit and community of help which is given to the saints; and not as we had hoped, but first gave themselves to the Lord, and then to us also, by the will of God."

Here one can well see with what inclined and willing hearts the churches were ready to keep community not only in spiritual but also in material things, for they desired to follow the master Christ, and become like Him and one with Him, who Himself went before us in such a way, and commanded us to follow Him.

Part 6

Revolution: Protestant Resistance in Germany, Scotland, France, and the Netherlands

Editor's note

The documents in Part 6 present revolutionary themes as developed by
First Reformation authors, both Protestant and Catholic. They provide
a counterbalance to the themes expounded by Second Reformation
writers (Parts 1–5) and serve as a bridge to our First and Second
Reformation testimonies concerning the Puritan Revolution in England.
Although they originated with the reluctantly revolutionary German
reformer Martin Luther, First Reformation revolutionary movements in
the latter part of the sixteenth century developed elsewhere than in
Germany, largely under Calvinist auspices, and culminated in the
Scottish, French, and Dutch national-religious revolutions against
entrenched Catholic regimes.

The German former monk, who originated the Reformation in a
dispute over the validity of indulgences and argued from a new
theological perspective of justification by faith, curtailed his attack on
the Roman Catholic Church when his radical associates, Carlstadt and
the Zwickau prophets, seemed to encourage violence against enemies of
the new Protestant cause (see Documents 5–9). Both from the perspective of his dualistic "Two Kingdoms" doctrine and from his political
situation in Saxony as a subject of Prince Frederick, Martin Luther
counseled obedience to secular authority even when Catholic policies
predominated. Until 1530, Luther sternly warned against resistance to
rulers; he attempted to distinguish between active and passive resistance,
allowing only the latter.[1] The Lutheran attempt to achieve confessional
status—the Augsburg Confession of 1530—was rejected by the
Catholic Emperor Charles V, who gave the Lutherans a year to submit
before he would war on them. Charles failed to carry out his threat for
years because of his own wars with the French, the pope, and the
Turks. In 1530, together with Justus Jonas and Melanchthon, Luther
allowed himself to be persuaded by his jurists into signing a resolution
which conceded that, according to secular laws, the German princes
had the right to resist the emperor with force.[2] A military League of
Schmalkalden was formed by Protestant princes and cities in 1531. In a

letter to Spengler in 1531, Luther reassured the more conservative
Nuernbergers that resistance to the emperor still lacked theological
justification, although he conceded to his jurists that is was legally
allowable. After this crisis had been peaceably resolved, the pope
reopened the issue, and as his disputation of 1539 shows, Luther at last
asserted, clearly but still cautiously, that active resistance to the
emperor might be permissible for Christian princes.

Martin Luther   Resistance Supported Legally,
                                    Not Theologically (Letter to
                                    Lazarus Spengler in
                                    Nuernberg, March 18, 1531)[3]

. . . We have placed this proposition before the jurists: If they find
(as some think they do) that the imperial law teaches resistance as
a matter of self-defense in such a case, we cannot check the course
of temporal justice.

For as theologians we are obliged to teach that a Christian is not
to offer resistance but to suffer everything. Nor is he to plead the
shift: It is permissible to repel force by force.

If, therefore, the jurists are right in saying that a Christian may
offer resistance, not as a Christian but as a citizen or member of the
body politic, we let that pass.

We speak about the members of Christ and the body ecclesiastical;
we know well enough that a Christian as a citizen or member of the
body politic may bear the sword and a temporal office. We have
often written of this matter.

But our office will not allow our advising a member of the body
politic to offer such resistance; nor are we acquainted with their
statute law. They will have to take this responsibility upon their
conscience. . . .

Martin Luther   Disputation Concerning the
                                    Right to Resist the Emperor
                                    (May 8–9, 1539)[4]

If one may resist the pope, one may also resist all the emperors and
dukes who contrive to defend the pope. . . . The pope . . . wishes
. . . every soul . . . to go to hell for his sake. Hence it is necessary
that one march against his soldiers that war under him and go out
to meet them even though it mean a revolution. For we can not

allow the damnation of souls. I am obliged to lay down my life for
the emperor, but not my soul.

If the emperor defends the pope, who is a wolf, one is not to
yield or stand for it, but one must attack him. . . . Self-defense is
the natural course.

The princes must resist the tyrants, a thing which the First Table
also requires. The emperor and Ferdinand are seeking first and foremost to get our goods, but still under the cover of the pope.

A Confession of the Magdeburg Pastors Concerning Resistance to the Superior Magistrate

Editor's note

Luther did not live to see what he had feared: the fiasco of the Schmalkaldic War, with the victory of the emperor at Muehlberg in 1547 and the disaster of the Interim. The leading Protestant princes, John Frederick of Saxony and Philip of Hesse, were imprisoned after their defeat at Muehlberg. The Augsburg Interim, which gave the Protestants a few concessions until the meeting of a general council, was promulgated in 1548. The German princes now lacked the power to resist the emperor that Luther had reluctantly conceded them. Many Protestant pastors were exiled when they failed to support the Interim.

The real center of Lutheran resistance was the city of Magdeburg, under the orthodox Lutheran pastors Nicholas Gallus, Nicholas Amsdorf, and Matthias Flacius Illyricus. In 1550, nine theologically conservative pastors of Magdeburg issued a confession presenting a full resistance doctrine, which was supported later by Calvinists. In it the people of Magdeburg justified the necessary resistance of their own magistrates to the emperor, who sought to destroy their religion. Gallus and his friends also argued that the princes were still bound to support the Magdeburgers against the forced oaths of the princes to execute the imperial ban against Magdeburg. They cautiously affirmed also that the magistrates were justified, although not required, to resist any higher authority which attempted unjustly to take away the peoples' lives, liberty, or property. The Magdeburg Confession thus was the first formal assertion of a theory of rightful resistance issued by orthodox Protestants.

Nicholas Gallus et al.   A Confession of the
Magdeburg Pastors Concerning
Resistance to the Superior
Magistrate (April 13, 1550)[5]

We will undertake to show that a Christian government may and should defend its subjects against a higher authority which should try to compel the people to deny God's Word and to practice idolatry.

We scarcely expect to convince the Catholics that subjects may resist their Lord and a lower magistrate may resist a higher if he seeks to uproot the Christian religion, for the Catholics do not admit that we have the Christian religion and consequently think they have the right to make war upon us.

Our object is primarily to allay the scruples of those who do adhere to the true Word of God. . . .

But first we would address ourselves to the Emperor and beg him not to let the Pope persecute the Lord, Christ. But if your Majesty will not concede that Lutherans are Christians, bear in mind that Christ was considered a blasphemer, and He has shown us one mark of the true Church, namely that it should not constrain anyone with the sword as the Roman Church does. Obedience to God and to Caesar are not incompatible, provided each stays within his own proper sphere. Your Majesty has gone beyond your office and encroached upon the Kingdom of Christ. Your present dissatisfaction with us is no one's fault but your own, and we may say to you in the words of Elijah to Ahab, "It is not I that troubles Israel but you."

We will show from Holy Scripture that if a higher magistrate undertakes by force to restore popish idolatry and to suppress or exterminate the pure teaching of the Holy Gospel, as in the present instance, then the lower godfearing magistrate may defend himself and his subjects against such unjust force in order to preserve the true teaching, the worship of God together with body, life, goods, and honor.

The powers that be are ordained of God to protect the good and punish the bad (Romans 13), but if they start to persecute the good, they are no longer ordained of God.

There are to be sure degrees of tyranny and if a magistrate makes unjust war upon his subjects contrary to his plighted oath, they may resist, though they are not commanded to do so by God.

But if a ruler is so demented as to attack God, then he is the very devil who employs mighty potentates in Church and State. When, for example, a prince or an emperor tampers with marriage against the dictates of natural law, then in the name of natural law and Scripture he may be resisted.

Praise be to God. Because He lives we also shall live and be exalted since now we suffer with Him and for his sake we are killed all the day long (Psalm 44).

[Signed by Nicholas Amsdorf, Nicholas Gallus, Lucas Rosenthal, John Stengel, H. Freden, A. Hitfeldius, I. Baumgarten, I. Wolterstorpius, and H. Gercken.]

Constitutional Magistrates Ought to Check the Tyranny of Kings

Editor's note

A generation younger than Luther, John Calvin from Noyon, France, became the second major reformer, directing his mission from exile in Geneva to the great French nation rather than confining his outreach to a single Swiss city, as did Zwingli in Zurich. Calvin not only strengthened the powerful Huguenot (Protestant) movement in France, but also helped change the whole religious and political configuration of Europe through his masterful exposition of biblical theology (the *Institutes*) and his ability to mold strenuous civic reform in Geneva.[6]

Like Luther, Calvin was reluctant to recommend resistance to tyrants. He consistently rejected any suggestion that a private citizen had a right to resist his ruler. From the first edition of the *Institutes* in 1536 until the last in 1559 he urged that Christians wait until intolerable governments are overturned by God's use of the wrath of men or by the actions of the lower magistrates, who are constitutional defenders of liberty. The latter, "ephors" argument (at the end of the *Institutes*, paragraph four of our excerpt) eventually had more influence in a revolutionary direction than all of Calvin's countless warnings against disobedience. Derived perhaps from the Zurich reformer Zwingli in 1524 or from the Strassburg reformer Butzer a bit later, Calvin's "magistrates of the people" argument needed only the proper context of armed conflict with the French king and the writings of eager Calvinist theorists to develop into a powerful revolutionary ideology, its animus against tyrants reaching in a secular form to the Estates General of 1789.

John Calvin   Constitutional Magistrates
                                 Ought to Check the Tyranny
                                 of Kings (1536 and 1559)[7]

. . . Let us then also call this thought to mind, that it is not for us
to remedy such evils; that only this remains, to implore the Lord's
help, in whose hand are the hearts of kings, and the changing of
kingdoms (Prov. 21:1). . . . Before his face all kings shall fall and
be crushed, and all the judges of the earth, that have not kissed his
anointed (Ps. 2:10–11). . . .

However these deeds of men are judged in themselves, still the
Lord accomplished his work through them alike when he broke the
bloody scepters of arrogant kings and when he overturned intolerable governments. Let the princes hear and be afraid.

But we must, in the meantime, be very careful not to despise or
violate that authority of magistrates, full of venerable majesty, which
God has established by the weightiest decrees, even though it may
reside with the most unworthy men, who defile it as much as they
can with their own wickedness. For, if the correction of unbridled
despotism is the Lord's to avenge, let us not at once think that it is
entrusted to us, to whom no command has been given except to
obey and suffer.

I am speaking all the while of private individuals. For if there are
now any magistrates of the people, appointed to restrain the willfulness of kings (as in ancient times the ephors were set against the
Spartan kings, or the tribunes of the people against the Roman
consuls, or the demarchs against the senate of the Athenians; and
perhaps, as things now are, such power as the three estates exercise
in every realm when they hold their chief assemblies), I am so far
from forbidding them to withstand, in accordance with their duty,
the fierce licentiousness of kings, that, if they wink at kings who
violently fall upon and assault the lowly common folk, I declare
that their dissimulation involves nefarious perfidy, because they dis-
honestly betray the freedom of the people, of which they know that
they have been appointed protectors by God's ordinance.

But in that obedience which we have shown to be due the authority of rulers, we are always to make this exception, indeed, to observe it as primary, that such obedience is never to lead us away
from obedience to him, to whose will the desires of all kings ought
to be subject, to whose decrees all their commands ought to yield,
to whose majesty their scepters ought to be submitted. . . . The Lord,

therefore, is the King of Kings, who, when he has opened his sacred mouth, must alone be heard, before all and above all men; next to him we are subject to those men who are in authority over us, but only in him. If they command anything against him, let it go unesteemed. And here let us not be concerned about all that dignity which the magistrates possess; for no harm is done to it when it is humbled before that singular and truly supreme power of God.

[1599 edition:] On this consideration, Daniel denies that he has committed any offense against the king when he has not obeyed his impious edict (Dan. 6:22–23). For the king had exceeded his limits, and had not only been a wrongdoer against men, but, in lifting up his horns against God, had himself abrogated his power. Conversely, the Israelites are condemned because they were too obedient to the wicked proclamation of the king (Hos. 5:13). For when Jeroboam molded the golden calves, they, to please him, forsook God's Temple and turned to new superstitions (I Kings 12:30). With the same readiness, their descendants complied with the decrees of their kings. The prophet sharply reproaches them for embracing the king's edicts (Hos. 5:11). Far, indeed, is the pretense of modesty from deserving praise, a false modesty with which the court flatterers cloak themselves and deceive the simple, while they deny that it is lawful for them to refuse anything imposed by their kings. As if God had made over his right to mortal men, giving them the rule over mankind! Or as if earthly power were diminished when it is subjected to its author, in whose presence even the heavenly powers tremble as suppliants!

[1536 edition:] I know with what great and present peril this constancy is menaced, because kings bear defiance with the greatest displeasure, whose "wrath is a messenger of death" (Prov. 16:14), says Solomon. But since this edict has been proclaimed by the heavenly herald, Peter—"We must obey God rather than men" (Acts 5:29)—let us comfort ourselves with the thought that we are rendering that obedience which the Lord requires when we suffer anything rather than turn aside from piety. . . .

Editor's note

Theodore Beza, a clergyman and Calvin's chief aide and successor in
Geneva, wrote a defense of the burning of heretics in 1554, attempting to
answer Castellio's denunciation of Calvin's burning of Servetus.[8] In the
course of proving to his satisfaction that magistrates have the right to
crush heresy by force, Beza analyzed the nature and function of
government and the limitations that can legitimately be applied to it.
He insisted that local government authorities have the right to defy
superior authorities on religious issues: he cited Magdeburg's defiance
of the emperor's Interim as an example. Slightly later, Beza's lawyer-
friend François Hotman was actively involved in the Amboise
Conspiracy against King Francis II.[9] And in 1562, Beza himself helped
to organize the revolt against Guise control of the monarchy, which
became the first French war of religion, by proposing the revolutionary
theory which French Calvinists then directed against the Catholic king.

Beza had enormous influence on his contemporaries. Huguenots,
Dutch, Germans, Scots, English Puritans, and American colonists all
quoted him or asked his counsel. John Whitgift, Queen Elizabeth's
anti-Puritan archbishop, complained to Beza about his seven publications
attempting to obtrude the Geneva discipline upon the churches and
bring back democracy in England and Scotland. An edition of Beza's
Latin Testament, teaching political Calvinism through its annotations,
appeared annually in England for a half-century. Beza thus had removed
Calvin's doctrinal restraint against resistance at a time when pressure
was mounting for military action among Calvinists, and consequently,
despite his doctrinal conservativism, he exerted notably radical influence
upon the religion and politics of his age.

Theodore Beza On the Authority of the
Magistrates to Punish
Heretics (1554)[10]

. . . Since therefore all councils and assemblies of men joined by
oath, which we call cities, have this ultimate goal, to help men live
the happiest possible lives; moreover in order to attain this goal,
certain laws must be maintained, some men [are] constituted cus-
todians and protectors of these laws, [these men] being called in the
general Greek vocabulary *archas* and in the Latin the Magistrate.

It is well known, unless I am mistaken, that the Magistrate is he
who by the public consent of the citizens is declared custodian of
that peace and tranquility. This peace depends on the observation
of laws which established the safety of all the citizens. . . .

Therefore, to define concisely the Magistrate, let us say that it is
he who is constituted in the Republic for the conservation of all
things public as well as private, sacred as well as profane, in order
that the citizens of the Republic which he superintends live the
happiest life possible. . . .

Furthermore, because it is necessary that these laws first gain the
assent of all the citizens, which cannot be done if they are not first
made intelligible to them, and moreover a work (to speak properly)
is best done by one person; for these reasons the Lord our God who
established this Church first of all wished to constitute certain duly
constituted interpreters of that civil law pertaining to the conscience.
Their duty in each assembly is to train the consciences of the citizens, partly by word, example, and oration, to lead them to the
knowledge and approval of these laws; partly also by dogma and its
enforcement by means of the Ecclesiastical Consistory which he
himself established, to keep opinion dutiful. . . .

Therefore, to express all these things in a few words: in each
assembly or Republic of the Christian Church, Magistrates are constituted as representatives of God, to serve as examples to the faithful in the declaring of glory and praise to God. . . .

What then if the Lord grant us princes who either through
apparent cruelty or through crass ignorance combat the reign of
Christ? First of all the Church should take refuge in prayers and
tears, and correct its life. For these are the arms of the faithful for
overcoming the rages of the world. However the inferior Magistrate
must, as much as possible, with prudence and moderation, yet con-

stantly and wisely, maintain pure religion in the area under his authority.

A signal example of this has been shown in our times by Magdeburg, that city on the Elbe . . . [aside against Castellio]. . . .

When then several Princes abuse their office, whoever still.feels it necessary to refuse to use the Christian Magistrates offered by God against external violence whether of the unfaithful or of heretics, I charge deprives the Church of God of a most useful, and (as often as it pleases the Lord) necessary defense. . . .

Editor's note

The refugee bishop of Winchester, John Ponet, in flight from the
restored Catholic regime of Mary Tudor, published his treatise on
political power in Strassburg.[11] Ponet argued that since God conferred
authority upon the community, an oppressed people might revoke the
authority of an unworthy prince. Calvinistic discipline was not the issue
for Ponet. Rather, his book may be compared with the Magdeburg
Confession (Document 27). Because Parliament, the English equivalent
of the lower magistrate, was controlled by Mary, Ponet searched
further for legitimate resisters. He hesitated to permit a private individual
to wield the sword against a ruler, finding biblical evidence that special
inspiration was required. Clergymen especially could excommunicate
rulers. Ponet's armor against tyrants, illustrated by Luther's
denunciation of Duke George, was repentance and prayer. Ponet
declared that it was a law of nature that evil rulers should be deposed
and tyrants punished with death. Thus, a private citizen could act
against an evil ruler, if all others were supine.

Ponet's book is an example of early Anglican tyrannicide doctrine
based on natural law and rooted in medieval Catholicism. It had little
direct influence upon England. Ponet's development of his tyrannicide
doctrine as a result of exasperation under Mary's Catholic yoke
resembles later developments in Huguenot France. Christina Garrett
claims that in 1554–55, from his exile in Strassburg, Ponet supported
the Anglican exile party at Frankfurt under Richard Cox. This view
contradicts the similarity of Ponet's resistance doctrine to that of John
Knox's competing Puritan teaching at Frankfurt.[12] Perhaps Calvinism
had not yet captured its special hold on tyrannicide doctrine by the
1550s. Various strands of continental Calvinism exerted great influence
upon Protestant theology in England until Charles I appointed the
Arminian William Laud archbishop of Canterbury in 1633. By that time
Puritan sentiment in England and Scotland could no longer be
suppressed, whatever the desires of the king and his clergy might be.

John Ponet   A Shorte Treatise of Politike
                                      Power (1556)[13]

And Christ pronounceth, that every tree which bringeth not furthe
good fruit, shall be cut down, and cast in to the fire: muche more
the evil tree, that bringeth furthe evil frute. And albeit some doo
helde, that the maner and meane to punishe evil and evil doers, is
not all one among Christianes (which be in dede that they professe
in worde) and Ethnikes, which thinke it lawful for every private
man (without respecte of ordre and time) to punishe evil.

Yet the lawes of many christiane regiones doo permitte, that
private men maie kil malefactours, yea though they were magistrates,
in some cases: as when a governour shall sodainly with his sworde
renne upon an innocent, or goo about to shoote him through with a
gonne, or if he should be founde in bedde with a mannes daughter;
muche more if [he] goo about to betraie and make awaie his countrey to forainers, etc.

Neverthles forasmuche as all things in every christen common
wealthe ought to be done decently and according to ordre and
charitie: I thinke it cannot be maintened by Goddes worde, that
any private man maie kill, except (wher execucion of iuste punishe-
ment upon tirannes, idolaters, and traiterous governours is either by the
hole state utterly neglected, or the prince with the nobilitie and
counsail conspire the subversion or alteracion of their contrey and
people) any private man have som special inwarde commandment
or surely proved mocion of God: as Moses had to kill the Egipcian,
Phinees the Lecherours, and Ahud king Eglon, with suche like: or
be otherwise commaunded or permitted by common autorities upon
iuste occasion and common necessitie to kill. . . .

Thou wilt say, what if the Nobility, and those that be called to
common Counsels, and should be the defenders of the people, wil
not, or dare not execute their autority: what then is to be done? The
people be not so destitute of remedy, but God hath provided another
mean, that is, to complaine to some Minister of the Word of God,
to whom the keyes be given to excommunicate, not onely common
people, for all notorious and open evils: but also Emperours, Kings,
Princes, and all Governours, when they spoile, rob, undo and kill
their poor subjects without justice and good laws. And whatsoever
such Ministers of Gods word bindeth upon those occasions here on
earth, it is fast bound in Heaven before the face of God. . . .

When *Iulian* the Emperor and Apostate had long persecuted the Chruch, at length when the people fell to *Repentance* and *Prayer*, he going into *Persia*, was slain, and none of the family of *Constantine* (whereof he came) after that was Emperor.

And in like manner not long since, when that Tyrant, *Duke George* of *Saxony*, persecuted all such as professed the Word of God, revived and pulled out of Purgatory by the worthy instrument of God *D. Luther*: and at length threatened, that he would burne and destroy the University of *Wittenberg*, which when Luther heard, he went into the Pulpit, and exhorted every man to put on his Armour: that is, *Repentance* and *Prayer* and soon after, God rid the world of that tyrant, and so not onely delivered his Church, but also augmented it with another University, called *Lipsia*, and all the whole countrey of this cruell Duke was converted to Christs Gospell.

These be the wonderfull works of Almighty God, whose power is as great and as ready at a pinch, as ever it was, and his mercy as willing to be shewed, if his poore, afflicted people would put on their armour: that is, be sorry for their sins, and desire him to withdraw his scourges, and to hold his mercifull hand over them. . . .

Some ther be that will have to littel obedience, as the ANABAPTISTES. For they bicause they beare of a christian libertie, wolde have all politike power taken awaye: and so indede no obedience.

Others (as thenglishe papistes) racke and stretche out obedience to muche, and wil nedes have civile power obeied in all things, and that what so ever it commanundeth, without respecte it ought and must be done. But bothe of them be in great errours. For the anabaptistes mistake christian libertie, thinking that men may live without sinne, and forget the fall of man, wherby he was brought in to suche miserie, that he is no more hable to rule himself by himself, than one beast is hable to rule an other: and that therfore God ordained civile power (his ministre) to rule him, and to call him backe, when so ever he should passe the limites of his duetie, and wold that an obedience should be geven unto him.

And the papistes neither consider the degrees of powers, nor over what thinges civile power hathe autoritie, ne yet how farre subiectes ought to obeye their governours, And this they doo not for lacke of knowledge, but of a spiritual malice, bicause it maketh against their purpose, that the truthe should be disclosed. . . .

The Anabaptistes wresting scripture to serve their madnesse, among other foule errours, have this: that all thinges ought to be common, they ymage man to be of that puritie that he was before the fall, that is, cleane without sinne, or that (if he will) he maie so be: and that as whan ther was no sinne, all thinges were common, so they ought now to be.

But this mingling of the state of man before the fall, and of him after the fall, muche deceaveth them. For by the fall, and ever after the fall, this corruptible fleshe of man is clogged with sinne, and shall never be ridde of sinne, as long as it is in this corrupt worlde, but shalbe alwaies disposed and prone to doo that is evil. And therfore as one meanes to be the rather uncombred of the heape of sinne, God ordained that man should get his living by the swette of his browes: and that he should be the more forced to labour, the distinction of thinges and propretie (MINE, and THINE) was (contrary to platoes opinion) ordained, as appeareth by these two lawes: THOU shalt Not Steale: Thou shall not covet thy neighbours wife, nor his maide, nor his oxe, nor asse, nor anything that is his. Afterwarde indede scripture speaketh of communion of things, not that they ought so to be (for so scripture should be directly against scripture) but that ther was such charitie among the people, that of their owne free will, they gave and solde all they had, to releve the miserie of their poore brethren: who for impotencie, or for multitude of children, were not with their labour hable to get sufficient to releve their necessitie. Nor of this so geven might every man take as muche as him lusted, but to every one (according to his necessitie) sufficient was distributed. So that it stode in the liberalitie of the gever, and not in the libertie of the taker.

But ther be some in these daies, not of the meanest or poorest sorte, but of the chiefest and richest: that is, many wicked governours and rulers, who in this errour excell the common Anabaptistes. For the common Anabaptistes doo not onely take other mennes goodes as common, but are content to let their owne also be common, which hathe som smacke of Charitie: for they themselves doo non other, but that they themselves are content to suffre.

But the evil governours and rulers will have all that their subiectes have, common to themselves, but they themselves will departe with nothing, but wher they ought not: no, not so muche as paie for those thinges, that in wordes they pretende to buie of their subiectes, nor paie those poore men their wages, whom they force to labour and toyle in their workes. But the maner of coming therby is so

diverse, that it maketh the iustenesse of their doings muche suspected. For some doo it under pretense to doo the people good:
some by craftie and subtil meanes, colour their doinges: and some
of right (but without right) claime them for their owne. . . .

Editor's note

Christopher Goodman was another Marian exile who had supported Knox against the English Prayer Book during the troubles of Frankfurt, and had helped to produce the Geneva Bible.[14] Goodman's exasperation in exile typified English Calvinism, and anticipated the attitudes of Puritan revolutionaries eighty years later. Like Knox, he regarded kings as elective. When kings as God's subjects abuse their power, they must be resisted and punished. Also like Knox, Goodman declared that when magistrates betray justice, common citizens become magistrates. If the prince and his magistrates will not punish idolatry, the people must do it themselves. In Goodman's opinion, Mary Tudor, the Jezebel, should be deposed and "punished with death" by the people.

Christopher Goodman   How Superior Powers Oght to be Obeyd (1558)[15]

Alas saye you, what is this we heare: Be not the people, of them-selves as sheepe without a pastor? If the Magistrates and other officers contemne their duetie in definding Gods glorie and the Lawes committed to their charge, lieth it in our power to remedie it? Shall we that are subjectes take the sworde in our handes?

It is in dede as you say, a great discouraging to the people when they are not stirred up to godlynesse by the good example of all sortes of Superiors, Magistrates and officers in the faithfull execut-ing of their office: and so muche more when they are not defended by them in their right and title, as wel concerning religion, as the freedome of their naturall countrie: but moste of all when they,

which shuld be their guydes and Capitayns, are become instrumentes
to inforce them to wicked impietie.

Nevertheles, all this can be no excuse for you, seing, that evil
doinges of others, whether they be Lordes, Dukes, Barons, knights
or any inferior officers, may not excuse you in evil. And thoghe you
had no man of power upon your parte: yet, it is a sufficient assurance for you, to have the warrant of Godds worde upon your side,
and God him self to be your Capitayne who willeth not onely the
Magistrates and officers to roote out evil from amongst them, beit,
idolatrie, blasphemie or open iniurie, but the whole multitude are
therwith charged also, to whom a portion of the sworde of iustice
is committed, to execute the judgementes which the Magistrates lawfully commande.

And therefore if the Magistrates would whollye despice and be-
traye the iustice and Lawes of God, you which are subiectes with
them shall be condemned except you mayntayne and defend the
same Lawes agaynst them, and all others to the uttermoste of your
powers, that is, with all your strength, with all your harte and with
all your soule, for this hath God requiured of you, and this have you
promised unto him not under condition (if the Rulers will) but
without all exceptions to do whatso ever your Lorde and God shall
commande you.

As touching idolatrie, it is worthie to be considered what Moyses
wrytethe, or rather the Spirite of God by him, how the Lorde in that
place chargeth the whole people to stone to death with out mercy
the false Prophet or dreamer, when anie shulde rise up amongst
them, yea thoghe the thinges came to pass which he before spake,
if that therby he sought to perswade them or drawe them to idolatrie.
And also howe he suffred such amongest his people to try and prove
them, whether they would love him with all their harte and with all
their soule, meaning (as every man may well perceave) that if they
shulde yelde for all their signes and wonders to idolatrie, and not
punishe such false Prophetes and dreamers as God had raysed up:
that then they loved him not, yea that they had playnly forsaken
and denied him, for that he commanded expresslye that everie such
Prophet shuld be put to death, and therfore chargeth to take the
evill from amongest them.

Which commandement as it is not geven onely to the Rulers and
Governours (thoghe I confesse it chieflie apperteyneth to their office
to see it executed, for which cause they are made Rulers) but also

is comon to all the people, who are likewise bownde to the observation of the same: evenso is the punishment appoynted of God, be-
longing to all mener of persons without exception, being found
transgressors.

For the Lorde is a iust punisher, with whom there is no respecte
of persons, who willeth his people to be like him in their iudgements.
In iudgement (saithe the Lorde) comitte no unrighteousness, nether
respect the face of the poore, nether be you afrayde at the counte-
naunce of the mightie, but iudge uprightly to your neighbour. . . .

32

The Appellation, The Interview
with Mary Queen of Scots,
and A Debate with Lethington

Editor's note

The Emperor Charles V failed to enforce the Interim in Germany, and after 1555 Lutherans had no further use for the right of rebellion. The Magdeburg doctrine now proved useful in Scotland, and a bit later in France and the Netherlands. John Knox adhered fervently to the Calvinist ideal of church-state organization, and very quickly moved beyond Calvin on resistance teaching.[16] Scotland was the first nation to present Calvinists with an opportunity to rebel successfully against constituted authority.

Captured by the French in 1547 after his early stand for the Reformation in Scotland, Knox endured imprisonment as a galley slave. After his release in 1549, he returned to England. He had to flee to the Continent after Mary's accession. He was a pastor to English refugees at Frankfurt in 1554 but was expelled when his Geneva-like ideas failed to convince those who wished to use the Prayer Book. In 1555 he returned to Scotland, where continuing persecution of Protestants led him in 1556 to exiled leadership of the English church in Geneva. There he published several tracts concerning the situation in Scotland.

Knox's *First Blast* of 1558 asserted the duty of deposing by force an impious ruler (Mary Tudor), because of the "curse pronounced against Woman."[17] Late that same year, feeling that rebellion against Mary of Guise, regent of Scotland, might succeed, Knox appealed for the commonality of Scotland to revolt, having himself been condemned to death in absence by the Scottish bishops. Knox's argument was that of Goodman in a simpler form. If magistrates suppress truth, God commissions subjects to resist.

Back in Scotland in 1559, Knox was able to establish a powerful national Presbyterian church in that country. By 1561 he recorded with satisfaction (impenetrable stupidity, J. W. Allen called it) his interview with the new queen, Mary Stewart. But Knox's narrowness was also a liberating force: no prince or vested interest may impede righteousness. In his debate with Lethington, Knox avoided advocating mere assassination of tyrants in favor of punishment of idolators by "the people of God." He referred to the Magdeburg Confession, and also cited the Dominicans of Bologna for resistance to the pope. The sixteenth century was especially ecumenical in its resistance theories.

John Knox   The Appellation (1558)[18]

The appellation of John Knox from the cruell and most uniust sentence pronounced against him by the false bishoppes and clergie of Scotland, with his supplication and exhortation to the nobilitie, estates, and communaltie of the same realme. Printed at Geneva, 1558. . . .

True it is, God hath commanded Kinges to be obeyed, but like true it is, that in things which they commit against his glorie, or when cruelly without cause they rage against theire brethren, the members of Christes body, he hath commanded no obedience, but rather he hath approved, year, and greatlie rewarded such as have opponed themselves to theyre ungodly commandementes and blind rage, as in the example of the Three children, of Daniel, and Abdemelech, it is evident. The Three children wold nether bowe nor stoupe before the golden image at the commandement of the great King Nabuchadnezar. . . .

But how acceptable in God's presence was this resistance to the ungodlie commandementes and determinations of theyr King, the end did witness. For the Three children were delivered from the fornace of fyer, and Daniel from the den of lions, to the confusion of their ennemies to the better instruction of the ignorant kinges, and to the perpetuall comfort of Goddes afflicted children. . . .

Advert and take hede, my Lordes, that the men, who had condemned the Prophet, were the King, his Princes, and Councill, and yet did one man accuse them all of iniquitie, and did boldly speak in the defense of him of whose innocencie he was persuaded. And the same, I say, is the duetie of every man in his vocation, but chefely of the Nobilitie, which is joyned with theyr Kinges, to bridel and represse theyr folie and blind rage. Which thing if the Nobilitie do not, neither yet labor to do, as they are traitors to their kings; so do they provoke the wrath of God against themselves and against the realme in which they abuse the auctoritie, which they have receaved of God, to mentaine vertue and to represse vice. For hereof I would your Honours were most certainly persuaded, that God will neither excuse Nobilitie nor People, but the Nobilitie least of al, that obey and folow theyr Kinges in manifest iniquitie.

But with the same vengeance will God punishe the Prince, People, and Nobilitie, conspiring togither against him and his holie ordenances; as in the punishment taken upon Pharao, Israel, Juda, and Babylon is evidently to be sene. For Pharao was not drowned alone, but his captayns, chareotes, and greate armie drank the same cup with him. The Kinges of Israel and Juda were not punished without compayny; but with them were murthered the councilers, theyre princes imprisoned, and their people ledd captive. And why? because none was found so faithful to God, that he durst enterprise to resist nor againstand the manifest impietie of theyr Princes. And therefore was God's wrath powred furth upon the one and the other. . . .

John Knox   The Interview with Mary
                                    Queen of Scots (1561)[19]

The Queen accused John Knox that he had raised a part of her subjects against her mother and against herself; that he had written a book against her just authority, —she meant the *First Blast against the Monstrous Regiment of Women*. . . .

John Knox. And, touching that Book which seemeth so highly to offend your Majesty, it is most certain that I wrote it. . . .

Queen Mary. Ye think then that I have no just authority? . . .

John Knox. If the Realm finds no inconvenience from the government of a woman, that which they approve shall I not further disallow than within my own breast, but shall be as well content to live under Your Grace as Paul was to live under Nero. My hope is, that so long as ye defile not your hands with the blood of the Saints of God, neither I nor that book shall either hurt you or your authority. In very deed, Madam, that book was written most especially against that wicked Jezebel of England [Queen Mary Tudor]. . . .

Queen Mary. But yet ye have taught the people to receive another religion than their Princes can allow. How can that doctrine be of God, seeing that God commandeth subjects to obey their Princes?

John Knox. Madam, as right religion took neither original strength nor authority from worldly princes, but from the Eternal God alone, so are not subjects bound to frame their religion according to the appetites of their princes. . . .

Queen Mary. Yea, but none of these men raised the sword against their princes.

John Knox. God, Madam, had not given them the power and the means.

Queen Mary. Think ye that subjects, having the power, may resist their princes?

John Knox. If their princes exceed their bounds, Madam, no doubt they may be resisted, even by power. . . .

Queen Mary. Well then, I perceive that my subjects shall obey you, and not me. They shall do what they list, and not what I command; and so must I be subject to them, and not they to me.

John Knox. God forbid that ever I take upon me to command any to obey me, or yet to set subjects at liberty to do what pleaseth them! God craves of Kings that they be foster-fathers to His Church, and commands Queens to be nurses to His people. . . .

Queen Mary. Yea, but ye are not the Kirk that I will nourish. I will defend the Kirk of Rome, for it is, I think, the true Kirk of God.

John Knox. Your *will*, Madam, is no reason; neither doth your *thought* make that Roman harlot to be the true and immaculate spouse of Jesus Christ. . . .

Queen Mary. My conscience is not so.

John Knox. Conscience, Madam, requireth knowledge; and I fear that right knowledge ye have none. . . .

Queen Mary. Ye interpret the Scriptures in one manner, and they in another. Whom shall I believe? . . .

John Knox. Ye shall believe God, that plainly speaketh in His Word. The Word of God is plain in itself. . . . I pray God, Madam, that ye may be as blessed within the Commonwealth of Scotland, if it be the pleasure of God, as ever Deborah was in the Commonwealth of Israel. . . .

[Commenting on the interview Knox said,] If there be not in her a proud mind, a crafty wit, and an indurate heart against God and His truth, my judgment faileth me.

John Knox   Debate with Lethington
                                            (1564)[20]

. . . I [Knox] am assured what I have proven, to wit:

1. That subjects have delivered an innocent from the hands of their king, and therein offended not God.

2. That subjects have refused to strike innocents when a king commanded, and in so doing denied no just obedience.

3. That such as struck at the commandment of the king, before God were reputed murderers.

4. That God has not only of a subject made a king, but also has armed subjects against their natural kings, and commanded them to take vengeance upon them according to his law.

And last, That God's people have executed God's law against their king, having no further regard to him in that behalf than if he had been the most simple subject within this Realm.

And therefore, albeit ye will not understand what should be concluded, yet I am assured that not only God's people may, but also that they are bound to do the same where the like crimes are committed, and when he gives unto them the like power.

Well, said Lethington, I think ye shall not have many learned men of your opinion.

My lord, said the other [Knox], the truth ceases not to be the truth, howsoever it be that men either misknow it, or yet gainstand it. And yet (said he), I praise my God, I lack not the consent of God's servants in that head. And with that he presented unto the Secretary the Apology of Magdeburg; and willed him to read the names of the ministers who had subscribed the defense of the town to be a most just defense; and therewith added, That to resist a tyrant, is not to resist God, nor yet his ordinance.

Which when he had read, he [Lethington] scripped [mocked] and said, Men of no note. The other [Knox] answered, Yet servants of God. . . .

At last, Mr. John Craig, fellow-minister with John Knox in the Kirk of Edinburgh, was required to give his judgment and vote, who said, I will gladly show unto your Honours what I understand. . . . But yet I shall not conceal from you my judgment, adhering first to the protestation of my Brother, to wit, That our voting prejudge not the liberty of the General Assembly. I was (said he), in the University of Bononia [Bologna], in the year of God 1554, where, in the place of the Black-Friars of the same town, I saw in the time of their General Assembly this Conclusion set forth: This same I heard reasoned, determined, and concluded:

"That is, All Rulers, be they supreme or be they inferior, may and ought to be reformed or deposed by them by whom they are chosen, confirmed, or admitted to their office, as oft as they break that promise made by the oath to their subjects: Because that their

Prince is no less bound by oath to the subjects, than are the subjects
to their Prince, and therefore ought to be kept and reformed equally,
according to the law and condition of the oath that is made of either
party."

This Conclusion, my Lords, I heard sustained and concluded, as
I have said, in a most notable auditure. The sustainer was a learned
man, Magister Thomas de Finola, the Rector of the University, a
man famous in that country. Magister Vincentius de Placentia affirmed the Conclusion to be most true and certain, agreeable both
with the law of God and man. The occasion of this disputation and
conclusion, was a certain disorder and tyranny that was attempted
by the Pope's governors, who began to make innovations in the
country against the laws that were before established, alleging themselves not to be subject to such laws, by reason that they were not
instituted by the people, but by the Pope, who was King of that
country; and therefore they, having full commission and authority
of the Pope, might alter and change statutes and ordinances of the
country, without all consent of the people. Against this their usurped
tyranny, the learned and the people opposed themselves openly:
and when that all reasons which the Pope's governors could allege
were heard and confuted, the Pope himself was feign to take up the
matter, and to promise to keep not only the liberty of the people,
but also that he should neither abrogate any law or statute, neither yet
make any new law without their own consent. And, therefore, my
Lord (said he), my vote and conscience is, that princes are not only
bound to keep laws and promises to their subjects, but also, that in
case they fail, they justly may be deposed; for the band betwix the
Prince and the people is reciprocal. . . .

33   The Powers of the Crown in Scotland

Editor's note

Around 1567, George Buchanan, a Scottish-French humanist scholar and poet, wrote a dialogue treatise on Scottish kingship, which related resistance theory to medieval doctrines, in probable dependence upon John Major, the Scottish scholastic and teacher of Buchanan, Calvin, and Knox.[21] The purpose of Buchanan's work was to justify the dethronement in 1567 of the Scottish queen, Mary Stewart. Buchanan had become a Calvinist in France and, after tutoring the young queen in Scotland, openly joined the Presbyterian Church. Also in 1567 Buchanan was appointed moderator of the Presbyterian general assembly. Though his reputation continued to emphasize scholarship rather than religion, Buchanan consistently exerted his influence against the Roman Catholic queen, who was finally beheaded by Queen Elizabeth in 1587 as a subversive fugitive.

In his *Powers of the Crown* Buchanan argued that political society originated from a natural tendency to associate with beings of one's own kind, and that the will of the people is naturally expressed through numerical majorities. Thus authority rests with the people, to whom kings are responsible. The traditional coronation promises of the Scottish kings bound them into a covenant with the people, Buchanan recalled. The people are obligated to the king only when he keeps his promises, and they may depose and even slay him if he proves faithless and tyrannical. Protestant revolution had restored traditional practices. In this work Buchanan partially anticipated the Huguenot *Defense of Liberty against Tyrants* (Document 36), although the Huguenots did not accept Buchanan's motion that majorities determine the will of the people. Nor was Buchanan's populist revolt Presbyterian: the Scottish Parliament condemned his writing in 1584 for the "offensive and extraordinary matters" therein contained.

George Buchanan The Powers of the Crown in
Scotland (1579, written
1567)[22]

Buchanan: There are many other points of difference between political and tyrannical governments, which, since anyone may easily
collect them out of Aristotle's writings, I pass over briefly. A royal
government is in accordance with nature; tyranny is contrary to
nature; the king governs subjects who willingly accept his authority;
the tyrant rules unwilling subjects; a royal and political government
is the leadership of free men by a free man, a tyranny is a lordship
over slaves. . . . Can he then be called a father who holds the citizens in servitude? Or a shepherd who does not feed his flock, but
devours it? Or a pilot who plans only barratry, and who, as the
proverb has it, bores a hole in the hull of every ship in which he
sails?
Maitland: No indeed!
Buchanan: What shall we call him, then, who does not govern in
order that he may attend to the interests of the people, but is concerned only for himself? Who does not vie with the good in excellence, but competes with criminals as to which can surpass the other
in disgraceful conduct? A ruler who leads his people into open
ambuscades?
Maitland: Truly he should be regarded as neither leader, nor
commander, nor governor. . . .
Buchanan: Within what limits do you define civilized society?
Maitland: . . . I observe that those who go outside the laws—as
robbers, thieves, and adulterers—are punished; and I regard this
as a just ground of their punishment, that they have placed themselves beyond the bounds of civilized society.
Buchanan: What of those who desire never to go within these
walls?
Maitland: They should be regarded as enemies of God and of
men; I think they should be regarded as wolves or other predatory
animals rather than as men. Monsters of such a sort that to nourish
them is to nourish one's own destruction; so that the man who kills
them benefits not only himself but also the whole community. . . .
What of a case in which a king would not willingly submit to
trial, and could not be compelled to do so?
Buchanan: Here he is in a common case with all criminals; for
no robber or poisoner submits to trial of his own accord. But you

know, I think, what the law provides—that anyone may slay a thief by night, and may slay him by day in self-defense. . . .

Maitland: This justification of war is generally regarded as valid when the war is waged against enemies, but the case is far otherwise with respect to making war against a people's own kings; for we are under obligation, by the taking of a most sacred oath, to obey them.

Buchanan: We are indeed obligated; but before we take the oath the kings first promise that they will maintain the law in justice and goodness.

Maitland: Precisely so.

Buchanan: There is, then, a mutual compact between king and citizens.

Maitland: So it appears.

Buchanan: Does not he who first withdraws from the covenant or does something contrary to the agreement break the covenant and the agreement?

Maitland: He does indeed break it.

Buchanan: I think moreover that in case the king has broken the bond which holds him and his people together, he who first breaks the agreement forfeits whatever rights belong to him under it.

Maitland: He forfeits them.

Buchanan: But the other party to the covenant would be in the same state as he was before the agreement, free.

Maitland: He clearly has the same rights and the same liberty.

Buchanan: If a king were to do something the effect of which would be to destroy orderly government, for the preservation of which he was made a king, what would we call him?

Maitland: A tyrant, of course.

Buchanan: But a tyrant has no rightful public authority; but is a public enemy.

Maitland: He is an enemy indeed.

Buchanan: And is it right to wage war against an enemy in case one suffers great and unendurable injury?

Maitland: It is absolutely right.

Buchanan: What of that war which is waged against a tyrant, the enemy of all humanity?

Maitland: It is the most just of all.

Buchanan: But once a just war is undertaken with an enemy, it is not only right for the whole people to destroy an enemy, but for the individual to do so. . . .

Maitland: I know that almost all nations share that opinion. . . .

Fulvius killed his own son who had gone with Cataline, and Brutus
slew his own sons and kinsmen when he learned that they were
setting on foot a plan to establish a tyranny. Public rewards and
honors were provided in many Greek states for those who killed
tyrants. For these Greeks, as was said earlier, were convinced that
there is no obligation to treat a tyrant as a human being. . . .

Maitland: One thing more seems to be necessary to resolve our
problem. . . . Tell me if the Church imposes any censure on tyrants.

Buchanan: You may, if you like, begin with the First Epistle of
Paul to the Corinthians, where the Apostle forbids the having any
fellowship, either by living or talking, with evil and dishonest men.
If this rule were observed among Christians, scoundrels, unless they
mended their ways, would perish of hunger, cold, or exposure.

Maitland: That is certainly a severe censure, and I doubt if the
people, accustomed as they are to yielding to their rulers in everything, will agree that kings ought to be included under this rule.

Buchanan: The Church Fathers certainly understood this passage
from Paul's writings to teach that they should be so included. For
Ambrose refused to admit the Emperor Theodosius to Christian
fellowship, and Theodosius obeyed the bishop. No action of which
I have ever heard on the part of any other bishop of the early
Church has received more praise; nor has the dignity of any other
emperor been commended more highly than that of Theodosius.
But what difference is there in a case of this sort between being expelled from the Christian commonwealth and being forbidden the
use of fire and water. For this last is the extremely severe sentence
imposed by secular rulers on those who refuse to do their commands;
and the first is the sentence of churchmen.

Now death is the penalty for refusing to accept either sovereignty,
but the one pronounces sentence upon the body, the other commands the destruction of the whole man. Does the Church, therefore
—which regards death as a punishment much lighter than that which
the criminal merits—not believe that that man deserves to die whom
she expels from the society of good men while he is alive and con-
signs to the society of unclean spirits when he is dead?

I think that I have said quite enough to show the justice of our
[the Scottish people's] case; and if I do not satisfy certain foreigners,
I ask them to consider how unfairly they are persecuting us. . . .
Ours, to be sure, is a poor nation, but for two thousand years now
we have held it, free from the domination of foreigners. From the

first, we have made our kings constitutional rulers. We have imposed
the same laws on them and on ourselves, and the passing centuries
have taught the value of the constitution principle. For this kingdom
owes its preservation more to the faithful observance of this principle than to strength of arms. . . .

Editor's note

Following the death of thousands of French Huguenots in the Massacre of St. Bartholomew (August 1572), the Protestants in France dropped all restraint in attacking the king. Among the treatises resulting, the most significant were those of Hotman, on the historical side, and of Mornay (or Languet) on the systematic side. François Hotman, a French jurist and friend of Calvin and Beza who narrowly escaped death in the massacre, published the *Franco-Gallia* the following year during his exile in Geneva.[23] Identifying pre-Roman Gaul with France, he regarded the Germanic Franks as deliverers from Roman tyranny. The popular sovereignty of Franco-Gallia, he argued, had later been usurped by the French kings at the end of the fifteenth century. As in the case of Buchanan, Hotman reappropriated medieval arguments in an effort to repudiate royal absolutism, advocate the rights of the Estates General, and promote a mutual contract between king and people. Hotman thus supplied strong historical support for the embattled Huguenot cause.

François Hotman   Francogallia (1573)[24]

. . . In constituting the kingdom of Francogallia our ancestors accepted Cicero's opinion that the best form of a commonwealth is that which is tempered by the mixture of the three kinds of government. This can be shown by a variety of proofs, especially from the speech of King Louis, known as the Pious, delivered to all the estates of Francogallia, and also from Ansegius' book on Frankish law, where an official report is quoted as follows: "Yet, however mighty this royal office may seem to be in our person, our office is known by both divine authority and human ordinance to be so divided throughout its parts that each one of you in his own place and rank may be recognized as possessing a piece. Hence it seems that we should be your counsellor, and all of you should be our deputies. And we are aware that it is fitting for each one of you to have a piece of authority vested in you."[25] Later Ansegius writes to the same effect: "And as we have said, each one of you is distinguished by having your part among the many segments of our office." Again, he says: "We urge your loyalty so that you may recall both your desire for the trust placed in us and the office which in part has been entrusted to you."

For this reason our ancestors accepted this mixed and tempered commonwealth embodying the three kinds of government, and very wisely laid it down that every year there should be a public council of the whole kingdom on the first of May, and that at this council the greatest affairs of the commonwealth should be dealt with through the general advice of all the estates. In this manner that ancient and golden law prevailed: "LET THE WELFARE OF THE PEOPLE BE THE SUPREME LAW."[26] The wisdom and utility of this practice is very apparent in three respects. First, the large number of men of prudence ensured that there would be an amplitude of advice, and advice of a kind to procure the welfare of the people, such as might satisfy Solomon (Prov. 11 and 15) and other wise men. Next, because it is an attribute of liberty that those at whose peril a thing is done should have some say and authority in arranging it, or, as it is customarily and commonly said, what touches all should be approved by all.[27] Lastly, those who have great influence with the king, and are foremost in great affairs of government, should, in the performance of their office, be held in fear of this council, in which the requests of the provinces are freely heard. When certain kingdoms are governed by the will and pleasure of a single king—as today the Turks are ruled—their government would lack the advice of free men and enlightened opinion and would be like that of cattle and beasts, as Aristotle rightly observes in his *Politics*.[28] For in such circumstances they are like cattle who are not controlled by one of their own kind, or like boys and youths, who are governed by someone of superior status rather than by one of their own age.

In the same way a multitude of men ought not to be ruled and governed by one of their own number, who, peradventure, sees less than others do when taken together, but rather by proven men of excellence, selected with the consent of all, who act by combined advice as if they possessed one mind composed from many. . . .

. . . Office, which ought to be the most sacred of human affairs, has

been made a piece of merchandise to be bought and sold for cash.
. . . Can anyone refrain from tears when he reflects that the clients
and beneficiaries of the Roman pontiff, those clerics bound to him
by oath, and those endowed with fat livings, acquire a large share of
these magistracies; and, in addition, that those who wish to be
known as laymen, and want benefices of this sort to be conferred
upon their children through the tyranny of this same pontiff, sell
their faith and religion?

. . . The more I track down the origin of this disease of petti-
foggery, which we can very truly call the French pox, the more I am
certain of the view I earlier advanced, namely that just as the plague
of superstition, and many other plagues beside, flowed out from the
workshop of the Roman pontiffs, so too did the practice of the art
of legal chicanery reach us from the court of Rome, because it is
known to have expanded to its full extent a few years after the
promulgation of the decretals. For in the decretals of Gratian[29] there
is reference to a letter from Pope Leo (whom they list in the calen-
dar of their saints) to Louis II, who was both king of France and
emperor. There it is stated that the pope submits to the edicts and
ordinances of the emperors and the law established by them. The
letter goes on to say that the pope begs that same emperor for his
clemency and wishes the constitutions of Roman Law everywhere to
be observed. Indeed, there exists a decretal of Pope Honorius III[30]
where it is clearly shown that right up to that time the popes had
obeyed the provisions of Roman Law and the constitutions of the
Christian emperors contained in Justinian's *Code*, and that these
were used in disputes on oath.

Someone may ask whether we have any remedy to suggest for
such ills. It is clear that the cause of all these troubles is in part
impiety, and in part the incredible superstition of our people, which
flowed in to us throughout those times from that same font. This
shrouded the whole Christian world like a huge fog, and, when the
single light of the Christian religion was extinguished as the holy
scriptures were obscured and buried, all things continued to be
weighed down by the thick darkness of superstition. Wherefore, if it
is permitted by those among us who fancy themselves for the rôle of
Alastor and in the midst of the crazed instigators of civil wars—or,
as we may more properly say, if it be granted us through the singular
charity of God—let the authority of the holy scriptures prevail in
France, and the youth of our country devote their energy to studying
them. Then without doubt the darkness would be put to flight by the

risen sun, and the arts of legal chicanery, together with the superstitions drawn from the same font, would be driven out. Since God,
the all-good and almighty, may grant this to our generation for the
glory of Christ his son and our saviour, it should be asked of Him
in earnest prayer.

FINIS.

**The Rights of Rulers
and Duty of Subjects**

Editor's note

J. H. Elliot has noted that there was a "general revolution of the 1560s" in seven or eight stages beginning with the 1559–60 Scottish revolt which culminated in the abdication of Mary Queen of Scots in 1567, and including most significantly the outbreak of the French civil wars in 1562 and the beginnings of revolt in the Netherlands in 1566.[31] Since the French and Dutch revolutions were intimately related, it is fair to suggest that France in the second half of the sixteenth century became, like Germany in the Thirty Years' War, a European battleground for the supranational struggle of the Reformation versus the Counter-Reformation.

Armed conflict had begun in France with the abortive conspiracy of Amboise in 1560 and erupted into open warfare in 1562. Only after the slaughter of Protestants on St. Bartholomew's Day in 1572 were French Calvinists willing to advocate revolution openly as a religiously justified teaching. Theodore Beza, Calvin's successor at Geneva, led the Huguenots into the changed teaching.[32] The bloody wars continued off and on until Henry IV was able to become king, having made peace with his Catholic enemies (including the counter-Huguenot revolutionaries within the Catholic League), and granted toleration to the French Protestants in 1598.

As we have seen in Document 29, Beza first proposed a revolutionary theory to the French Protestants in 1554. Following the St. Bartholomew's Massacre, his lectures on the rights of rulers were refused publication by the Geneva authorities in 1573. A French version appeared anonymously the following year in Lyon, its title page indicating (falsely) that the work was the Magdeburg Confession. Beza wished to present a systematic argument, anticipating Morney, for the encouragement of French Huguenot resistance to the king, giving evidence for resistance from doctrinal, ethical, and legal standpoints. He made full use of covenant theology, which activated man without controlling God. When the ruler breaks his covenant, those who have

entered into agreement with him have a right to depose him. Beza
developed fully the revolutionary implications of the inferior magistrate
doctrine, and he calmly asserted that Christian martyrs included not only
passive sufferers but also heroes who actively oppose tyrants in defense
of God's laws.

Theodore Beza   The Rights of Rulers and Duty
of Subjects (1574)[33]

. . . I could never approve of the view of those who without any
distinction or exception at once and indiscriminately condemn all
tyrannicides on whom the Greeks formerly bestowed such exceptional rewards. As little does the view of those command itself to
whom the majority of liberations recorded in the Book of Judges
seem so foreign and strange that they are of opinion that these can
in no way be adduced as examples. For however true it may be that
those Judges of the people of Israel were moved and stirred to the
performance of those famous deeds by some divine and exceptional
instinct, yet it does not immediately follow that the Israelites themselves, without holding office or even as private citizens, could not
in accordance with their ordinary right have expelled the tyranny of
strangers who had been neither elected nor approved by the people.

But that those liberations were effected by means of those men
alone whom God summoned forth in a special way does not go to
disprove my contention, but rather demonstrates that the spirit of
the Israelites had for their transgressions been stunned and broken
by the just judgment of God. Therefore . . . if anyone strives to seize
or has already usurped an unjust tyranny over others, whether he be
a stranger or whether as a viper he leaps from the womb of his
country that by his birth he may cause her death, then shall private
citizens before all else approach their legitimate magistrates in order
that if it may be the public enemy be cast forth by the public
authority and common consent of all.

But if the magistrate connives [at the attempt] or in some way
refuses to perform his duty, then let each private citizen bestir himself with all his power to defend the lawful constitution of his country, to whom after God he owes his entire existence, against him who
cannot be deemed a lawful magistrate since he either has already
usurped that rank in violation of the public laws or is endeavouring
to usurp it. . . .

. . . THE ORDERS OR ESTATES, ESTABLISHED TO CURB THE SUPREME MAGISTRATES, CAN AND SHOULD IN EVERY WAY OFFER RESISTANCE TO THEM WHEN THEY DEGENERATE INTO TYRANTS. . . .

The people existed before there was any magistrate and the magistrates were made for the sake of the people and not vice versa the people for the sake of the magistrates.

. . . Hence it follows that the authority of all magistrates, however supreme and powerful they be, is dependent upon the public authority of those who have raised them to this degree of dignity, and not contrariwise. And let no one urge the objection that such was indeed the first beginning of magistracies but that the people subsequently completely subjected themselves to the power and arbitrary will of those whom they had received as their supreme magistrates and that they gave up their liberty to them wholly and without any reserve whatever. In the first place I deny that there is any certain proof of this complete renunciation; nay, on the contrary I maintain that as long as right and justice have prevailed no nation has either elected or approved its kings without laying down specific conditions. And if these kings violate these, the result is that those who had the power to confer this authority upon them have retained no less power again to divest them of that authority. . . .

The purport therefore of all that has been said above is as follows, namely that the highest authority rests with kings or other supreme rulers with this proviso that if they violate the noblest laws and sworn conditions and degenerate into unabashed tyranny nor give heed to sound counsels, it shall be lawful and permitted to the subordinate magistrates to take precautions for themselves and for those over whom they exercise guardianship, and to offer resistance to the tyrant of the people.

But the Estates or Orders of the realm upon whom this authority has been conferred by the laws, can and must so far oppose the tyrant and even, if need be, inflict just and deserved punishment upon him until matters have been restored to their former condition. And if they do so, so far from deserving to be regarded as guilty of sedition or high treason, they should on the contrary only then be deemed to have carried out conscientiously their duty and their oath by which they were bound towards God and their country. And though by means of the clearest examples of kingdoms and empires both ancient and modern we have already above demonstrated the practice in these matters, yet to answer the objection that (the matter) should be judged by legal arguments rather than by examples, I shall add as many other grounds as possible to lend greatest support to our point of view.

1. Argument from Natural Law
and Equity

I maintain that there are two propositions which justice as such, or that law of nature upon which alone the maintenance of all human society depends, does not allow to be called in question; the first of these is that in all compacts and covenants which are contracted by mutual and sole agreement between the parties, those by whom the obligations were entered into can of themselves cancel and annul it, whenever reason so demands. Accordingly those who possess authority to elect a king will also have the right to dethrone him. The second [proposition] is that if there is any just occasion for the annulment of a compact or covenant by reason of which the obligation would of itself disappear and be held as naught, it never arises but when the essential conditions, for which particularly the obligation was entered upon, are manifestly violated.

. . . Finally the ruler will be fully occupied in rendering the true religion secure by means of good and noble decrees against those who assail and resist it out of pure obstinacy, as we have seen done in our times in England, Denmark, Sweden, Scotland, and the greater part of Germany and Switzerland against the Papists, the Anabaptists and other heretics. If the other nations preferred following their example rather than trusting and obeying that bloodstained whore of Rome, could greater tranquillity indeed be seen in the whole world in the sphere of religion as well as of politics?

What therefore will subjects have to do if on the other hand they are compelled by their ruler to worship idols? Assuredly reason does not permit them to force their ruler to a complete change in their condition; nay, rather, they will consider it needful patiently to bear with him even to persecution, while they worship God purely in the meantime, or altogether to go into exile and seek new abodes. But if the free exercise of the true religion has once been granted by means of decrees lawfully passed and settled and confirmed by public authority, then I declare that the ruler is so much the more bound to have them observed as a matter of religion is of greater moment compared with all others, so much so that he has no right to repeal

them upon his own arbitrary decision, and without having heard
the case, but only with the intervention of that same authority by
which they were in the first instance enacted. . . .

If he acts otherwise I declare that he is practicing manifest tyranny; and with due allowance for the observations made above,
(his subjects) will be all the more free to oppose him as we are
bound to set greater store and value by the salvation of our souls
and the freedom of our conscience than by any other matters however desirable. It should therefore now be no cause of surprise to
anyone that Our Lord Jesus Christ, the Prophets and the Apostles,
too, or the other martyrs, since they were men in private station,
confined themselves within the limits of their calling.

And as regards those who held public office or those legions which
in the midst of battle suffered martyrdom with their commanders
without offering any resistance even though their attackers were
acting in violation of the decrees previously passed in favour of the
Christians, as happened especially under the Emperors Diocletian
and Julian, there is, I say, a twofold answer. Firstly, although certain
emperors before Diocletian had made the persecutions somewhat less
severe, as it is certain that Hadrian, Antonius and Alexander did,
yet none of them had ever permitted the public exercise of the Christian religion.

Next, I also repeat the well-known saying that whatever is lawful
is not always expedient as well. For I should not be inclined to assert
that a religion made lawful by public decrees must needs always be
defended and held fast by means of arms against manifest tyranny,
but that even so that is the right and lawful course especially for
those upon whom this burden rests and to whom God has granted
the opportunity, as the example of the people of Libnah against
Jehoram and of the people of Jerusalem against Amaziah[34] and the
war of Constantine against Maxentius undertaken at the request of
the citizens of Rome as described above abundantly prove.

Hence I conclude that among the martyrs should be counted not
only those who have defeated the tyranny of the enemies of the truth
by no other defense than patience, but those also who, duly supported by the authority of laws or of those whose right it is to defend the laws, devoted their strength to God in defense of the true
religion. . . .

Editor's note

The final and most eloquent French resistance document is the *Defense of Liberty against Tyrants*, probably produced in collaboration by Philip Duplessis-Mornay, a Huguenot nobleman and lawyer who from 1573 was chief adviser to Henry of Navarre, and Hubert Languet, a Burgundian disciple of Melanchthon and emissary of German princes.[35] The defense distinguished two covenants: the first between God, the king, and the people, the other between the king and the people. Thus the magic of kingship was broken. The ruler was placed upon the same level with all Christians, to be judged by how well he performed his duties. A tyrannical king was to be judged by the inferior magistrates. The people were to act through their representatives, although any local community could take the initiative against an idolatrous tyrant. On the one hand, this treatise represents a backward-looking aristocratic federalism. On the other, it influenced a more successful revolutionary tradition in the Netherlands and England, and helped originate parliamentary democracy.

The *Defense of Liberty*, with its ringing affirmation of the priority of the political community over against the king, was quickly repudiated by Henry IV and the Stuart monarchs in England, who sponsored the powerful doctrine of the "divine right of kings." It was the French political philosopher Jean Bodin who formulated this contrasting theory most effectively in his *Republique* of 1576.[36] Bodin repudiated Mornay's insistence than sovereignty is limited by the law of nature, by the community's moral consciousness, by positive law, and by the Scriptures. Instead, Bodin went back to the Justinian tradition of Roman law, holding that sovereignty could never be mixed but must have a clearly defined center of authority. Bodin's theory appealed to the times and won a short-range victory. But ultimately Mornay's theory contributed greatly to the emergence of modern democracy and liberty.

Philip Mornay   A Defense of Liberty against
                                   Tyrants (1579) [37]

Whether Private Men May Resist
by Arms

. . . What then shall private men do, if the king will constrain them
to serve idols? If the magistrates into whose hands the people have
consigned their authority, or if the magistrates of the place where
these particulars dwell, do oppose these proceedings of the king, let
them in God's name obey their leaders, and employ all their means
(as in the service of God) to aid the holy and commendable enterprises of those who oppose themselves lawfully against his wicked
intention. Amongst others they have the examples of the centurions,
and men at arms, who readily and cheerfully obeyed the princes of
Judah, who, stirred up by Jehoidas, purged the church from all profanation, and delivered the kingdom from the tyranny of Athaliah.[38]
But if the princes and magistrates approve the course of an outrageous and irreligious prince, or if they do not resist him, we must lend
our ears to the counsel of Jesus Christ, to wit, retire ourselves into
some other place. We have the example of the faithful mixed among
the ten tribes of Israel, who, seeing the true service of God abolished
by Jereboam, and that none made any account of it, they retired
themselves into the territories of Judah, where religion remained in
her purity.[39] Let us rather forsake our livelihoods and lives, than
God, let us rather be crucified ourselves, than crucify the Lord of
Life: fear not them (saith the Lord) who can only kill the body.
He Himself, His apostles, and an infinite number of Christian martyrs, have taught us this by their examples; shall it not then be
permitted to any private person to resist by arms? What shall we
say of Moses, who led Israel away in despite of King Pharaoh? . . .
Were not these particulars? I answer, that if they be considered
in themselves, they may well be accounted particular persons, insomuch as they had not any ordinary vocation. But, seeing that we
know that they were called extraordinarily, and that God Himself
has (if we may so speak) put His sword into their hands, be it far
from us to account them particular or private persons: but rather
let us esteem them by many degrees, excelling any ordinary magistrates whatsoever.

The calling of Moses is approved by the express word of God,
and by most evident miracles. . . . But where God Almighty does
not speak with His own mouth, nor extraordinarily by His prophets,

it is there that we ought to be exceedingly cautious, and to stand upon our guard; for if any, supposing he is inspired by the Holy Ghost, do attribute to himself the before-mentioned authority, I would entreat him to look that he be not puffed up with vain glory, and lest he make not a God to himself of his own fancy, and sacrifice to his own inventions. . . . Let the people also be advised on their parts, lest in desiring to fight under the banner of Jesus Christ, they run not to their own confusion to follow the army of some Galilean Thendas, or of Barcozba: as it happened to the peasants and Anabaptists of Munster, in Germany, in the year 1323. . . .[40]

Whether It Be Lawful to Resist
a Prince Who Doth Oppress or
Ruin a Public State. . . .

Princes are chosen by God, and established by the people. As all particulars considered one by one are inferior to the prince; so the whole body of the people and officers of state, who represent that body, are the prince's superiors. In the receiving and inauguration of a prince, there are covenants and contracts passed between him and the people, which are tacit and expressed natural or civil; to wit, to obey him faithfully whilst he commands justly, that he serving the commonwealth, all men shall serve him, that whilst he governs according to law, all shall be submitted to his government, etc. The officers of the kingdom are the guardians and protectors of these covenants and contracts. He who maliciously or wilfully violates these conditions, is questionless a tyrant by practice. And therefore the officers of state may judge him according to the laws. And if he support his tyranny by strong hands, their duty binds them, when by no other means it can be effected by force of arms to suppress him.

Of these officers there be two kinds, those who have generally undertaken the protection of the kingdom: as the constable, marshals, peers, palatines, and the rest, every one of whom, although all the rest do either connive or consort with the tyranny, are bound to oppose and repress the tyrant; and those who have undertaken the government of any province, city, or part of the kingdom, as dukes, marquesses, earls, consuls, mayors, sheriffs, etc., they may according to right, expel and drive tyranny from their cities, confines, and governments.

But particular and private persons may not unsheathe the sword against tyrants by practice, because they were not established by particulars, but by the whole body of the people. But for tyrants, who, without title intrude themselves for so much as there is no contract or agreement between them and the people, it is indifferently permitted all to oppose and depose them; and in this rank of tyrants may those be ranged, who abusing the weakness and sloth of a lawful prince, tyrannously insult over his subjects. Thus much for this.

Whether Neighbour Princes May . . . Aid the Subjects of Other Princes, Persecuted for True Religion, or Oppressed by Manifest Tyranny

. . . If a prince outrageously overpass the bounds of piety and justice, a neighbour prince may justly and religiously leave his own country, not to invade and usurp another's, but to contain the other within the limits of liberty and equity. And if he neglect or omit his duty herein, he shews himself a wicked and unworthy magistrate. . . .

As there have ever been tyrants distressed here and there, so also all histories testify that there have been neighbouring princes to oppose tyranny, and maintain the people in their right. The princes of these times by imitating so worthy examples, should suppress the tyrants both of bodies and souls, and restrain the oppressors both of the commonwealth, and of the church of Christ: otherwise, they themselves may most deservedly be branded with that infamous title of tyrant.

To conclude this discourse in a word, piety commands that the law and church of God be maintained. Justice requires that tyrants and destroyers of the commonwealth be compelled to reason. Charity challenges the right of relieving and restoring the oppressed. Those who make no account of these things, do as much as in them lies to drive piety, justice, and charity out of this world, that they may never more be heard of.

An Apology against the King of Spain

Editor's note

The Scottish revolution developed and triumphed quickly. The French rebels met effective resistance and the struggle was prolonged; the Huguenot fate was on the whole tragic, in spite of effective help from the French nobility and Calvinist clergy. In the Netherlands, a protest movement by the high nobility was followed in 1566 by a popular revolt, and an incredibly complex struggle developed. The apocalyptic Dutch Anabaptists had been crushed earlier by a united ruling class. Now the people of the Netherlands were led by trained Calvinist ministers whose resistance theories enabled them to secure immediate objectives through practical means, associated as they were with a governing class in open opposition to the Spanish crown.

The Dutch revolt produced a notable leader: William the Silent, count of Nassau and prince of Orange.[41] After the capture of Brill in 1572, William was able to take and hold Holland and Zealand for the revolutionaries, and the modern Netherlands eventually resulted, although Brabant and Flanders failed to stay Protestant because of military power used against them. Ambiguously Protestant, tenacious and tolerant, William of Orange wrote a ringing apology against King Philip, which testified to his liberating zeal. Three years later he was murdered, and the king of Spain paid a 25,000 ecus reward to the assassin's family. Despite his death, after eighty years (1568–1648) the Dutch revolt succeeded, although modern Belgium and the Netherlands were united only from the Congress of Vienna in 1815 until Belgium declared its independence in 1830. The founder of the Dutch Republic, William of Orange has been praised as "the wisest, gentlest and bravest man who ever led a nation" (G. M. Trevelyan).

. . . What in this world can be more acceptable and that specially
to him who hath enterprised so great and excellent a work, as is the
liberty of so good a people, oppressed by so wicked a people, than
to be deadly hated of his enemies, yea such enemies as are withal
the enemies of the country, & by their own very mouth and confession, to receive a sure testimony of his faithfulness towards his own
people, and of constancy against tyrants & disturbers of common
peace? In so much that the Spaniards and their adherents, thinking
in deede to do my displeasure, have done me many pleasures, as by
this infamous Proscription they have thought to hurt me more than
before, and yet they have made me more rejoice, and given me more
contentedness of minde. For I have not only thereby receaved that
profit, but they have opened unto me a more large field to defend
my selfe, than I durst ever be bolde to desire, that so I might cause
all the world to know the equity and justice of my enterprises. . . .

[If in reviewing my life I am forced to praise myself and blame
others] attribute the same rather to the necessity so to do (which
my enemies have layde upon me) than to my nature, & by that
means to unburden me, and to laye the faulte wholly, upon their
own shamelessness & importunity. And I will pray you (my Lords)
to remember that I am falsely accused to be "unthankfull, unfaithful, an heretic, an hypocrite, like unto Judas and Cain, the disturber
of the country, rebellious, a stranger, an enemy of mankind, the
public plague of the Christian commonwealth, a traitor, and a wicked
person, that I am set out to be slain as a beast, with reward to all
murderers, and to all persons which will attempt the same," leaving
you to judge (my Lords) whether it be possible to purge myself
from such slanders, without ripping up in some matters the ordinary
course of my life, and without exceeding the custom in speaking of
myself and other men. . . .

Seeing that the special foundation and groundwork of this [accu-
sation] is that I have taken and born arms against my Superior, I
am likewise content to enter into this matter where they shall find
themselves to have as good foundations as in other places. In the
first place I would have them tell me by what title King Philipp, the
heir of the bastard Henry of Castille, possesses the Kingdom of Castille
and of Leon? For it is most manifest that Henry his predecessor was

a bastard who rebelled against the lawful heir, who was his own
brother and Lord, whom also he slew with his own hand. What right
then or title had this bastard being the King's great-grandfather?
They answer that Don Pedro was a tyrant, and indeed I confess that
commonly they give him the name of the Cruel. But if by this title
Philipp holds Castille, why does he not perceive that men may by
the same measure drive him out, who has chased away others? And
if there has never been any more cruel tyrant, who has more proudly
and with less consideration, violated the privileges of the country
than Philipp himself, shall not he be much more unworthy to bear
and to wear the Crown of Castille than Don Pedro? . . .

Do you not see, I say, that if the Nobles, according to their oath
and bond, do not force the Duke to yield equity and justice to the
country, that they themselves should be condemned of perjury, unfaithfulness, and rebellion against the Estates of the country? As
concerning myself, I have indeed a particular reason which touches
me yet more nigh, that is, that contrary to all the said privileges,
I was deprived of all my goods, without observing any form or order
of justice therein. But that which fell out in the person of my son,
the Count of Buren, is so evident a testimony of the enemy's dis-
loyalty and unfaithfulness, and of the transgression or breach of the
privileges, that no man can with any good reason doubt why I have
taken up arms.

In that I was not able at the first time to take fast footing in the
country, which he upbraids about, what new thing has happened to
me, which has not fallen out unto the greatest Captains of the world?
Yes, even unto himself, who has so oftentimes entered into Holland
and Zealand with such great and mighty armies, and yet with a hand-
full of people, and by the aid of my Lords the Estates of the same
provinces, he has been shamefully driven out of the said country,
and that great Captain, the Duke of Alva, and his successors, without having at this day, in the said countries, one foot of land under
his disposition and government, as by your good aid, I hope that
shortly he shall not have any in all the rest of the country.

To be short, in his oath he states that in case we repudiate it, we
should no longer be bound to him, neither yield him any service
nor obedience, as appears in the last article. If then I be not bound
unto him: If I owe him not any more service or obedience, why is
he so rash as to say that I have taken up arms against my Lord?
Certainly between all lords and vassals there is a mutual bond, and

this saying of a certain Senator to a Consul shall always be praised: If you do not account me for a Senator, I will not account you for a Consul.

But between vassals there is very great difference, some remaining without comparison in far greater liberty than others, as we are in Brabant, having such large privileges and rights that we may freely make and give grants in our lands, so that, excepting the homage we owe, we cannot have anything more than we have. And among other rights and privileges we have this, to have the same power over against our Dukes that the Ephori at Sparta had over against their Kings, that is to say, to keep the Kingdom sure, in the power of a good Prince, and to cause him to yield equity, who took a position against his oath. . . .

My enemies object that I have "established liberty of conscience." I confess that the glow of fires in which so many poor Christians have been tormented is not an agreeable sight to me, although it may rejoice the eyes of the Duke of Alva and the Spaniards; and that it has been my opinion that persecutions should cease in the Netherlands. I will confess, too, in order that my enemies may know that they have to do with one who speaks out roundly and without circumlocution, that when the king was leaving Zealand he commanded me to put to death several worthy persons suspected on account of their religion. I did not wish to do this, and I could not with a clear conscience, so I warned them myself, since one must obey God rather than men. Let the Spaniards say what they please, I know several nations and peoples who are quite their equals who will approve and praise my conduct, for they have learned that nothing is to be accomplished by fire and sword. . . .

They denounce me as a hypocrite, which is absurd enough, since I have never resorted to dissimulation. As their friend, I told them quite frankly that they were twisting a rope to hang themselves when they began the barbarous policy of persecution. If their unbounded passion and their contempt for me had not prevented their following my advice, they would never have come out where they did. When later I became their opponent and enemy in the interest of your freedom, I do not see what hypocrisy they could discover in me, unless they call it hypocrisy to wage open war, take cities, chase them out of the country, and inflict upon them, without disguise, all the harm that the law of war permits. But, gentlemen, if you will reread my "Justification," published thirteen years ago, you will find there the letters of a deceitful and hypocritical king, who thought

to deceive me by his false and honeyed words, just as now he would
stun me by his threats and the thunder of his denunciations. . . .

They cast also infinite blames and slanders upon our religion and
they call us heretics. But it is a long time since they took upon
themselves to prove it, and yet were never able to bring it to purpose
or effect. I say that these injuries (being like unto the words of
women, provoked and chased with bad temper) do not deserve any
answer, much less that beastliness to say that I never trusted any
priest or friar unless he were married, and that I forced them to
marry. For who does not know, that without choice or discretion,
they cast at my head everything that they find in the way, so great
is their fury, and their passion so outrageous and unmeasurable?
And albeit that these things were true, as indeed they are not, neither
yet reasonable (for we learn by our religion that marriage ought to
be free, and should not be either enforced or forbidden), yet so it is,
that this fault should not be comparable with that tyranny over
consciences which has forbidden marriage to a great part of Christendom, against which forbidding not only the Eastern churches opposed themselves, but also the churches of Germany and France. . . .

As for me personally, you see, gentlemen, that it is my head that
they are looking for, and that they have vowed my death by offering
such a great sum of money. They say that the war can never come
to an end so long as I am among you. Might it please God that my
perpetual exile, or even my death, should bring you a true deliverance from all the evils and calamities which the Spaniards are preparing for you and which I have so often seen them considering in
council and devising in detail! How agreeable to me would be such
a banishment! How sweet death itself! . . . Why have I so often
endangered my life, what reward shall I expect for my long labors
for you, which have extended into old age, and for the loss of my
goods, if it be not to obtain and purchase your liberty, even at the
cost of my blood if necessary?

If, then, gentlemen, you believe that my exile, or even my death,
may serve you, I am ready to obey your behests. Here is my head,
over which no prince or monarch has authority save you. Dispose
of it as you will for the safety and preservation of our commonwealth. But if you judge that such little experience and energy as I
have acquired through long and assiduous labors, if you judge that
the remainder of my possessions and of my life can be of service
to you, I dedicate them to you and to the fatherland. . . .

Editor's note

The written thought stemming from the Dutch revolt was conceptually
uninspired and artistically insignificant compared to comparable documents of the English, American, and French revolutions. Yet the Dutch
declaration of independence was an important milestone on the road of
European liberty. The summer vapors of the Amsterdam canals
encouraged the Estates General to complete its work in the Hague, an
aristocratic country town, which became the capital of the nation.
Separated from Spain on July 24, the Dutch representatives proclaimed
William head of the government until such time as a new sovereign
should be found, and feted him at a banquet. The argument of the
Abjuration was that of Mornay's *Defense*, published only eighteen months
before. The formula of abjuration made independence complete. William
appealed for the union to be kept in effect as well as in words, "so that
you may execute that which your sheaf of arrows, tied with one band
only, doth mean" (from William of Orange's *Apology*).

The Estates General of the *United Netherlands*	An Act of Abjuration [Declaration of Independence], July 26, 1581[43]

. . . A prince is constituted by God to be a ruler of a people, to defend them from oppression and violence, as the shepherd of his sheep; and whereas God did not create the people slaves to their prince, to obey his commands, whether right or wrong, but rather the prince for the sake of the subjects, to love and support them as a father for his children, or a shepherd his flock . . . and when he does not behave thus but . . . oppresses them, seeking opportunities to infringe their ancient customs, exacting from them slavish compliance, then he is no longer a prince but a tyrant, and they may not only disallow his authority, but legally proceed to the choice of another prince for their defence. . . .

The Estates General of the *United Netherlands*	A Formula of Abjuration, July 29, 1581[44]

. . . I solemnly swear that I will henceforward not respect nor obey nor recognize the king of Spain as my prince and master; but that I renounce the king of Spain, and abjure the allegiance by which I may have formerly been bound to him. At the same time I swear fidelity to the United Netherlands—to wit, the provinces of Brabant, Flanders, Friesland, Gelderland, Groningen, Holland, Malines, Overissel, Utrecht, and Zealand, and also to the national council established by the estates of these provinces; and promise my assistance according to the best of my abilities against the king of Spain and his adherents. . . .

Part 7

Roman Catholic Resistance in England and Spain

Editor's note

Roman Catholic resistance teaching was ancient and powerful, including
the right to depose unfaithful rulers. In 1570, for example, Pope Pius V
had excommunicated Queen Elizabeth and absolved her subjects from
obedience to her. William Cecil's pamphlet of 1583 argued that the pope
was the leader of an international political conspiracy and that Jesuit
colleges at Douai and Rheims, which sent a hundred priests to England
before 1580, were treasonable.[1] A leading English Jesuit exile, Dr. (later
Cardinal) William Allen, answered Cecil in 1584, hoping thereby to
prepare suffering English Catholics for a great revolt to come against
Elizabethan government.[2]

In 1568, Allen had founded the College of Douai, in Flanders, to
educate English Roman Catholic clergy. By 1600 it had sent nearly three
hundred priests to England, almost one-third of whom were executed.
In effect, Allen set up a network of treason against Protestant rule in
England, and the government retaliated; 357 Catholics were executed in
England during the sixteenth and seventeenth centuries, over one-third of
them during Elizabeth's reign. (Mary Tudor had martyred 285
Protestants during her four-year effort to re-establish the Catholic faith.)
In 1970, Pope Paul VI completed canonization ceremonies for forty
English and Welsh martyrs from this period, including Allen's Jesuit
colleague Edmund Campion.[3] Allen ended his days at the English College
at Rome, which he had founded with the aid of Pope Gregory XIII.

In his *Defense*, Cardinal Allen quoted Thomas Aquinas and canon
law, of course, but he based most of his argument upon Scripture and the
church fathers. He did not fail to recapitulate Protestant resistance
theories, turning them against their owners. His accurate catalog of
Protestant theories served admirably his own polemical purposes. That
game now seemed to be played by every one except Anabaptists.

William Allen, S.J.   A True, Sincere, and Modest
                                       Defence of English Catholics
                                       (1584)[4]

. . . But first before we come to the declaration of Catholique doctrine concerning churches authoritie in censuring and deposing
Princes for matter of Religion, it shal not be amisse perhappes to
set doune the iudgment and practize of Protestants in the same case:
which though it weigh little or nothing with us as being altogether
both done and spoken of seditious and partial affection to their
Heresie, and against the lawful Magistrate of God: yet the adver-
sarie seing his owne Masters against him, shal wel perceave that the
resisting of Princes and Magistrates in cause of Religion, as also
the subjects taking armes for their defence in such a case, is no way
to be accounted treason; but most lawful, according to their new
Ghospel.

And first their grand-maister, Io. Calvin putteth doune his oracle,
as a conclusion approved of their whole sect and confraternitie in
thes wordes. "Earthlie Princes doe bereave them selves of al authoritie when they doe erect themselves against God, yea they are unworthy to be accompted in the number of men: and therfore we
must rather spit upon their heades, than obey them; when they
become so proude, or perverse, that they wil spoile God of his right;
& to the same place I further referre the reader for his instruction."[5]

For declaration of which text, and for cutting of al cavillation
about the interpretation of his wordes, their brother Beza shal speake
next who alloweth & highly commenndeth in writing, the fighting in
France for religion, against the lawes and lawful K. of that Countrie;
saying in his epistle dedecatorie of his new testament to the Q. of
England herself; "That the Nobilitie of France (under the noble
Prince of Condey) laid the first foundation of restoring true Christian religion in France, by consecrating most happilie their blood to
God in the batail of Druze [Dreux]."[6]

Whereof also the Ministers of the reformed French Churches (as
their phrase is) doe give their common verdict, in the confession
of their faith, thus, "We affirme that subjiects must obey the lawes,
pay tribute, beare al burthens imposed, and susteine the yoke even
of infidel Magistrates; so far al that, that the supreme dominion
and due of God be not violated."[7]

Zwinglius likewise a cater-cosen to the Calvinistes in religion,
writeth thus. "If the Empire of Rome, or what other Soveraigne so

ever, should oppresse the sincere religion, and we necligentlie suffer
the same; we shal be charged with contempt, no lesse than the oppressors thereof themselves; whereof we have an example in the
fiftenth of Ieremie, wher the destruction of the people is prophecied;
for that they suffred their K. Manasses, being impious and ungodly,
to be unpunished."[8]

. . . And what our English Protestants writ or thinke of this matter,
you shal wel perceive, by their opinion & high approbation of Wiats
rebellion in Q. Maries dayes: whereof one of their cheefe Ministers
called Goodman thus speaketh in his Treatise entituled; "How superior magistrats ought to be obeyed:" "Wiat did but his dutie, and
it was the dutie of al others that professe the Gospel, to have risen
with him, for maintenance of the same. His cause was just, and they
al were traitors that tooke not part with him. O Noble Wiat thou
art now with God, & thos worthie men that died for that happie
enterprise etc."[9]

What the Scottish Ministerie defineth in this question, is plaine,
by the vedict of John Knokes their mightiest Prophet; the argument
of a treatise of this matter being set doune by himself, thus: "If the
people have either rashelie promoted anie manifest wicked person,
or els ignorantlie chosen such an one, as after declareth himself
unworthie of regiment above the people of God (and such be al
Idolators and cruel persecutors) most surlie may the same men depose and punish him."[10]

So Luther also the Protestants Elias being asked his opinion of
the Almans confederacie, made at Smalcalde against Charles the
fift their lawful & noble Emperour; answered: "That in deed he was
in doubt for a time, whether they might take armes against their
Supreme Magistrate or no; but afterward seing the extremitie of
things, and that Religion could not otherwise be defended, nor themselves; he made no conscience of the matter, but ether Caesar, or
anie, waging warres in his name, might be resisted."

Sledan also recordeth that the Duke of Saxonie & the Lantzgrave,
gave this reason, of their taking armes against their supreme Magistrate: "For as much (say they) as Caesar intendeth to destroy the
true religion and our ancient libertie; he giveth us cause inough,
why we may with good conscience resist him, as both by prophane
and sacred histories may be prooved."

The same writer reporteth the like of the Ministers of Magde-
burge; declaring how the inferiour may defend himself against the

superior, compelling him to doe against the truth and rule of Christes
lawes.[11]

By al which you see; that to resist the Magistrat, defend themselves in cases of conscience, and to fight against the superiour for
religion, is a cleere and ruled case; and no treasonable opinion at al
against the Prince, if we wil be judged by Protestants; wherein their
knowen facts be far more notorious, then their writinges. For that
Beza and other the cheefe ministers of the French Calvinical Congregations, were themselves in feeld, against two or three of their
natural leige lordes and kinges.

. . . Thus both Schooles and Lawes speake and resolve for the
matter in hand: both Catholiques and Protestants agreing, that Princes
may for some causes, and especiallie for their defection in Faith and
Religion, be resisted and forsaken: though in the maner of executing
the sentence and other needful circumstances, Protestants folowe
faction and popular mutinie; we reduce al, to lawe, order and
judgement.

Editor's note

Many Jesuits defended popular sovereignty from a medieval perspective
as a means of weakening royal against papal authority. A leading
Spanish Jesuit, Juan de Mariana, who was a teacher of Cardinal
Bellarmine, took that line also.[12] His book of 1599 on the education of
the king aroused an international furor because of Mariana's defense of
individual tyrannicide, which was said to have encouraged the assassination of Henry IV, and resulted in Jesuit condemnation of Mariana's
teachings. The Catholic Mariana and the Protestant Buchanan were
unusual in allowing the individual the right of tyrannicide. Yet for
Mariana the initiative for assassination lay with the estates, not with the
individual. He thus summed up Huguenot teaching on the conditional
character of all human authority, as well as maintaining the conviction
of the French Catholic League that national unity is dependent upon
unity of religion. The natural basis of Mariana's thought was medieval.
It was his moral scruples that got him into trouble because of his
incautious statements about murdering tyrants. Mariana also looked
forward, somewhat skeptically, towards the dominance of the national,
secular state.

Mariana's more celebrated Jesuit contemporary, Cardinal Robert
Bellarmine of Italy, led the Jesuits in a less extreme, more legalistic
position than that of Mariana.[13] Distinguishing between the indirect
power of the papacy in secular matters, with the people standing
between canon law and worldly magistrates, and direct papal power in
the religious realm, Bellarmine allowed for deposition of a tyrant solely
by the pope, and only when a tyrant actually endangered people's souls.
In spite of its official status, Bellarmine's teaching had less immediate
influence than Mariana's in its effect on the Catholic League resistance
in France, and less far-range influence than the *politique* tendency of
Chancellor L'Hôpital, King Henry IV, and Jean Bodin to place national
monarchies above religious factions and claims.

Juan de Mariana, S.J.   Whether It Is Right to Destroy
a Tyrant? (1599)[14]

. . . Tyranny, which is the most evil and disadvantageous type of
government, as compared with the kingly, exercises an oppressive
power over its subjects, and is built up generally by force. . . . Although the duties of a real king are to protect innocence, punish
wickedness, provide safety, to enlarge the commonwealth with every
blessing and success, on the contrary the tyrant establishes his maxi-
mum power on himself—abandonment to boundless licentiousness
and the advantages therefrom, thinks no crime to be a disgrace to
him, no villany so great that he may not attempt it; through force
he brings blemish to the chaste, he ruins the resources of the powerful, violently snatches life away from the good, and there is no kind
of infamous deed that he does not undertake during the course of
his life. . . .

Such are the character and habits of a tyrant, hated equally by
Heaven and men. Though he may seem very fortunate, his shameful
acts become his punishment. Like bodies cut with the whip, his dis-
torted mind and conscience are tortured by his savagery, caprice
and fear. . . . Many examples, both ancient and modern, are avail-
able to demonstrate how great is the strength of a multitude angered
with hatred for a ruler, and that the ill will of the people results in
the destruction of the prince. . . .

Henry III, King of France, lies dead, stabbed by a monk in the
intestines with a poisoned knife, a detestable spectacle and one especially to be remembered; but also by this princes are taught that
impious attempts by no means go unpunished, and that the power
of princes is weak once reverence has departed from the minds of
the subjects.[15]

Henry III was planning, since he had no heir, to leave the kingdom to Henry of Vendôme, husband of his sister, although the
brother-in-law from an early age had been infected with wrong ideas
of religion, being at that time under an excommunication from the
Roman Pontiffs and cut off from the succession by law; though now
he is King of France, after a change of heart.

When the plan became known a great part of the nobles, after
the matter had been talked over with the other princes, both in
France and abroad, took up arms for the safety of the fatherland
and for their religion; from everywhere came aid. The leader was

Guise, in whose manliness and family the hopes and fortunes of
France in this storm were resting.

The designs and plans of kings remain constant. Henry, preparing
to punish the attempts of the nobles, resolved on killing Guise, and
called him to Paris. Since the plan did not go well, as the people
were enraged and incited to take up arms, he quickly departed from
the city, and after a short interval he pretended that he was won
over to better counsels and wanted a public consultation on the
common safety.

After all classes had come together at his summons, he killed at
Blois on the Loire, in his palace, Guise and his brother the cardinal,
who felt safe in the good faith of the meeting. Nevertheless after the
killing the crimes of treason were imputed to them, in order that it
might seem to have been done justifiably. They were accused with
no one defending them, and it was decreed that they were punished
under the law of treason. He seized others, among them the Bourbon
cardinal, upon whom, although in an advanced age, the next hope of
ruling rested by the law of blood.

This matter stirred up the minds of a large part of France; and
many cities, after having renounced Henry, publicly renewed the
fight for the common safety. At the head was Paris, to which no city
in Europe is comparable in resources, extent and pursuit of wisdom.
But the insurrection of a people is like a torrent; it is swollen for
but a short time.

As the people were quieting down, while Henry had his camp
about four miles out, still looking forward to punishing the city, and
though matters were almost despaired of, the audacity of one young
man in a short time definitely restored them. Jacques Clement, born
among the Aedui in the obscure district of Sorbon, was studying
theology in the Dominican college of his order. He was told by the
theologians, whom he had consulted, that a tyrant may be killed
legally. . . . Keeping his own counsel, he resolved to kill the king.
He then went out into his camp on July 31, 1589. There was no
delay. On the ground that he wished to tell secrets of the citizens
to the king, he was admitted at once. After he had delivered the
letters that he was carrying, he was directed to wait till the next day.

On August 1, which is sacred to the feast of Peter the Apostle in
Chains, after Clement had performed the service, he was summoned
by the king. He went in as the king was arising and was not yet fully
dressed. They had some conversation. As he approached under color

of handing over some letters into his hands, he inflicted a deep wound above the bladder with a knife treated with poison which he was concealing in his hand—a deed of remarkable resolution and an exploit to be remembered. Grievously wounded, the king struck back at the murderer, wounding him in the eye and breast with the same knife, crying out against the traitor and king-killer. . . .

By the death of the king [Clement] made a great name for himself. A killing was expiated by a killing, and at his hands the betrayal and death of the Duke of Guise were avenged with the royal blood. Thus Clement died, an eternal honor to France, as it has seemed to very many, twenty-four years of age, a young man of simple temperament and not strong of body; but a greater power strengthened his normal powers and spirit. . . .

There was no unanimity of opinion about the deed of the monk. While many praised him and deemed him worthy of immortality, others, eminent in their reputations for wisdom and learning, condemned him, denying that it is right for anyone on his own private authority to kill a king, . . . even though he be profligate in his morals and also has degenerated into tyranny. . . .

The protectors of the people have no fewer and lesser arguments. Assuredly the republic, whence the regal power has its source, can call a king into court, when circumstances require and, if he persists in senseless conduct, it can strip him of his principate. . . . Besides, we reflect, in all history, that whoever took the lead in killing tyrants was held in great honor. What indeed carried the name of Thrasybulus in glory to the heavens unless it was the fact that he freed his country from the oppressive domination of the Thirty Tyrants? . . . Many conspired against Domitius Nero with luckless result, and yet without censure, but rather with the praise of all ages. . . . The praetorians slew Elagabalus, a monstrosity and disgrace of the empire—his sin atoned for by his own blood. . . .[16]

Would you leave to the tyrant your native land, to which you owe more than to your parents, to be harassed and disturbed at his pleasure? Out with such iniquity and depravity! Even if life, safety, fortune are imperiled, we will save our country from destruction. . . .

In this I see that both the philosophers and theologians agree, that the Prince who seizes the State with force and arms, and with no legal right, no public, civic approval, may be killed by anyone and deprived of his life and position. Since he is a public enemy and afflicts his fatherland with every evil, since truly and in a proper sense he is clothed with the title and character of tyrant, he may be removed by any means and gotten rid of by as much violence as he used in seizing his power. Thus meritoriously did Ehud (Judges 3:12–30), having worked himself by gifts into the favor of Eglon, King of the Moabites, stab him in the belly with a poniard and slay him; he snatched his own people from a hard slavery, by which they had been oppressed for then eighteen years. . . .

So the question of fact remains, who justly may be held to be a tyrant, for the question of law is plain that it is right to kill one. . . . Out of so great a number of tyrants, such as existed in the ancient times, one may count only a few that have perished by the swords of their own people; in Spain, hardly more than one or two, though this may be due to the loyalty of the subjects and the mildness of the princes, who got their power with the best right and exercised it modestly and kindly.

Nevertheless, it is a salutary reflection that the princes have been persuaded that if they oppress the state, if they are unbearable on account of their vices and foulness, their position is such that they can be killed not only justly but with praise and glory. Perhaps this fear will give some pause lest they deliver themselves up to be deeply corrupted by vice and flattery; it will put reins on madness. . . .

Part 8

Puritan Religious Revolution in England

41   To the True and Faithful Congregation of Christ's Universal Church

Editor's note

Not to be confused with George Fox (b. 1624), the seventeenth-century founder of the Quakers, and author of Document 52, the Anglican John Foxe (b. 1516) joined the Protestant exiles abroad during Mary Tudor's reign.[1] He sympathized with the more radical Knoxians at Frankfurt and Basel, but continued to work with the central Edwardian group associated with Cranmer, Ridley, and Latimer. A graduate of Oxford, his *Acts and Monuments* ("Foxe's *Book of Martyrs*"), a history of Christian persecutions in support of Edwardian Reformation principles, was first published at Strassburg and Basel in Latin. The first English edition in 1563 created a sensation. The second edition of 1570 doubled the length of text and revised its point of view, shifting the beginning of the millennium from the time of Christ to that of Constantine.

Like Thomas Brightman and John Napier (b. 1550), Foxe explained the millennium as occurring between Constantine and Wycliffe.[2] All three praised the Christian Emperor Constantine, but only Foxe praised the post-Constantinian church. Thus Foxe influenced the development of Puritan millennialism in the seventeenth century. The Puritans moved beyond Foxe in radicalism. Brightman, for example, identified the Elizabethan church with the church of Laodicea in the book of Revelation, vulnerable because of its lukewarmness to more thorough reformation. Joseph Mead or Mede (b. 1568), under the influence of Johannes Alsted (b. 1588) of Germany, moved beyond Brightman in introducing the new premillennialism of the seventeenth century, which claimed that the literal Second Advent of Christ would precede the millennium.[3] An earthly kingdom was imminent, when the saints would rule politically with Christ. Thomas Goodwin (Document 43) was a representative of this premillennial position. Foxe had helped create Puritan revolutionary theology, but the apocalptic revolutionaries of the 1640s were more radical than Foxe.

John Foxe's *Book of Martyrs* has influenced the English Protestant mind almost as much as the Bible, which it attempted to bring up to

date. Himself a defender of Elizabethan royal supremacy and an
Erasmian opponent of separatism, John Foxe at the same time set forth
the standard Puritan providential interpretation of history, which was to
arm revolutionary freedom-fighters against a visible, powerful,
persecuting church, supported in their opinion by an ungodly monarch,
first Catholic and later Anglican. Foxe's preface to the faithful outlined
the meaning of history plainly. The early church was the true church.
After the apostles had brought the Gospel to England, the English-born
Emperor Constantine saved the church from pagan persecution and
Roman wiles. (Here he differed from the Anabaptists, who saw the fall
as originating with Constantine.) A minority of faithful preachers and
teachers kept the true church alive in the middle ages, amidst clerical
Roman dominance. Wycliffe had restored the Gospel, which was now
being preached in 1570. Threats abounded however. The Marian
martyrs had testified to the same heroic faith as the early Christians.
Christ was about to return. He would complete his redemptive drama
with the end of history. It behooved believers to patch up strife among
themselves. If Satan were to be loosed among them, the faithful would
act against him bravely, knowing that their days of suffering would be
brief. The premillennialists added to this picture the glories of the
thousand-year reign of the saints with Christ on earth. For all Puritans,
Christ's return was imminent.

John Foxe   To the True and Faithful
                                     Congregation of Christ's
                                     Universal Church (1570)[4]

. . . Most humbly would I crave of almighty God . . . that as the
prayers of them which prayed in the outward temple were heard, so
all true disposed minds which shall resort to the reading of this
present history, containing the acts of God's holy martyrs and monuments of his church, may, by example of their life, faith, and doctrine, receive some such spiritual fruit to their souls, through the
operation of his grace, that it may be to the advancement of his
glory and profit of his church, through Christ Jesus our Lord.
Amen. . . .

    As for me and my history, my purpose hath been simple. . . .
First, to see the simple flock of Christ, especially the unlearned
sort, so miserably abused, and all for ignorance of history, not
knowing the course of times and true descent of the church, it pitied
me that [this] part of diligence [had] so long been unsupplied in
this my-country church of England. Again, considering the multitude
of chronicles and storywriters, both in England and out of England,
of whom the most part have been either monks or clients to the See

of Rome, it grieved me to behold how partially they handled their
stories. . . .

Which history therefore I have here taken in hand, that as other
storywriters heretofore have employed their travail to magnify the
church of Rome, so in this history might appear to all Christian
readers the image of both churches, as well of the one as of the other;
especially of the poor oppressed and persecuted church of Christ.
Which persecuted church, though it hath been of long season
trodden under foot by enemies, neglected in the world, nor regarded
in histories, and almost scarce visible or known to worldly eyes, yet
hath it been the true church only of God, wherein he hath mightily
wrought hitherto in preserving the same in all extreme distresses,
continually stirring up from time to time faithful ministers by whom
always have been kept some sparks of his true doctrine and religion.
. . .

In Christ's time who would have thought but [that] the congregation and councils of the Pharisees had been the right church? And
yet had Christ another church in earth besides that; which, albeit it
was not so manifest in the sight of God. Of this church meant Christ,
speaking of the temple which he would raise again the third day;
and yet after that the Lord was risen, he showed not himself to the
world but only to his elect, which were but few. The same church,
after that, increased and multiplied mightily among the Jews; yet
had not the Jews eyes to see God's church, but did persecute it till
at length all their whole nation was destroyed.

After the Jews, then came the heathen emperors of Rome, who
having the whole power of the world in their hands did what the
world could do to extinguish the name and church of Christ. Whose
violence continued the space of three hundred years. . . . For although many then of the Christians did suffer death, yet was their
death neither loss to them nor detriment to the church; but the more
they suffered, the more of their blood increased. In the time of these
emperors God raised up then in this realm of Britain divers worthy
preachers and witnesses . . . in whose time the doctrine of faith,
without men's traditions, was sincerely preached. After their death
and martyrdom it pleased the Lord to provide a general quietness
to his church, whereby the number of his flock began more to increase. . . . All this while, about the space of four hundred years,
religion remained in Britain uncorrupt, and the word of Christ truly
preached, till, about the coming of Augustine and of his companions
from Rome [(A.D. 597)], many of the said Britain-preachers were

slain by the Saxons. After that began [the] Christian faith to enter
and spring among the Saxons after a certain Romish sort, yet notwithstanding somewhat more tolerable than were the times which
after followed, through the diligent industry of some godly teachers
which then lived amongst them—as Aidan, Finian, Colman the
archbishop of York, Bede [et al.]. . . .

And thus hitherto stood the condition of the true church of
Christ, albeit not without some repugnance and difficulty, yet in
some mean state of the truth and verity, till the time of Pope
Hildebrand, called Gregory VII, which was near about the year
1080, and of Pope Innocent III in the year 1215: by whom all
together was turned upside down, all order broken, discipline dissolved, true doctrine defaced, Christian faith extinguished; instead
whereof was set up preaching of men's decrees, dreams, and idle
traditions. And whereas before, truth was free to be disputed amongst
learned men, now liberty was turned into law, argument into authority. . . . During which space the true church of Christ, although it
durst not openly appear in the face of the world, [was] oppressed
by tyranny; yet neither was it so invisible or unknown, but, by the
providence of the Lord, some remnant always remained from time
to time which not only showed secret good affection to sincere doctrine, but also stood in open defense of truth against the disordered
church of Rome. In which catalogue . . . a learned multitude of
sufficient witnesses here might be produced, whose names neither
are obscure nor doctrine unknown—as Joachim abbot of Calabria,
. . . the Waldenses or Albigenses which to a great number segregated
themselves from the church of Rome, . . . Gulielmus Ockham, . . .
Dantes Aligerius, an Italian who wrote against the pope, monks, and
friars and against the donation of Constantine, A.D. 1330; Taulerus,
a German preacher, [etc., etc.]. . . .

To descend now somewhat lower in drawing out the descent of
the church. What a multitude here cometh of faithful witnesses in the
time of John Wickliff, as Ocliff, Wickliff (A.D. 1379), . . . Chaucer,
. . . John Huss, Jerome of Prague (a schoolmaster), with a number
of faithful Bohemians and Thaborites not to be told; with whom I
might also adjoin Laurentius Valla and Joannes Picus (the learned
Earl of Mirandula). But what do I stand upon recital of names,
which almost are infinite? Wherefore if any be so far beguiled in his
opinion [as] to think the doctrine of the church of Rome as it now
standeth to be of such antiquity, and that the same was never im-

pugned before the time of Luther and Zwingli now of late, let him
read these histories. . . .

Let us now proceed further as we began, deducing this descent
of the church unto the year 1501. In which year the Lord began to
show in the parts of Germany wonderful tokens and bloody marks
of his passion; as the bloody cross, his nails, spear, and crown of
thorns, which fell from heaven upon the garments and caps of men
and rocks of women. . . . By the which tokens Almighty God, no
doubt, presignified what grievous afflictions and bloody persecutions
should then begin to ensue upon his church for his gospel's sake,
according as in this history is described; wherein is to be seen what
Christian blood hath been spilt, what persecutions raised, what tyranny exercised, what torments devised, what treachery used against
the poor flock and church of Christ; in such sort as since Christ's
time greater hath not been seen.

And now by revolution of years we are come from that time of
1501 to the year now present, 1570. In which the whole seventy
years of the Babylonish captivity draweth now well to an end if we
count from the first appearing of these bloody marks above mentioned. Or if we reckon from the beginning of Luther and his persecution, then lacketh yet sixteen years. Now what the Lord will do
with this wicked world, or what rest he will give to his church after
these long sorrows—he is our Father in heaven, his will be done in
earth as seemeth best to his divine Majesty.

In the meantime let us, for our parts, with all patient obedience
wait upon his gracious leisure, and glorify his holy name, and edify
one another with all humility. And if there cannot be an end of our
disputing and contending one against another, yet let there be a
moderation in our affections. And forsomuch as it is the good will
of our God, that Satan thus should be let loose among us for a short
time; yet let us strive in the meanwhile what we can to amend the
malice of the time with mutual humanity. They that be in error, let
them not disdain to learn. . . .

No man liveth in that commonwealth where nothing is amiss; but
yet because God hath so placed us Englishmen here in one commonwealth, also in one church, as in one ship together, let us not mangle
or divide the ship, which being divided, perisheth; but every man
serve in his order with diligence wherein he is called—they that sit
at the helm keep well the point of the needle to know how the ship
goeth and whither it should; whatsoever weather betideth, the needle,

well touched with the stone of God's word, will never fail. Such as labor at the oars start for no tempest but do what they can to keep from the rocks. Likewise they which be in inferior rooms, take heed they move no sedition nor disturbance against the rowers and mariners. . . .

The Lord of peace, who hath power both of land and sea, reach forth his merciful hand to help them up that sink, to keep them up that stand, to still these winds and surging seas of discord and contention amongst us; that we, professing one Christ, may, in one unity of doctrine, gather ourselves into one ark of the true church together; where we, continuing steadfast in faith, may at the last luckily be conducted to the joyful port of our desired landing-place by his heavenly grace. . . . Amen.

Editor's note

In the seventy years between Foxe's preface and the outbreak of
revolution in 1640, the English Puritans pursued two objectives. They
failed in the first—namely, to reform the government, worship, and
discipline of the church beyond what the Elizabethan Settlement
allowed. But their second activity, preaching the Word,[5] had never been
suppressed completely, as point 5 of this document indicates. In
November 1640, during the early days of the Long Parliament, all
restraints on pulpit and press suddenly came to an end. The Root and
Branch Petition was the result. It touched off a train of events which
disrupted church government, brought on civil war, and gave one
faction of preachers the opportunity to replace the bishops with an
English version of presbyterianism. Yet these events were not
anticipated in the petition itself. The only prescription the preachers had
for governing was "according to God's Word." They were asking first
for liberty to preach. The opportunity to govern came later.

The background of the Root and Branch Petition is that of a
prehistory of revolution.[6] Charles I enjoyed personal popularity when
he became king in 1625, but Parliament was already in a strong
political position, having declared its rights and ready to act upon them.
Severe conflict followed. Charles affirmed the divine right of kings;
Parliament stood on its prerogatives. After Scotland rebelled against the
king's effort to enforce high church ritual in their churches, the Long
Parliament (from 1640 through 1653) held power over the king,
attacking his ministers through its power of impeachment. Parliament
was divided, however, into religious-political factions, with the Puritan
party unsuccessfully demanding abolition of episcopacy "root and
branch." The massacre of thirty thousand Protestants in Ulster in 1641
made revolt against Charles inevitable. Two civil wars followed, with
Charles encouraging the Scots and Irish in a second rising, set off by
Scottish dissatisfaction with English toleration of religious sects. Oliver
Cromwell, the parliamentary general, again crushed the rebellion,
making the army supreme. The largely Independent or Congregationalist

army, which tolerated all religious sects, then clashed with Parliament
(chiefly Presbyterians) and Commons was purged of those unsympathetic
with the army. Charles was brought to trial and beheaded in 1649.

The Puritans were not able to sustain effective political government
over a long period of time in England. But the Root and Branch
Petition spelled out the kind of minute concern which turned seeming
religious cranks into revolutionaries. A whole series of petitions
followed, from all over England. Church government had come to be
the burning political issue of the day. England thus had become a
commonwealth, the first modern written constitution was put into effect,
and Cromwell was named lord protector. Cromwell improved the
English navy, restored England's international prestige, and established
religious toleration at home. He ruled absolutely, but advanced
England's interests with his power. Military despotism increased under
Richard, Cromwell's son, and in 1660 the Stuart kings returned to
power. But the Puritans led the way from church government to political
democracy. Seldom in modern times has religious enthusiasm so
positively developed into political democracy as in the England of
the 1640s.[7]

Isaac Pennington (?)   The Root and Branch Petition,
                                   December 11, 1640[8]

The humble Petition of many of His Majesty's subjects in and about
the City of London, and several Counties of the Kingdom,

Showeth,

That whereas the government of archbishops and lord bishops, deans
and archdeacons, etc., with their courts and ministrations in them,
have proved prejudicial and very dangerous both to the Church and
Commonwealth, they themselves having formerly held that they have
their jurisdiction or authority of human authority, till of these later
times, being further pressed about the unlawfulness, that they have
claimed their calling immediately from the Lord Jesus Christ, which
is against the laws of this kingdom, and derogatory to His Majesty
and his state royal. And whereas the said government is found by
woeful experience to be a main cause and occasion of many foul
evils, pressures and grievances of a very high nature unto His Majesty's subjects in their own consciences, liberties and estates, as in
a schedule of particulars hereunto annexed may in part appear:

We therefore most humbly pray, and beseech this honorable assembly, the premises considered, that the said government, with all
its dependencies, roots and branches, may be abolished, and all laws
in their behalf made void, and the government according to God's

Word may be rightly placed amongst us: and we your humble suppliants, as in duty we are bound, will daily pray for His Majesty's long and happy reign over us, and for the prosperous success of this high and honorable Court of Parliament.

A Particular of the manifold
evils, pressures, and grievances
caused, practiced and occasioned
by the Prelates and their
dependents.

1. The subjecting and enthralling all ministers under them and their authority, and so by degrees exempting them from the temporal power; whence follows,

2. The faint-heartedness of ministers to preach the truth of God, lest they should displease the prelates; as namely, the doctrine of predestination, of free grace, of perseverance, of original sin remaining after baptism, of the sabbath, the doctrine against universal grace, election for faith foreseen, free-will against antichrist, non-residents, human inventions in God's worship; all which are generally witheld from the people's knowledge, because not relishing to the bishops.

3. The encouragement of ministers to despise the temporal magistracy, the nobles and gentry of the land; to abuse the subjects, and live contentiously with their neigmbors, knowing that they, being the bishops' creatures, shall be supported.

4. The restraint of many godly and able men from the ministry, and thrusting out of many congregations their faithful, diligent, and powerful ministers, who lived peaceably with them, and did them good, only because they cannot in conscience submit unto and maintain the bishops' needless devices; nay, sometimes for no other cause but for their zeal in preaching, or great auditories.

5. The suppressing of that godly design set on foot by certain saints, and sugared with many great gifts by sundry well-affected persons for the buying of impropriations, and placing of able ministers in them, maintaining of lectures, and founding of free schools, which the prelates could not endure lest it should darken their glories, and draw the ministers from their dependence upon them.

6. The great increase of idle, lewd and dissolute, ignorant and erroneous men in the ministry, which swarm like the locusts of Egypt over the whole kingdom; and will they but wear a canonical coat, a surplice, a hood, bow at the name of Jesus, and be zealous of

superstitious ceremonies, they may live as they list, confront whom they please, preach and vent what errors they will, and neglect preaching at their pleasures without control.

7. The discouragement of many from bringing up their children in learning; the many schisms, errors, and strange opinions which are in the Church; great corruptions which are in the Universities; the gross and lamentable ignorance almost everywhere among the people; the want of preaching ministers in very many places both of England and Wales; the loathing of the ministry, and the general defection to all manner of profaneness.

8. The swarming of lascivious, idle, and unprofitable books and pamphlets, play-books and ballads; as namely, Ovid's "Fits of Love," "The Parliament of Women," which came out at the dissolving of the last Parliament; Barns's "Poems," Parker's "Ballads," in disgrace of religion, to the increase of all vice, and withdrawing of people from reading, studying, and hearing the Word of God, and other good books.

9. The hindering of godly books to be printed, the blotting out or perverting those which they suffer, all or most of that which strikes either at Popery or Arminianism; the adding of what or where pleaseth them, and the restraint of reprinting books formerly licensed, without relicensing.

10. The publishing and venting of popish, Arminian, and other dangerous books and tenets; as namely, "That the Church of Rome is a true Church, and in the worst times never erred in fundamentals"; "that the subjects have no propriety in their estates, but that the king may take from them what he pleaseth"; "that all is the king's, and that he is bound by no law"; and many other, from the former wherof hath sprung.

11. The growth of popery and increase of papists, priests and Jesuits in sundry places, but especially about London since the Reformation; the frequent venting of crucifixes and popish pictures both engraven and printed, and the placing of such in Bibles.

12. The multitude of monopolies and patents, drawing with them innumerable perjuries; the large increase of customs and impositions upon commodities, the ship-money, and many other great burthens upon the Commonwealth, under which all groan.

13. Moreover, the offices and jurisdictions of archbishops, lord bishops, deans, archdeacons, being the same way of church government, which is in the Romish Church, and which was in England in the time of popery, little change thereof being made (except only

the head from whence it was derived), the same arguments supporting the pope which do uphold the prelates, and overthrowing the
prelates, which do pull down the pope; and other reformed Churches,
having upon their rejection of the pope cast the prelates out also as
members of the beast. Hence it is that the prelates here in England,
by themselves or their disciples, plead and maintain that the pope is
not Antichrist, and that the Church of Rome is a true Church, hath
not erred in fundamental points, and that salvation is attainable in
that religion, and therefore have restrained to pray for the conversion of our Sovereign Lady the Queen. Hence also hath come:

14. The great conformity and likeness both continued and increased of our Church to the Church of Rome, in vestures, postures,
ceremonies and administrations, namely as the bishop's rochets and
the lawn-sleeves, the four-cornered cap, the cope and surplice, the
tippet, the hood, and the canonical coat; the pulpits clothed, especially now of late, with the Jesuits' badge upon them every way.

15. The standing up at *Gloria Patri* and at the reading of the
Gospel, praying towards the East, the bowing at the name of Jesus,
the bowing to the altar towards the East, cross in baptism, the kneel-
ing at the Communion.

16. The turning of the Communion table altar-wise, setting images,
crucifixes, and conceits over them, and tapers and books upon them,
and bowing or adoring to or before them; the reading of the second
service at the altar, and forcing people to come up thither to receive,
or else denying the sacrament to them; terming the altar to be the
mercy-seat, or the place of God Almighty in the church, which is a
plain device to usher in the Mass.

17. The christening and consecrating of churches and chapels,
the consecrating fonts, tables, pulpits, chalices, churchyards, and
many other things, and putting holiness in them; yea, reconsecrating
upon pretended pollution, as though everything were unclean without their consecrating; and for want of this sundry churches have
been interdicted, and kept from use as polluted.

18. The Liturgy for the most part is framed out of the Romish
Breviary, Rituals, Mass-Book, also the Book of Ordination for archbishops and ministers framed out of the Roman Pontifical.

19. The multitude of canons formerly made, wherein among other
things excommunication, *ipso facto*, is denounced for speaking of a
word against the devices above-said, or subscription thereunto,
though no law enjoined a restraint from the ministry without subscription, and appeal is denied to any that should refuse subscription

or unlawful conformity, though he be never so much wronged by the inferior judges. Also the canons made in the late sacred Synod, as they call it, wherein are many strange and dangerous devices to undermine the Gospel and the subjects' liberties, to propagate Popery, to spoil God's people, ensnare ministers, and other students, and so to draw all into an absolute subjection and thralldom to them and their government, spoiling both the King and the Parliament of their power.

20. The countenancing of plurality of benefices, prohibiting of marriages, without their license, at certain times almost half the year, and licensing of marriages without banns asking.

21. Profanation of the Lord's Day, pleading for it, and enjoining ministers to read a Declaration set forth (as it is thought) by their procurement for tolerating of sports upon that day, suspending and depriving many godly ministers for not reading the same out of conscience, because it was against the law of God so to do, and no law of the land to enjoin it.

22. The pressing of the strict observation of the saints' days, whereby great sums of money are drawn out of men's purses for working on them; a very high burthen on most people, who getting their living on their daily employments, must either omit them, and be idle, or part with their money, whereby many poor families are undone, or brought behind-hand; yet many churchwardens are sued, or threatened to be sued by their troublesome ministers, as perjured persons, for not presenting their parishioners who failed in observing holydays.

23. The great increase and frequency of whoredoms and adulteries, occasioned by the prelates' corrupt administration of justice in such cases who taking upon them the punishment of it, do turn all into monies for the filling of their purses; and lest their officers should defraud them of their gain, they have in their late canon, instead of remedying these vices, decreed that the commutation of penance shall not be without the bishops' privity.

24. The general abuse of that great ordinance of excommunication, which God hath left in His Church as the last and greatest punishment which the Church can inflict upon obstinate and great offenders; and the prelates and their officers who of right have nothing to do with it, do daily excommunicate men, either for doing that which is lawful, or for vain, idle, and trivial matters, as working, or opening a shop on a holyday, for not appearing at every beck

upon their summons, not paying a fee, or the like; yea, they have
made it, as they do all other things, a hook or instrument wherewith
to empty men's purses, and to advance their own greatness; and so
that sacred ordinance of God, by their perverting of it, becomes
contemptible to all men, and is seldom or never used against notorious offenders, who for the most part are their favorites.

25. Yea further, the pride and ambition of the prelates being
boundless, unwilling to be subject either to man or laws, they claim
their office and jurisdiction to be *Jure Divino*, exercise ecclesiastical
authority in their own names and rights, and under their own seals,
and take upon them temporal dignities, places and offices in the
commonwealth, that they may sway both swords.

26. Whence follows the taking commissions in their own courts
and consistories, and where else they sit in matters determinable of
right at common law, the putting of ministers upon parishes, without the patron's and people's consent.

27. The imposing of oaths of various and trivial articles yearly
upon churchwardens and sidesmen, which they cannot take without
perjury, unless they fall at jars continually with their ministers and
neighbors, and wholly neglect their own calling.

28. The exercising of the oath *ex officio*, and other proceedings
by way of inquisition, reaching even to men's thoughts, the appre-
hending and detaining of men by pursuivants, the frequent suspending and depriving of ministers, fining and imprisoning of all sorts
of people, breaking up of men's houses and studies, taking away
men's books, letters, and other writings, seizing upon their estates,
removing them from their callings, separating between them and
their wives against both their wills, the rejecting of prohibitions with
threatenings, and the doing of many other outrages, to the utter
infringing the laws of the realm and the subjects' liberties, the ruin-
ing of them and their families; and of later time the judges of the
land are so awed with the power and greatness of the prelates, and
other ways promoted, that neither prohibition, *Habeas Corpus*, nor
any other lawful remedy can be had, or take place, for the distressed
subjects in most cases; only papists, Jesuits, priests, and such others
as propagate popery or Arminianism, are countenanced, spared, and
have much liberty; and from hence followed amongst other these
dangerous consequences.

1. The general hope and expectation of the Romish party, that
their superstitious religion will ere long be fully planted in this king-

dom again, and so they are encouraged to persist therein, and to practice the same openly in divers places, to the high dishonor of God, and contrary to the laws of the realm.

2. The discouragement and destruction of all good subjects, of whom are multitudes, both clothiers, merchants and others, who being deprived of their ministers, are overburdened with these pressures, have departed the kingdom to Holland, and other parts, and have drawn with them a great manufacture of cloth and trading out of the land into other places where they reside, whereby wool, the great staple of the kingdom, is become of small value, and vends not; trading is decayed, many poor people want work, seamen lose employment, and the whole land is much impoverished, to the great dishonor of this kingdom and blemishment to the government thereof.

3. The present wars and commotions happened between his Majesty and his subjects of Scotland, wherein his majesty and all his kingdoms are endangered, and suffer greatly, and are like to become a prey to the common enemy in case the wars go on, which we exceedingly fear will not only go on, but also increase to an utter ruin of all, unless the prelates with their dependences be removed out of England, and also they and their practices, who, as we under your honor's favors, do verily believe and conceive have occasioned the quarrel.

All which we humbly refer to the consideration of this honorable assembly, desiring of Lord of heaven to direct you in the right way to redress all these evils.

Editor's note

The Puritan saints saw the predicted millennium of Foxe, Napier, Brightman, and Mead come still closer when the Long Parliament met. The tension produced by the Reformation combined with nationalism, Protestant literalism, Calvinist elitism, and perhaps Lollard tradition to produce widespread apocalyptic or millenarian struggle, intensifying earlier excitement. Millenarianism was the most striking and fundamental characteristic of the formal preaching before the Long Parliament, the majority of the preachers being Presbyterian.[9] The millenarian wave caught up large numbers of ministers, of Presbyterian, Independent, and Baptist views alike. Of some 112 ministers in this period who published three new works apiece, 78 or just under 70 percent can be identified as millenarians: they believed in an imminent kingdom of glory on earth, either a literal thousand years' reign, or (often in the case of the Presbyterians) a period of latterday glory, and often explained the civil war as its precursor.[10]

The notable sermon *Syons Glory* (1641) showed clearly that Christ's reign would begin in 1650 and by 1695 would be completed. Daniel and Revelation provided the evidence. The poor and humble saints would bring about Christ's triumph. Often attributed to the Baptist chiliast, Hanserd Knollys, it has recently been argued that the sermon was preached at the gathering of a congregation in Holland by Thomas Goodwin, a leading Independent or Congregationalist minister, who back in England helped to wreck Presbyterian hopes for ecclesiastical and political control with the help of his five "dissenting brethren" in Parliament and kindred preachers in the army, city, and country (1645).[11]

Since millenarian ideas were widespread in Parliament and especially among the sects and in the army, millenarianism became activistic: God's wish was for the saints to throw down Babylon and to establish the New Jerusalem, not merely to await some divine intervention. Muenster now could be repeated on English soil, without all the old notoriety. Eager preachers called for zealous prosecution of the civil war. The millennium, the war, and the cause of God had all become part of the same cosmic and terrestial struggle. Goodwin's use of millennial and popular imagery indicates how respectable vivid apocalyptic expectations were in the universities of his day and especially at the right hand of Cromwell's growing political power.

Thomas Goodwin   A Glimpse of Syons Glory
                                                        (1641)[12]

Rev. 19:6: "And I heard as it were the voice of a great multitude, and as the voice of many waters, and as the voice of mighty thunderings, saying: Hallelujah, for the Lord God Omnipotent reigneth."

At the pouring forth of the first vial, there was a voice saying: "Babylon is fallen, it is fallen." At the pouring forth of the sixth, John hears a voice as the voice of many waters, and as the voice of thunderings, saying: "Hallelujah, the Lord God Omnipotent reigneth," immediately following the other. Babylon's falling is Syon's raising. Babylon's destruction is Jerusalem's salvation. The fourth vial was poured upon the sun, which is yet doing, namely upon the Emperor and that house of Austria, and will be till that house be destroyed. . . .

This is the work that is in hand. As soon as ever this is done, the Antichrist is down, Babylon fallen, then comes in Jesus Christ reigning gloriously; then comes in this "Hallelujah, the Lord God Omnipotent reigneth." . . . It is the work of the day to cry down Babylon, that it may fall more and more; and it is the work of the day to give God no rest till he sets up Jerusalem as the praise of the whole world. Blessed is he that dasheth the brats of Babylon against the stones. Blessed is he that hath any hand in pulling down Babylon. And beautiful likewise are the feet of them that bring glad tidings unto Jerusalem, unto Syon, saying, "The Lord God Omnipotent reigneth." This is the work of this exercise: to show unto you how, upon the destruction of Babylon, Christ shall reign gloriously, and how we are to further it. . . .

From whence came this hallelujah? "I heard as it were the voice of a great multitude, and as the voice of many waters." By waters we are to understand people: the voice of many waters, of many people. . . . The voice of Jesus Christ reigning in his Church comes first from the multitude, the common people. The voice is heard from them first, before it is heard from any others. God uses the common people and the multitude to proclaim that the Lord God Omnipotent reigneth. As when Christ came at first the poor receive[d] the Gospel —not many wise, not many noble, not many rich, but the poor—so in the reformation of religion, after Antichrist began to be discovered, it was the common people that first came to look after Christ. . . .

The business, brethren, concerning the Scots, it is a business in the issue whereof we hope there will be great things. Where begin it? At the very feet, at the very soles of the feet. You that are of the meaner rank, common people, be not discouraged; for God intends to make use of the common people in the great work of proclaiming the kingdom of his Son: "The Lord God Omnipotent reigneth." The voice that will come of Christ's reigning is like to begin from those that are the multitude, that are so contemptible, especially in the eyes and account of Antichrist's spirits and the prelacy: the vulgar multitude, the common people—what more condemned in their mouths than they? . . .

Though the voice of Christ's reign came first from the multitude; yet it comes but in a confused manner, as the noise of many waters. Though the multitude may begin a thing, and their intention may be good in it, yet it is not for them to bring it to perfection: that which they do commonly is mixed with much confusion and a great deal of disorder. . . . The people had a hint of something: Down with Antichrist, down with popery. Not understanding distinctly what they did, their voice was but as the voice of many waters. Therefore it follows: "And as the voice of mighty thunderings." . . .

After the beginning of this confused noise among the multitude, God moves the hearts of great ones, of noble, of learned ones; and they come in to the work, and their voice is as the voice of mighty thundering, a voice that strikes terror, and hath a majesty in it to prevail. . . . This is the work of the day, for us to lift up our voice to heaven, that it might be mighty to bring forth more and more the voices of our Parliament as a voice of thunder, a terrible voice to the Anti-christian party, that they may say, "The Lord God Omnipotent reigneth." And let us not be discouraged, for our prayers, though they be poor and mean, and scattered, they may further the voice of thunderings. . . . It may be, it is to be a stumbling block to wicked and ungodly men in his just judgment, that they should see and not understand. And it was upon this ground that God suffered his kingdom to be darkened hitherto, that Antichrist might prevail: because of much glory that he is intending to bring out of the prevailing of Antichrist in the world, therefore in his providence he hath so permitted it as that the kingdom of his Son for many years should be darkened. . . . But God in his providence, because he would permit Antichrist to rise and to rule for a long time—and he had many things to bring out of the kingdom of Antichrist, to work for his glory—therefore God hath left this truth to be so dark: the setting up of Christ in his kingly office.

Thirdly, because God would exercise the faith and other graces of his Spirit in his children, that they might believe in, and love Jesus Christ for his spiritual beauty, though no outward beauty, no outward kingdom doth appear, but he be as a spiritual king only. . . . And the less Christ doth reign outwardly in the world, the less glorious his kingdom doth appear outwardly, the more let us labor to bring our hearts under his spiritual reign. . . . For yet the voice is not heard much, that the Lord God Omnipotent reigneth, abroad in the world, though lately some noise we have heard. But blessed be God, in our congregations amongst us we may hear that the Lord God Omnipotent reigneth. It is through our wretched wickedness if his kingly power be not fully set up amongst us in all his ordinances. . . .

But though it be dark for a while, certainly he shall reign, and the voice will be glorious and distinct one day, saying, "Hallelujah, the Lord God Omnipotent reigneth." He shall reign first personally; secondly, in his Saints. First, personally. We will not fully determine of the manner of his personal reigning. But thus far we may see there is . . . a probability, in his person, God and Man, he shall reign upon the earth, here in this world, before that great and solemn day. There are divers scriptures that have somewhat of this in them. . . . 2 Thessalonians 2:8: "Antichrist shall be destroyed by the brightness of Christ's coming, the brightness of his personal coming." And that place (Rev. 20) where it is said, "The Saints shall reign with him a thousand years," which cannot be meant reigning with him in heaven. It is made as a proper peculiar benefit unto such as had refused Antichrist's government, especially to the Christian Church. It is likely divers of the prophets and patriarchs may come in, but especially it belongs to the Christian Church. Now the reigning with Christ a thousand years is not meant reigning with him in heaven. For after these thousand years there shall be many enemies raised against the Church; Gog and Magog shall gather themselves together. If it were meant of heaven, that could not be; and therefore it must be meant of Jesus Christ coming and reigning here gloriously for a thousand years. And although this may seem to be strange, yet heretofore it hath not been accounted so. It hath been a truth received in the primitive times. Justin Martyr, that lived presently after John, he spake of this as a thing that all Christians acknowledged; and likewise Lactantius hath such expressions in divers places of his seventh book. . . .

God intends to honor Christ and the Saints before the world. . . . And God is pleased to raise the hearts of his people to expect it; and those that are most humble, most godly, most gracious, most spiritual, searching into the scriptures, have their hearts most raised in expectation of this. And it is not like, that that work of the Spirit of theirs shall be in vain. But God is beginning to clear it up more and more. God is beginning to stir in the world, and to do great things in the world, the issue whereof (I hope) will come to that we speak of. . . .

The first thing wherein the happiness of the Church consists is this: that it shall be delivered from all the enemies of it, and from all molesting troubles, and so be in a most blessed safety and security. The God of peace shall tread down Satan shortly, and all that are of Satan. Christ is described in this Revelation 19, with his garment dyed in blood, when he doth appear to come and take the kingdom. And he appeared with many crowns on his head; that notes his many victories, and his name was King of Kings and Lord of Lords. And the Saints appeared triumphing with him, clothed with white linen and set upon white horses. Is that a clothing for soldiers? Yes, for the army of Christ, that rather comes to triumph than for to fight. Christ fighteth and vanquisheth all these enemies; and they come triumphing in white. . . . And this city that is described in the Revelation shall have the gates always open, in regard of the security that is there—no danger at all of any enemy.

Secondly, there shall be a wonderful confluence of people to this church: both Jew and Gentile shall join together to flow to the beautifulness of the Lord. Daniel 2:35: Christ is compared to the stone that shall break the image and shall become a mountain, and fill the whole heaven. Isaiah 60:8: "They shall come as doves to the windows." And when John came to measure the city, the Church, it was a great and mighty city.

Thirdly, because where there is much confluence, there useth to be a contraction of much filthiness; therefore, in the third place, it shall be most pure—a pure church, yea, in great part, if not altogether; nay, we may almost affirm, altogether to be delivered from hypocrites. "Without there shall be dogs, and whosoever shall work or make a lie." Not without, in hell; but without the church. Hypocrites shall be discovered and cast out from the church. . . . It is a most pure church, and therefore is described: the walls to be precious stones, the city to be as clear as glass, and the pavement to be pure gold.

Fourthly, there shall be abundance of glorious prophecies fulfilled, and glorious promises accomplished. When you read the Prophets, you have prophecies of many glorious things; and the knowledge of this truth will help to understand those prophecies. . . .

Fifthly, abundance of hidden mysteries of godliness will be cleared then, that are now exceeding dark. . . . Revelation 11:19: "There was seen the Ark of the Testament"; whereas the Ark stood before in the Holy of Holies that was shut up, that none was to come into it but the High Priest. But now it is opened to all. In the Ark were the secrets, a type of the secrets that shall be opened at this time, that were shut up before. Glorious truths shall be revealed, and above all the mystery of the Gospel and the righteousness of faith shall be discovered. Before, what a little of the mystery of the Gospel and the righteousness of faith was discovered! But this will grow brighter and brighter till that time, which is the great design of God for his glory to all eternity.

Sixthly, the gift of the Saints shall be abundantly raised. He that is weak shall be as David; and he that is strong, as the Angel of the Lord (Zech. 12:8). And then shall be accomplished that promise that "God will pour his Spirit on them; and their young men shall see visions, and their old men shall dream dreams." It was fulfilled in part upon the Apostles, but the full is not till that time knowledge shall be increased.

Seventhly, the graces of the Saints shall be wonderfully enlarged, even in a manner glorified; though not so full as afterwards in the highest heaven, but mightily raised. The Saints shall be all clothed in white linen, which is the righteousness of the Saints; that is, the righteousness they have by Christ, whereby they shall be righteous before God, and holy before men. Holiness shall be written upon their pots, and upon their bridles: upon every thing their graces shall shine forth exceedingly to the glory of God. . . .

The people of God have been, and are, a despised people. But their reproach shall be for ever taken away, and they shall not be ashamed of religion, for it shall be glorified before the sons of men. . . . There are notable texts of scripture to show the great honor that shall be in the ways of religion. Isaiah 49:23: "Kings shall be thy nursing fathers, and queens thy nursing mothers; they shall bow down to thee, and lick up the dust of thy feet." What a high expression is this for the honor of godliness! . . . The second place is in Zechariah 12:5: "The governors of Judah shall say in their hearts: The inhabitants of Jerusalem shall be my strength in the Lord of Hosts, their God."

We know that now in many places the governors of Judah, the great ones of the country, their spirits have been set against the Saints of God. We know what reproachful names they have put upon them, and how they have discountenanced them. Though the governors of Judah have counted them factious, and schismatics, and Puritans, there is a time coming when the governors of Judah shall be convinced of the excellency of God's people, so convinced as to say in their hearts that the inhabitants of Jerusalem, that is, the Saints of God gathered together in a church, are the best commonwealth's men: not seditious men, not factious, not disturbers of the state. . . . This shall be when the Lord God Omnipotent reigneth in his Church. And through God's mercy we see light peeping out this way. . . .

In the ninth place, the presence of Jesus Christ and of God shall be exceeding glorious in the Church: then the name of it shall be called Jehovah Shammah, "The Lord is there." They shall follow the Lamb wheresoever he goeth; they shall see the King in his beauty and glory. And such a presence of Christ will be there as it is questionable whether there shall be need of ordinances, at least in that way that now there is. And therefore some interpret that place so: "They shall be all taught of God, and shall not need to teach one another." . . . The presence of Christ shall be there and supply all kind of ordinances. . . .

In the tenth place, . . . many of the worthies of God, that have lived in former times, shall rise again. . . .

The eleventh is this: there shall be most blessed union of all the churches of the world. . . . Blessed will the time be when all dissensions shall be taken away; and when there shall be a perfect union of all, and not any distinction of Calvinists or Lutherans, or the like, but all shall come and serve God and be called by one name.

And twelfth is the resurrection of the creatures of the world: and so in that regard there shall be abundance of outward glory and prosperity. . . . When the fulness of the glory of the adoption of the sons of God shall come, the creatures shall be delivered to them. The whole world is purchased by Christ, and purchased for the

Saints, that is Christ's aim. "All is yours," says the Apostle, "the whole world"; and therefore (Rev. 21:7) it is said, "The Saints shall inherit all things." You see that the Saints have little now in the world; now they are the poorest and the meanest of all; but then when the adoption of the sons of God shall come in the fulness of it, the world shall be theirs; for the world is purchased for them by Jesus Christ. "Not only heaven shall be your kingdom, but this world bodily." . . .

But you will say, Are these things true? To that we answer: For the truth of them I will go no further than this chapter, verse 9, "These are the true sayings of God." . . .

But how can they be? Zechariah 8:9: "If it be marvellous in your eyes, should it also be marvellous in my eyes? saith the Lord of Hosts." . . . It is God Omnipotent that shall do these things, by that power, "whereby he is able to subdue all things unto himself." Mountains shall be made plain, and he shall come skipping over mountains and over difficulties. Nothing shall hinder him. . . .

But when shall these things be? Truly, brethren, we hope it is not long before they shall be; and the nearer the time comes, the more clearly these things shall be revealed. . . . No place in scripture gives us so much light to know when this shall be an Daniel 12:11. "And from the time that the daily sacrifices shall be taken away, and the abomination that maketh desolate set up, there shall be a thousand, two hundred and ninety days." What is the meaning of this? The light that I have from this, I acknowledge to be from that worthy instrument of God, Mr. Brightman. A day is usually taken for a year, and so many days as were set, so many years it should be. All the question is about the beginning of the time. This abomination of desolation was in Julian's time, in 360, because then Julian would set up the Temple again (that was destroyed), in despite of the Christians, and would set up the Jewish religion again. That was the abomination of desolation says he; and the whole Jewish religion was not consumed till that time.

Now reckon so many years according to the number of the days, it comes to 1650; and it is now 1641, and that place for the abomination of desolation is like to be it as any that can be named. But it is said, "Blessed is he that comes to another number": 1335 days; that is 45 years more added. That is, says he, in 1650 they shall begin; but it shall be 45 years before it comes to full head, and blessed is he that comes to this day. And he hath hit right in other things, as never the like, in making Sardis to be the church of Germany, and foretold from thence how things would fall out, and we see now are. Now we have also a voice from the multitude as from the waters, and it begins to come from the thunderings. . . .

If God hath such an intention to glorify his Church, and that in this world, oh, let every one say to his own heart: What manner of persons ought we to be? . . . Because you are beginning this despised work, gathering a church together, which way God will honor. Certainly, the communion of Saints, and independency of congregations, God will honor. And this work is a foundation of abundance of glory that God shall have, and will continue till the coming of Christ. And blessed are they that are now content to keep the word of God's patience. And do you keep the word of God's patience though you suffer for it, as you now do. . . .

Editor's note

Civil war broke out when King Charles and Archbishop Laud attempted to force the Presbyterian Scots to use the Anglican Book of Common Prayer. Charles convened the Long Parliament (1640) in order to appropriate money to drive the invading Scots out of England. Instead, Parliament imprisoned and later executed Laud. Finally, war broke out between Charles and Parliament. Their forces in trouble, Parliament turned for help to the Scots, signing in 1643 the Solemn League and Covenant, which promised to work toward uniformity of religion in the Britich Isles and toward abolishing both popery and episcopacy in England. It appeared as if the Church of England would become Presbyterian as the proceedings of the Westminster Assembly indicated. Anglicanism was dead.[13] Yet the alliance of Parliament with the Presbyterians did not please the more radical Puritan advocates of independency and toleration. With radical sentiment growing in the powerful army, the Presbyterian position of Parliament became precarious.

Oliver Cromwell, the parliamentary leader who rose to become an extraordinary general, led an army of "saints," the New Model of volunteer officers, "agitators," chaplains, and cavalry, together with infantry and dragoons, which was largely Independent or Congregational in religion but allowed toleration and a wide variety of sects.[14] A revolutionary military force emerged based upon preaching the Word of God and using a radical Protestant organizational principle. The army became a training ground for democracy and religious freedom, as the army debates at Putney in 1647 reveal. By covenanting together in voluntary groups, the parliamentary forces opened a new way for organizing politics and religion in modern society. The revolutionary army, fighting for personal religious devotion and biblically covenanted communities, easily defeated the forces supporting divine right monarchy. Thomas Muentzer's abortive peasant revolutionary covenant emerged victorious amid the more middle-class English Puritan New Model army.

Alexander Henderson (?) A Solemn League and Covenant (House of Commons), September 25, 1643[15]

A solemn league and covenant for Reformation and Defense of Religion, the honor and happiness of the King, and the peace and safety of the three kingdoms of England, Scotland and Ireland.

We noblemen, barons, knights, gentlemen, citizens, burgesses, ministers of the Gospel, and commons of all sorts in the kingdoms of England, Scotland, and Ireland, by the providence of God living under one King, and being of one reformed religion; having before our eyes the glory of God, and the advancement of the kingdom of our Lord and Savior Jesus Christ, . . . and calling to mind the treacherous and bloody plots, conspiracies, attempts and practices of the enemies of God against the true religion and professors thereof in all places, especially in these three kingdoms, ever since the reformation of religion, . . . have (now at last) after other means of supplication, remonstrance, protestations and sufferings, for the preservation of ourselves and our religion from utter ruin and destruction, . . . resolved and determined to enter into a mutual and solemn league and covenant, . . . [and] with our hands lifted up to the most high God, do swear,

I. That we shall sincerely, really and constantly, through the grace of God, endeavor in our several places and callings, the preservation of the reformed religion in the Church of Scotland, in doctrine, worship, discipline and government, according to the Word of God, and the example of the best reformed Churches; and we shall endeavor to bring the Churches of God in the three kingdoms to the nearest conjunction and uniformity in religion, confession of faith, form of Church government, directory for worship and catechising, that we, and our posterity after us, may, as brethren, live in faith and love, and the Lord may delight to dwell in the midst of us.

II. That we shall in like manner, without respect of persons, endeavor the extirpation of Popery, prelacy (that is, Church government by Archbishops, Bishops, their Chancellors and Commissaries, Deans, Deans and Chapters, Archdeacons, and all other ecclesiastical officers depending on that hierarchy), superstition, heresy, schism, profaneness, and whatsoever shall be found to be contrary to sound doctrine and the power of godliness, lest we partake in other men's sins, and thereby be in danger to receive of their plagues; and that the Lord may be one, and His name one in the three kingdoms.

III. We shall with the same sincerity, reality and constancy, in our several vocations, endeavor with our estates and lives mutually to preserve the rights and privileges of the Parliaments, and the liberties of the kingdoms, and to preserve and defend the King's Majesty's person and authority, in the preservation and defense of the true religion and liberties of the kingdoms, that the world may bear witness with our consciences of our loyalty, and that we have no thoughts or intentions to diminish His Majesty's just power and greatness.

IV. We shall also with all faithfulness endeavor the discovery of all such as have been or shall be incendiaries, malignants or evil instruments, by hindering the reformation of religion, dividing the King from his people, or one of the kingdoms from another, or making any faction or parties amongst the people, contrary to the league and covenant, that they may be brought to public trial and receive condign punishment, as the degree of their offenses shall require or deserve, or the supreme judicatories of both kingdoms respectively, or others having power from them for that effect, shall judge convenient.

V. And whereas the happiness of a blessed peace between these kingdoms, denied in former times to our progenitors, is by the good providence of God granted to us, and hath been lately concluded and settled by both Parliaments: we shall each one of us, according to our places and interest, endeavor that they may remain conjoined in a firm peace and union to all posterity, and that justice may be done upon the willful opposers thereof, in manner expressed in the precedent articles.

VI. We shall also, according to our places and callings, in this common cause of religion, liberty and peace of the kingdom, assist and defend all those that enter into this league and covenant, in the maintaining and pursuing thereof; and shall not suffer ourselves, directly or indirectly, by whatsoever combination, persuasion or terror, to be divided and withdrawn from this blessed union and conjunction. . . .

And because these kingdoms are guilty of many sins and provocations against God, and His Son Jesus Christ, as is too manifest by our present distresses and dangers, the fruits thereof: we profess and declare, before God and the world, our unfeigned desire to be humbled for our own sins, and for the sins of these kingdoms; especially that we have not as we ought valued the inestimable benefit of the Gospel; that we have not labored for the purity and power thereof and that we have not endeavored to receive Christ in our hearts, nor to walk worthy of Him in our lives, which are the cause of other sins and transgressions so much abounding amongst us; and our true and unfeigned purpose, desire and endeavor, for ourselves and all others under our power and charge, both in public and private, in all duties we owe to God and man, to amend our lives, and each one to go before another in the example of a real reformation, that the Lord may turn away His wrath and heavy indignation, and establish these Churches and kingdoms in truth and peace. . . .

Editor's note

Samuel Rutherford (1600?–1661), like some other Scottish
Presbyterian ministers, expressed hopeful millenarian views about the
meaning of the civil war.[16] Later he played a prominent part in the
Westminster Assembly. Rutherford's *Lex Rex*, disputing the just
prerogatives of king and people, supplanted Buchanan's *Powers of the
Crown* as a handbook for resistance by Scotsmen to tyrannical
monarchs.

By entering into a contract, Rutherford argued, the king remains
strictly a servant of the people. Family constitutes no claim to the
throne, for the origin of monarchy was elective. Nor may Parliament
resist the people any more than the king. The people's cause is the same
in all countries, and one country has the duty to go to the aid of
another.

Yet Rutherford limited freedom. Though the people as a collective
entity should have its way, individuals may not do and think as they
will. Rutherford wrote against liberty of conscience from a Presbyterian
perspective, and Milton attacked him for it in a sonnet. Rutherford
represents most fully the radical political thought of the northern
Presbyterians at the time of optimistic resistance during the Civil War.

Samuel Rutherford   Lex Rex: The Law and the
Prince (1644)[17]

Who doubteth (Christian reader) but innocency must be under the courtesy and mercy of malice, and that it is a real martyrdom to be brought under the lawless inquisition of the bloody tongue? Christ, the Prophets, and Apostles of our Lord went to heaven with the note of traitors, seditious men, and such as turned the world upside down. Calumnies of treason to Caesar were an ingredient in Christ's cup, and therefore the author is the more willing to drink of that cup that touched his lip, who is our glorious forerunner. What if conscience toward God and credit with men cannot both go to heaven with the Saints? The author is satisfied with the former companion and is willing to dismiss the other. Truth to Christ cannot be treason to Caesar, and for his choice he judgeth truth to have a nearer relation to Christ Jesus than the transcendent and boundless power of a mortal prince. . . .

[The Presbyterians] hold (I believe with the warrant of God's word): if the king refuse to reform religion, the inferior judges and assembly of godly pastors and other church officers may reform; if the king will not . . . do his duty in purging the House of the Lord, may not Eli[j]ah and the people do their duty and cast our Baal's priests? Reformation of religion is a personal act that belongeth to all, even to any one private person according to his place. . . .

For the lawfulness of resistance in the matter of the king's unjust invasion of life and religion, we offer these arguments. That power which is obliged to command and rule justly and religiously for the good of the subjects, and is only set over the people on these conditions, and not absolutely, cannot tie the people to subjection without resistance, when the power is abused to the destruction of laws, religion, and the subjects. But all power of the law is thus obliged (Rom. 13:4; Deut. 17:18–20; II Chron. 19:6; Ps. 132:11–12; 89: 30–31; II Sam. 7:12; Jer. 17:24–25), and hath, and may be abused by kings to the destruction of laws, religion, and subjects. . . .

Much is built to commend patient suffering of ill, and condemn all resistance of superiors, by Royalists, on the place (I Pet. 2:18) where we are commanded, being servants, to suffer buffet, not only for ill-doing, of good masters, but also undeservedly. . . . But it is clear, the place is nothing against resistance. . . . One act of grace and virtue is not contrary to another. Resistance is in the children of God an innocent act of self-preservation, as is patient suffering, and therefore they may well subsist in one. . . .

We hold that the law saith with us that vassals lose their farm if they pay not what is due. Now what are kings but vassals to the state, who, if they turn tyrants, fall from their right? . . .

Let Royalists show us any act of God making David king, save this act of the people making him formally king at Hebron, and therefore the people as God's instrument transferred the power, and God by them in the same act transferred the power, and in the same they chose the person. . . . This power is the people's radically, naturally. . . . And God hath revealed (in Deut. 17:14–15) the way of regulating the act of choosing governors and kings, which is a special mean of defending and protecting themselves; and the people is as principally the subject and fountain of royal power, as a fountain is of water. . . .

Editor's note

Roland H. Bainton has shown how Puritan Congregationalists moved away from the traditional just-war theory toward a crusading mentality in England.[18] No clearly distinguishable religious and political parties had yet appeared in the England of 1640. Presbyterianism contended mightily in 1643 because of Parliament's alliance with the Scots. The Independents then became the more radical Puritan opposition, taking over leadership after the army and Parliament split in 1647. Coming out of Anglicanism, both Presbyterians and Congregationalists were steeped in traditional just-war theory. As Calvinists, both parties also tended toward a crusading stance against the enemies of God. The third Christian attitude toward war (pacifism), which many Anabaptists had advocated, was scarcely discernible among the Puritans. The Congregationalists squared their just-war theory with revolutionary or crusading zeal against the king by calling upon Calvin's old *ephors* argument for constitutional government. This doctrine that inferior magistrates might restrain the superior now meant that the English Parliament (or army) might curb the king, just as it had suggested in Germany that the princes might resist the emperor and in France that the nobles might coerce the crown. The English revolutionaries had revived, in a Calvinist establishment form, the teachings of Thomas Muentzer and the Muensterites.

Robert Ram, clergyman son of an Anglican bishop in Ireland, came to accept the viewpoint of the revolutionary Independent army, with considerable danger to his own person because of lay opposition to his views in a neighboring parish.[19] In 1644, Ram published a *Soldier's Catechism*, which gave the ordinary soldier an opportunity to confess his holy-war faith. The theory behind Ram's catechism remained conservative: the king is the highest person, but the parliament is the highest power, and every soul is bound to be subject to the higher powers. The Old Testament doctrine of holy war now found fervent advocates. The reign of King Jesus in England was about to begin.

Robert Ram   The Souldiers Catechisme
                                (1644)[20]

Q. What Profession are you of?

A. I am a Christian and a souldier.

Q. Is is lawful for Christians to be souldiers?

A. Yea doubtlesse: we have Arguments enough to warrant it. . . .

   1. God calls himself a man of war, and Lord of Hosts.

   2. Abraham had a Regiment of 318. Trained men. David was imployed in fighting the Lords battels. . . .

   7. The New Testament mentioneth two famous Centurions. . . .

Q. What side are you of? . . .

A. I am for King and Parliament: or in plainer terms: I fight to recover the King out of the hands of a Popish Malignant Company, that have seduced His Majesty with their wicked Counsels, and have withdrawne him from his Parliament.

   2. I fight for the Lawes and Liberties of my Countrey, which are now in danger to be overthrowne by them that have long laboured to bring into this Kingdome an Arbitrary, and Tyrannicall Government.

   3. I fight for the preservation of our Parliament. . . .

   4. I fight in defence and maintenance of the true Protestant Religion. . . . Almighty God declares himselfe a friend to our Party. . . . God now calls upon us to avenge the blood of his Saints. . . .

Q. Who do you thinke were the Authors, and occasioners of this unnaturall Warre?

A. The Jesuits. . . .

   2. The Bishops. . . .

   3. The Delinquents. . . .

Editor's note

Oliver Cromwell became the genius of the Puritan Revolution through his personal combination of practical military leadership and a rugged faith in "providences."[21] Born of a gentry family and educated under Puritan influence at Cambridge, Cromwell supported Puritanism when he became a member of Parliament. Inconspicuous at first, he rose rapidly to leadership during the first Civil War because of his genius for organizing and inspiring light-horse troops in the parliamentary armies. Having reorganized the New Model army during conflict between Parliament and the military in 1644, Cromwell won a decisive victory over the king. When Parliament and the army quarreled again, Cromwell supported his soldiers in a purge of Parliament and in the execution of Charles in 1649. He had no doubt that executing Charles was just, considering the principles of Mariana and Buchanan: "a breach of trust ought to be punished more than any other crime whatever." The Rump Parliament abolished monarchy and the House of Lords and declared England a commonwealth. But when the political situation worsened, the army made Cromwell lord protector. In that quasi-monarchical role, Cromwell had to compromise his ideal of representative government because he wished even more to rule a godly nation that would at the same time be religiously tolerant.

Leaning toward religious independency, Cromwell was close to the radical Levellers, Diggers, and Fifth Monarchy Men, although he repudiated their anarchic extremes.[22] His solution to the problem of religious division was a radical one for that age: he abandoned the state-church idea in favor of a national religion resting on Presbyterian, Independent, and Baptist bases. Although he could massacre the Irish in response to barbarous provocation, most of his contemporaries were horrified at the degree of tolerance he expressed. He fully acquiesced in Foxe's idea of providence. As his letter to the speaker of the House of Commons shows, Cromwell regarded his Civil War victory at Bristol as a crusading result of a holy cause, under a righteous God. And since he "looked unto providences," he was willing to trust whatever results history brought him. Like most who trust in providence, he ended his career with less than complete confidence and success; yet the protectorate he built was religiously tolerant and politically viable. Cromwell had introduced the first modern revolution, integrating religion and politics.

Oliver Cromwell   A Letter from Bristol,
                                          September 14, 1645[23]

For the Honorable William Lenthall, Speaker of the Commons House of Parliament: These

Sir, It hath pleased the General to give me in charge to represent unto you a particular account of the taking of Bristol, the which I gladly undertake.

After the finishing of that service at Sherborne, it was disputed at a council of war, whether we should march into the West or to Bristol. Amongst other arguments, the leaving so considerable an enemy at our backs, to march into the heart of the Kingdom; the undoing of the country about Bristol, which was exceedingly harassed by the Prince his being but a fortnight thereabouts; . . . these considerations, together with the taking so important a place, so advantageous for the opening of trade to London, did sway the balance, and begat that conclusion.

When we came within four miles of the city, we had a new debate, whether we should endeavor to block it up, or make a regular siege. The latter being overruled, Colonel Welden with his brigade marched to Pile Hill, on the south side of the city, being within musket-shot thereof, where in a few days they made a good quarter, overlooking the city. . . .

By sallies (which were three or four) I know not that we lost thirty men, in all the time of our siege. Of officers of quality, only Colonel Okey was taken, by mistake going to the enemy, thinking them to be friends, and Captain Guilliams slain in a charge. We took Sir Bernard Asteley; and killed Sir Richard Crane, men very considerable with the Prince.

We had a council of war concerning the storming of the town, about eight days before we took it; and in that there appeared great unwillingness to the work, through the unseasonableness of the weather, and other apparent difficulties. . . . The day and hour of our storm was appointed to be Wednesday morning, the tenth, about one of the clock. . . . The general signal unto the storm was the firing of straw, and discharging four piece of cannon at Prior Hill Fort. The signal was very well perceived by all, and truly the men went on with great resolution, and very presently recovered the line, making way for the horse to enter. . . .

By this, all the line from Prior Hill Fort to Avon, which was a full mile, with all the forts, ordinance and bulwarks, were possessed by us but one, wherein there were about 120 men of the enemy which the General summoned, and all the men submitted. . . .

Being possessed of thus much as hath been related, the town was fired in three places by the enemy, which we could not put out; and this begat a great trouble to the General and us all, fearing to see so famous a city burnt to ashes before our faces. Whiles we were viewing so sad a spectacle, and consulting which way to make further advantage of our success, the Prince sent a trumpet to the General to desire a treaty for the surrender of the town, to which the General agreed. . . .

On Thursday about two of the clock in the afternoon, the Prince marched out; having a convoy of two regiments of horse from us; and making election of Oxford for the place he would go to, which he had liberty to do by his Articles. . . .

The Prince had foot of the garrison (as the mayor of the city informed me), two-thousand five-hundred, and about one thousand horse, besides the trained bands of the town, and auxiliaries 1200, some say 1500. I hear but one man hath died of the plague in all our army, although we have quartered amongst and in the midst of infected persons and places. We had not killed of ours in this storm, nor all this siege, 200 men.

Thus I have given you a true, but not a full account of this great business; wherein he that runs may read, that all this is none other than the work of God. He must be a very Atheist that doth not acknowledge it.

It may be thought that some praises are due to these gallant men, of whose valor so much mention is made: their humble suit to you and all that have an interest in this blessing, is, that in the remembrance of God's praises they may be forgotten. It's their joy that they are instruments to God's glory, and their country's good; it's their honor that God vouchsafes to use them.

Sir, they that have been employed in this service know that faith and prayer obtained this city for you. I do not say ours only, but of the people of God with you and all England over, who have wrestled with God for a blessing in this very thing. Our desires are, that God may be glorified by the same spirit of faith by which we asked all our sufficiency, and having received it, it's meet that He have all the praise. Presbyterians, Independents, all had here the same spirit of faith and prayer; the same pretense and answer; they agree here, know no names of difference: pity it is it should be otherwise anywhere.

All that believe, have the real unity, which is most glorious, because inward and spiritual, in the Body, and to the Head. As for being united in forms, commonly called Uniformity, every Christian will for peace-sake study and do, as far as conscience will permit; and from brethren, in things of the mind we look for no compulsion, but that of light and reason.

In other things, God hath put the sword into the Parliament's hands, for the terror of evil-doers, and the praise of them that do well. If any plead exemption from it, he knows not the Gospel: if any would wring it out of your hands, or steal it from you under what pretense soever, I hope they shall do it without effect. That God may maintain it in your hands, and direct you in the use thereof, is the prayer of

Your humble servant,
Oliver Cromwell.

Editor's note

Oliver Cromwell was admired and feared by Englishmen, and
respected abroad more than any English king. John Lilburne, the leader
of the Levellers, who spent two-thirds of his mature life in prison, was
the most popular man in England.[24] As the revolution developed,
Lilburne moved beyond his early religious separatism to a secular
political program, embodied in a constitution based on the sovereignty of
the people. Here was the first real popular European movement led by
laymen, representing an important element (radical democratic idealism)
within Cromwell's victorious army. Suppressed by Cromwell, the 1647
draft constitution of the Levellers survived and reappeared prior to the
American war for independence and the achievement of English
democracy. Not yet including common laborers, servants, and women in
their reforms, the Levellers nevertheless represented the finest hour of
English rhetorical inspiration, and showed that a revolution had really
taken place.

Like most revolutions, the Puritan revolt fizzled quickly after
Cromwell was gone. But it bequeathed a permanent legacy of human
rights and freedoms to mankind. The doctrines of the Agreement of the
People were not forgotten. Underneath the still aristocratic constitutions
of the seventeenth and eighteenth centuries, they survived. When the
time was ripe for their full implementation, human rights and freedoms
doctrines supplied much of the background for the American War of
Independence and for the constitutional reforms that made Great
Britain a democracy in the nineteenth century. It is the great contribution
of the Puritan Revolution to have developed a fully modern democratic
political program based on the notion of the sovereignty of the people.
In seventeenth century-England (still somewhat prematurely) the
radical free-church revolution resulted in the precious development
of successful modern democracy.

John Lilburne   The Agreement of the People,
                                   October 28, 1647[25]

Having by our late labors and hazards made it appear to the world at how high a rate we value our just freedom, and God having so far owned our cause as to deliver the enemies thereof into our hands, we do now hold ourselves bound in mutual duty to each other to take the best care we can for the future to avoid both the danger of returning into a slavish condition and the chargeable remedy of another war; for, as it cannot be imagined that so many of our countrymen would have opposed us in this quarrel if they had understood their own good, so may we safely promise to ourselves that, when our common rights and liberties shall be cleared, their endeavors will be disappointed that seek to make themselves our masters. Since, therefore, our former oppressions and scarce-yet-ended troubles have been occasioned, either by want of frequent national meetings in Council, or by rendering those meetings ineffectual, we are fully agreed and resolved to provide that hereafter our representatives be neither left to an uncertainty for the time nor made useless to the ends for which they are intended. In order whereunto we declare:

I. That the people of England, being at this day very unequally distributed by Counties, Cities, and Boroughs for the election of their deputies in Parliament, ought to be more indifferently proportioned according to the number of the inhabitants. . . .

II. That, to prevent the many inconveniences apparently arising from the long continuance of the same persons in authority, this present Parliament be dissolved upon the last day of September which shall be in the year of our Lord 1648.

III. That the people do, of course, choose themselves a Parliament once in two years. . . .

IV. That the power of this, and all future Representatives of this Nation, is inferior only to theirs who choose them, and does extend, without the consent or concurrence of any other person or persons, to the enacting, altering, and repealing of laws, to the erecting and abolishing of offices and courts, to the appointing, removing, and calling to account magistrates and officers of all degrees, to the making of war and peace, to the treating with foreign states, and, generally, to whatsoever is not expressly or impliedly reserved by the represented to themselves:

Which are as follows.

1. That matters of religion and the ways of God's worship are not at all entrusted by us to any human power, because therein we cannot remit or exceed a tittle of what our consciences dictate to be the mind of God without wilful sin: nevertheless the public way of instructing the nation (so it be not compulsive) is referred to their discretion.

2. That the matter of impressing and constraining any of us to serve in the wars is against our freedom; and therefore we do not allow it in our Representatives. . . .

3. That after the dissolution of the present Parliament, no person be at any time questioned for anything said or done in reference to the late public differences. . . .

4. That in all laws made or to be made every person may be bound alike, and that no tenure, estate, charter, degree, birth, or place do confer any exemption from the ordinary course of legal proceedings whereunto others are subjected.

5. That as the laws ought to be equal, so they must be good, and not evidently destructive to the safety and well-being of the people.

These things we declare to be our native rights, and therefore are agreed and resolved to maintain them with our utmost possibilities against all opposition whatsoever. . . .

49   The Tenure of Kings and
                                          Sonnet: To the Lord
                                          General Cromwell

Editor's note

John Milton, the most distinguished English poet, is an outstanding
example of a politically engaged artist.[26] Indeed, the middle years of his
life were largely occupied by his religious and political hopes for
revolution. Milton's greatest poetry was written after Cromwell's death
had tempered those hopes; his final poetic drama, *Samson Agonistes*,
employed the story of Samson to inspire the defeated Puritans with
courage to triumph through sacrifice. A convinced Puritan, Milton early
supported the revolution, at first on the side of the Presbyterians until
he became disillusioned with Presbyterian reluctance to execute the
king and with their opposition to liberty of conscience. As a noted
pamphleteer, he wrote prolifically in support of personal freedom,
including four pamphlets upholding the morality of divorce for
incompatibility. (Milton's wife had left him the same year they were
married, although they were later reunited.) Like other Puritans, Milton
exemplified a new view of marriage based on companionship and
loyalty rather than traditional sacramental or romantic norms. When the
victorious Puritan Parliament issued its own ordinance for control of
the press directed against his embarrassing writings, Milton published
his classic protest and plea for freedom of the press, *Areopagitica*, in
1644. Always an advocate of religious toleration, Milton also addressed
an admiring ode to Cromwell, although the lord protector did not
completely fulfill Milton's hopes for encouraging varieties of religious
beliefs in England.

By 1649, Milton had followed the power center into alliance with
Cromwell and the Independents. Thus his *Tenure of Kings* boldly
asserted the right of revolution, which had been accomplished with the
execution of the king. This work secured him a position in Cromwell's
government as secretary for foreign tongues, and he continued to defend
Cromwell and the Commonwealth government in several writings. One
of them, *The Tenure of Kings*, argued that men are by nature free, and
rulers are subject to law. Even untyrannical kings may be deposed by
the right of free men to govern as seems best to them.

After becoming completely blind in 1652, Milton carried on his responsibilities heroically. Milton, the bold revolutionary, remained a hierarchical aristocrat, loyal to his leader, Cromwell. His personal sacrifice for the cause was considerable, and he did not betray his principles. To Europe's intellectuals, Milton was *the* spokesman for revolutionary England. It was said that the two agencies most responsible for raising the reputation of the Commonwealth abroad were Cromwell's battles and Milton's books. Escaping the scaffold when the Restoration came, Milton wrote his greatest poems, including *Paradise Lost*, and a bold treatise on Christian doctrine as a blind old man essentially faithful to a Puritan vision but at the same time passing over into freethinking liberalism.

John Milton   The Tenure of Kings (1649)[27]

No man who knows ought, can be so stupid to deny that all men naturally were born free, being the image and resemblance of God himself, and were by privilege above all the creatures, born to command and not to obey: and that they lived so. 'Till from the root of *Adam*'s transgression, falling among themselves to do wrong and violence, and foreseeing that such courses must needs tend to the destruction of them all, they agreed by common league to bind each other from mutual injury, and jointly to defend themselves against any that gave disturbance or opposition to such agreement. Hence came Cities, Towns and Commonwealths.

And because no faith in all was found sufficiently binding, they saw it needful to ordain some authority, that might restrain by force and punishment what was violated against peace and common right. This authority and power of self-defense and preservation being originally and naturally in every one of them and unitedly in them all, for ease, for order, and lest each man should be his own partial Judge, they communicated and derived either to one, whom for the eminence of his wisdom and integrity they chose above the rest, or to more than one whom they thought of equal deserving: the first was called a King; the other Magistrates.

Not to be their Lords and Masters, . . . but to be their Deputies and Commissioners, to execute, by virtue of their entrusted power, that justice which else every man by the bond of nature and of Covenant must have executed for himself, and for one another. And to him that shall consider well why among free Persons, one man by civil right should bear authority and jurisdiction over another, no other end or reason can be imaginable. These for a while governed well, and with much equity decided all things at their own arbitre-

ment: till the temptation of such a power left absolute in their hands
perverted them at length to injustice and partiality.

Then did they who now by trial had found the danger and inconveniences of committing arbitrary power to any, invent Laws either
framed, or consented to by all, that should confine and limit the
authority of whom they chose to govern them: that so man, of
whose failing they had proof, might no more rule over them, but law
and reason abstracted as much as might be from personal errors and
frailties. While as the Magistrate was set above the people, so the
Law was set above the Magistrate. When this would not serve, . . .
they were constrained from that time, the only remedy left them, to
put conditions and take Oaths from all Kings and Magistrates at
their first installment to do impartial justice by Law: who upon
those terms, and no other, received Allegiance from the people, that
is to say, bond or Covenant to obey them in execution of those
Laws which they the people had themselves made, or assented to. . . .
They added also Counselors and Parliaments, nor to be only at his
beck, but with him or without him, at set times, or all times, when
any danger threatened to have care of the public safety. Therefore
saith *Claudius Seysell*, a French Statesman, "The Parliament was set
as a bridle to the King"; which I instance rather, not because our
English Lawyers have not said the same long before, but because
that French Monarchy is granted by all to be a far more absolute
than ours. . . . [28]

But I spare long insertions, appealing to the known constitutions
of both the latest Christian Empires in Europe, the Greek and
German, besides the French, Italian, Aragonian, English, and not
least the Scottish Histories: not forgetting this only by the way, that
William the Norman though a Conqueror, and not unsworn at his
Coronation, was compelled the second time to take oath at *St.
Albans*, ere the people would be brought to yield obedience.

It being thus manifest that the power of Kings and Magistrates is
nothing else, but what is only derivative, transferred and committed
to them in trust from the People, to the Common good of them all,
in whom the power yet remains fundamentally, and cannot be taken
from them, without a violation of their natural birthright, and seeing
that from hence *Aristotle* and the best of Political writers have defined a King, him who governs to the good and profit of his People,
and not for his own ends, it follows from necessary causes, that the
Titles of Sovereign Lord, natural Lord, and the like, are either
arrogancies, or flatteries, not admitted by Emperors and Kings of

best note, and disliked by the Church both of Jews, *Isaiah* 26:13, and ancient Christians, as appears by *Tertullian* and others. Although generally the people of Asia and with them the Jews also, especially since the time they chose a King against the advice and counsel of God, are noted by wise Authors much inclinable to slavery.

We may pass therefore hence to Christian times. And first our Savior himself, how much he favored Tyrants, and how much intended they should be found or honored among Christians, declares his mind not obscurely; accounting their absolute authority no better than Gentilism, yea though they flourished it over with the splendid name of Benefactors; charging those that would be his Disciples to usurp no such dominion; but that they who were to be of most authority among them, should esteem themselves Ministers and Servants to the public. *Matthew* 20:25. . . . So far we ought to be from thinking that Christ and his Gospel should be made a Sanctuary for Tyrants from justice, to whom his Law before never gave such protection. . . .

Surely it is not for nothing that tyrants by a kind of natural instinct both hate and fear none more than the true Church and Saints of God, as the most dangerous enemies and subverters of Monarchy, though indeed of tyranny; hath not this been the perpetual cry of Courtiers, and Court Prelates? Whereof no likelier cause can be alleged, but that they well discerned the mind and principles of most devout and zealous men, and indeed the very discipline of Church, tending to the dissolution of all tyranny. No marvel then if since the faith of Christ received, in purer or impurer times, to depose a King and put him to death for Tyranny, hath been accounted so just and requisite, that neighbor Kings have both upheld and taken part with subjects in the action. . . .

And to prove that some of our own Monarchs have acknowledged that their high office exempted them not from punishment, they had the Sword of *St. Edward* borne before them by an officer who was called Earl of the Palace, even at the times of their highest pomp and solemnities, to mind them, saith *Matthew Paris*, the best of our Historians, that if they erred, the Sword had power to restrain them.[29] And what restraint the Sword comes to at length, having both edge and point, if any *Skeptic* will doubt, let him feel. It is also affirmed from diligent search made in our ancient books of Law, that the Peers and Barons of England had a legal right to judge the King: which was the cause most likely, for it could be no slight cause, that they were called his Peers, or equals. . . .

Whence doubtless our Ancestors who were not ignorant with what rights either Nature or ancient Constitution had endowed them, when Oaths both at Coronation, and renewed in Parliament would not serve, thought it no way illegal to depose and put to death their tyrannous Kings. Insomuch that the Parliament drew up a charge against *Richard the second*, and the Commons requested to have judgment decreed against him, that the realm might not be endangered. And *Peter Martyr*, a Divine of foremost rank, on the third of *Judges* approves their doings. Sir *Thomas Smith*, also a Protestant and a Statesman, in his *Commonwealth of England*, putting the question whether it be lawful to rise against a Tyrant, answers that the vulgar judge of it according to the event, and the learned according to the purpose of them that do it.[30]

But far before these days, *Gildas*, the most ancient of all our Historians, speaking of those times wherein the Roman Empire decaying quitted and relinquished what right they had by Conquest to this Island, and resigned it all into the peoples' hands, testifies that the people thus re-invested with their own original right, about the year 446, both elected them Kings, whom they thought best (the first Christian British Kings that ever reigned here since the Romans) and by the same right, when they apprehended cause, usually deposed and put them to death. . . . [31]

Thus we have here both domestic and most ancient examples that the people of Britain have deposed and put to death their Kings in those primitive Christian times. And to couple reason with example, if the Church in all ages, Primitive, Romish, or Protestant, held it ever no less their duty than the power of their Keys, though without express warrant of Scripture, to bring indifferently both King and Peasant under the utmost rigor of their Canons and Censures Ecclesiastical, even to the smiting him with a final excommunion, if he persist impenitent, what hinders but that the temporal Law both may and ought, though without a special Text or precedent, extend with like indifference the civil Sword, to the cutting off without exemption him that capitally offends. Seeing that justice and Religion are from the same God, and works of justice ofttimes more acceptable.

There is nothing that so actually makes a King of *England*, as rightful possession and Supremacy *in all causes both civil and Ecclesiastical*: and nothing that so actually makes a Subject of *England*, as those two Oaths of Allegiance and Supremacy observed *without equivocating, or any mental reservation*. Out of doubt then

when the King shall command things already constituted in Church,
or State, obedience is the true essence of a subject, either to do, if
it be lawful, or if he hold the thing unlawful, to submit to that
penalty which the Law imposes, so long as he intends to remain a
Subject.

Therefore when the people or any part of them shall rise against
the King and his authority executing the Law in any thing established
civil or Ecclesiastical, I do not say it is rebellion, if the thing commanded though established be unlawful, and that they sought first
all due means of redress (and no man is further bound to Law) but
I say it is an absolute renouncing both of Supremacy and Allegiance,
which in one word is an actual and total deposing of the King, and
the setting up of another supreme authority over them.

John Milton   Sonnet: To the Lord General
                                       Cromwell (1652)[32]

Cromwell, our chief of men, who through a cloud
   Not of war only, but detractions rude,
   Guided by faith and matchless fortitude,
   To peace and truth thy glorious way hast ploughed,
And on the neck of crownéd fortune proud
   Hast reared God's trophies, and his work pursued,
   While Darwen stream with blood of Scots imbrued,
   And Dunbar field re-sounds thy praises loud,
And Worcester's laureate wreath. Yet much remains
   To conquer still; peace hath her victories
   No less renowned than war: new foes arise
Threatening to bind our souls with secular chains:
   Help us to save free conscience from the paw
   Of hireling wolves, whose gospel is their maw.

**The True Levellers' Standard
Advanced and The Diggers'
Mirth**

Editor's note

On the sectarian front of the revolution, a significant utopian communist emerged—Gerrard Winstanley, the leader of the Diggers or True Levellers.[33] With Winstanley we have returned to where we began, to the economic concerns of the peasants and a social theology like that of Thomas Muentzer. Winstanley attempted to explain the contemporary order through a unitary principle—ownership of the earth. His work beautifully combined political liberty and economic equality, in theological dress. Most scholars claim that Winstanley at last made the transition from chiliastic expectancy to rationalistic communism, which came to predominate in the Enlightenment. Yet Winstanley's digging project on St. George's Hill, which so incensed his contemporaries, might be accepted as what Winstanley said it was, a biblical, eschatological sign, taken from Ezekiel. When his people's park had been obliterated, Winstanley, like Muentzer, urged his prince, Cromwell, to complete the magisterial reformation so that God could finally restore His kingdom. Cromwell failed to heed the plea. Winstanley seems to have ended his life as a Quaker, having failed as a merchant possibly because of his communist ideals. Winstanley was the culmination of the rhetorical magnificence and ethical seriousness at the heart of the English Revolution.

Gerrard Winstanley   The True Levellers' Standard
Advanced (1649)[34]

In the beginning of time, the great Creator, Reason, made the earth
to be a common treasury, to preserve beasts, birds, fishes, and man,
the lord that was to govern this creation. For man had domination
given to him over the beasts, birds, and fishes. But not one word
was spoken in the beginning, that one branch of mankind should
rule over another. . . .

But since human flesh . . . began to delight himself in the objects
of the creation more than in the Spirit Reason and Righteousness,
who manifests himself to be the indweller in the five senses . . . ;
then he fell into blindness of mind and weakness of heart, and runs
abroad for a teacher and ruler, and so selfish imaginations, taking
possession of the five senses, and ruling as king in the room of
Reason therein, and working with covetousness, did set up one man
to teach and rule over another. . . .

And hereupon the earth, which was made to be a common treasury of relief for all, both beasts and men, was hedged into enclo-
sures by the teachers and rulers, and the others were made servants
and slaves. . . . And thereby the Spirit is killed in both. The one
looks upon himself as a teacher and ruler, and so is lifted up in
pride over his fellow creature. The other looks upon himself as
imperfect, and so is dejected in his spirit, and looks upon his fellow
creature, of his own image, as a lord above him. . . .

Now the great Creator, who is the Spirit Reason, suffered himself
thus to be rejected and trodden under foot by the covetous, proud
flesh, for a certain time limited. . . . For wherefore is it that there
is such wars and rumors of wars in the nations of the earth? And
wherefore are men so mad to destroy one another? But only to
uphold civil propriety of honor, dominion and riches one over
another, which is the curse the creation groans under, waiting for
deliverance. But when once the earth becomes a common treasury
again—as it must; for all the prophecies of scriptures and reason
are circled here in this community, and mankind must have the law
of righteousness once more writ in his heart, and all must be made
of one heart and one mind—then this enmity in all lands will
cease. . . .

Therefore you powers of the earth, or Lord Esau, the elder
brother, because you have appeared to rule the creation, first take
notice that the power that sets you to work is selfish covetousness,

and an aspiring pride to live in glory and ease over Jacob, the meek spirit. . . . And the time is now come for thy downfall; and Jacob must rise, who is the universal spirit of love and righteousness that fills, and will fill, all the earth. . . .

The work we are going about is this: to dig up George's Hill and the waste ground thereabouts, and to sow corn, and to eat our bread together by the sweat of our brows. And the first reason is this. That we may work in righteousness, and lay the foundation of making the earth a common treasury for all, both rich and poor. That every one that is born in the land may be fed by the earth, his mother that brought him forth, according to the reason that rules in the creation, not enclosing any part into any particular hand, but all as one man working together, and feeding together as sons of one father, members of one family; not one lording over another, but all looking upon each other as equals in the creation. . . .

And that this civil propriety is the curse, is manifest thus. Those that buy and sell land and are landlords, have got it either by oppression or murder or theft; and all landlords live in the breach of the Seventh and Eighth Commandments, "Thou shalt not steal, nor kill." First by their oppression. They have, by their subtle, imaginary, and covetous wit, got the plain-hearted poor, or younger brethren, to work for them for small wages, . . . or else by their covetous wit, they have outreached the plain-hearted in buying and selling, and thereby enriched themselves but impoverished others. Or else by their subtle wit, having been alifted up into places of trust, they have enforced people to pay money for a public use, but have divided much of it into their private purses, and so have got it by oppression.

Then, secondly, for murder. They have by subtle wit and power pretended to preserve a people in safety by the power of the sword. And what by large pay, much free-quarter, and other booties which they call their own, they get much moneys, and with this they buy land and become landlords. And if once landlords, then they rise to be justices, rulers, and state governors, as experience shows. But all this is but a bloody and subtle thievery, countenanced by a law that covetousness made; and is a breach of the Seventh Commandment, "Thou shalt not kill." And likewise, thirdly, a breach of the Eighth Commandment, "Thou shalt not steal." But these landlords have thus stolen the earth from their fellow creatures, that have an equal share with them by the law of reason and creation, as well as they. . . .

It is showed us, that all the prophecies, visions and revelations of
scriptures, of Prophets and Apostles, concerning the calling of the
Jews, the restoration of Israel, and making of that people the in-
heritors of the whole earth, doth all seat themselves in this work of
making the earth a common treasury.

And when the Son of Man was gone from the Apostles, his Spirit
descended upon the Apostles and Brethren as they were waiting at
Jerusalem; and the rich men sold their possessions and gave part to
the poor, and no man said that aught that he possessed was his own,
for they had all things common (Acts 4:32). Now this community
was suppressed by covetous, proud flesh, which was the powers that
ruled the world. And the righteous Father suffered himself thus to
be suppressed for a time, times and dividing of time, or for forty-
two months, or for three days and an half, which are all but one
and the same term of time.

And the world is now come to the half day; and the Spirit of
Christ, which is the Spirit of universal community and freedom, is
risen, and is rising, and will rise higher and higher, till those pure
waters of Shiloa, the well-springs of life and liberty to the whole creation, do overrun . . . those banks of bondage, curse, and slavery. . . .

Another voice that was heard was this: "Israel shall neither take
hire nor give hire." And if so, then certainly none shall say, "This
is my land; work for me and I'll give you wages." For the earth is
the Lord's; that is man's, who is lord of the creation, in every branch
of mankind. . . .

That which does encourage us to go on in this work is this. We find
the streaming out of love in our hearts towards all, to enemies as
well as friends. We would have none live in beggary, poverty, or
sorrow, but that every one might enjoy the benefit of his creation.
We have peace in our hearts, and quiet rejoicing in our work, and
[are] filled with sweet content though we have but a dish of roots and
bread for our food. And we are assured that, in the strength of this
Spirit that hath manifested himself to us, we shall not be startled,
neither at prison nor death, while we are about his work. . . .

For by this work, we are assured, and reason makes it appear to
others, that bondage shall be removed, tears wiped away, and all
poor people by their righteous labors shall be relieved and freed
from poverty and straits. For in this work of restoration there will
be no beggar in Israel. For surely, if there was no beggar in literal
Israel, there shall be no beggar in spiritual Israel, the antitype,
much more. . . .

Gerrard Winstanley et al.   The Diggers' Mirth (1650)[35]

A hint of that Freedom which shall come,
When the Father shall reign alone in his Son.

    The Father he is God alone;
       nothing beside him is.
    All things are folded in that One;
       by him all things subsist.

    He is our light, our life, our peace,
       whereby we our being have;
    From him all things have their increase,
       the tyrant and the slave.

    And when the Father seeth it good,
       and his set time is come,
    He takes away the tyrant's food,
       and gives it to the Son.

    Then Esau's pottage shall be eat,
       for which he sold his right;
    The blessing Jacob shall obtain,
       which Esau once did slight.

    And Jacob he shall then arise
       although he be but small,
    Which Esau once did much despise,
       and Esau down must fall.

    For there must rise a root of Jess,
       a righteous branch indeed;
    Who setteth free him that's opprest,
       and Esau down must tread. . . .

    And thou that as a lord hast reign'd
       over God's heritage,
    Thy part thou hast already play'd;
       therefore come off the stage.

    For when thou think'st thyself most safe
       and riches thou has got;
    Then in the middest of thy peace,
       torment shall be thy lot.

And of this, long time thou has been told,
   but much thou didst it slight;
Therefore, Esau, we must be bold
   now for to claim our right.

For now['s] the Father's 'pointed time,
   which he did fore-intend,
To set up Freedom, and pull down
   the man which did offend:

The time, I say, it is now come,
   in which the Lord will make
All tyrants servants to the Son,
   and he the power will take.

This worldly strength wherewith thou didst
   all times thyself repose,
Shall prove but as a broken reed,
   for thou the field shalt lose.

For there shall rise a mighty Stone,
   which without hands is cut;
Which shall thy Kingly powers break;
   he shall be free from shot.

The first at which this Stone shall smite,
   shall be the head of Gold;
A mortal wound he shall them give.
   Now mind, thou hast been told.

51   A Vindication of the Continued
                                        Succession of the Primitive
                                        Church

Editor's note

As the viewpoints of Winstanley and the English Diggers resembled
those of the social theology of Muentzer, so the Fifth Monarchy Men in
England (who saw their time as the fifth and final era foretold in
Daniel 7) paralleled the Muenster effort to erect the millennial New
Jerusalem on earth. For the first time since the unanimous repudiation
of the Muensterite fanatics in the 1530s, seventeenth-century
millennialists in the army and the sects (aided by the respectable
academic millenarianism of Mead and Alsted) openly used Muentzer,
Storch, and John of Leiden (Becold) as their models for revolutionary
activism. Although millennial beliefs in England were widespread in the
1640s, the Fifth Monarchists emerged only after 1649.[36] Their hopes
had been aroused by the execution of King Charles, but they formed
their own elitist revolutionary movement only when the Rump
Parliament and the army failed to set up Christ's kingdom on earth.
Having proposed social revolution and confiscation of the lands of the
ungodly, the Fifth Monarchists were put down in panic in 1653, and
once again reaction flowed through the Protectorate into the Restoration.

After Cromwell had established the Protectorate, he imprisoned and
silenced fifth monarchy critics in the army (for instance, Major-
Generals Thomas Harrison and Robert Overton). Lesser fifth monarchy
figures then opposed Cromwell. John More (d. 1702) published a letter
denouncing Cromwell as the little horn (Dan. 7:8) and beast of
Revelation. A former soldier in charge of military security, John
Spittlehouse (d. 1659) proposed with More a revolutionary
eschatology based explicitly upon Muentzerite and Muensterite
restoration of the true church.[37] Spittlehouse repudiated the teaching of
John Brayne, a Seeker, that continuity with the primitive church had
been lost from 406 A.D. to the present. Spittlehouse insisted that the true
church had been continuously visible in the world since its persecution
by the red dragon (Nero). Constantine was the man or dragon of
Revelation 13 who gave his (imperial) power to the beast (the popes),
after which the primitive church was in the wilderness 1,260 years,

from 283 (Constantine's birth) to 1543 (three years before the death of
Luther). Contrary to Luther's desire, the church came out of the
wilderness (of national churches and infant baptism) through the efforts
of Muentzer, Storch, and John of Leiden (the radical Anabaptists). They
cut down the tree and root of Antichrist, not just some of the leaves.
Papists, prelates, and presbyteries who led the primitive church captive
would themselves be overcome, and the true primitive church would be
restored so as to spread itself over the face of the whole earth. Thus,
the Anabaptists preserved the true primitive church for 1,260 years in
Germany, "inasmuch as Muentzer, etc. there discovered themselves at
the previous time indicated." Spittlehouse then urged his readers to
repudiate their meaningless "sprinkling" and ordination. More than any
other writing, the *Vindication* shows the continuity between the
religious views of Muentzer/Muenster and those of the later radical
revolutionaries in England.

John Spittlehouse and	A Vindication of the
John More	Continued Succession of the
	Primitive Church (1652)[38]

A vindication of the continued Succession of the Primitive Church
of Jesus Christ (now scandalously termed Anabaptists) from the
Apostles unto this present time. Answer to three following asser-
tions, extracted out of the writings of Mr. John Brain, and chiefly
out of his book, entituled, The Churches going in, and coming out
of the Wilderness, Viz.,

1. That the Gospel-frame of the Primitive Church hath been
devolved into the Antichristian Estate, and condition, since from
about the year 406, unto this present time.

2. That during the aforesaid time, there hath not been a true
Church-frame of Gospel-government.

3. That the Gospel-frame of the Gospel-government, is to be restored again by some one Man, who shall have Authoritie given him
from above, to restore Baptism, and all other lost Ordinances of
the Church.

And may also serve as a further Caveat, to the present deluded
People of this Nation, that are yet seduced by the crafy Demetriousses
of the Times, who for love of Gain, still indeavour to cry up their
Diana of Rome whom England, and all they call Christendom yet
Worship.

Matth. 28:19–20. Goe ye therefore and teach all Nations baptizing them, and Teaching them to observe all things, etc. And loe I am
with you alwayes, even unto the end of the World. Amen.

John 10:1, 7, 8, 9, 10, 16.

Published by John Spittlehouse and John More.
London, Printed by Gartrude Dawson, 1652. . . .

Having thus clearly proved a continuation of the Primitive Church
and frame of Gospel-government . . , I shall in the next place by
the same assistance prove the first approach of its visibility into the
world, after its aforesaid persecution under the Dragon and the
Beast mentioned, Rev. chap. 12 and 13.

And first of its persecution under the aforesaid red Dragon, whose
Originall I take to be the Emperor Nero, and that for these insuing
Reasons, Viz.

In that it is reported of him by Eusebius (lib. 2 ch. 24, 25 fol 34)
"That when he had reigned for the space of 8 years, etc. and being
settled in his Throne, he fell into abominable facts, and took armour
against the service due unto the universal and almighty God, etc." . . .

Again, it behoved us to take notice of this one thing of him above
the rest, Viz. "That he was counted the First Enemie of all the
Emperors unto the service of God, by which we may conclude, That
Nero was the first that began the persecution in the Gentile Church
of Christ." . . .

Having thus found out the Originall of the aforesaid Red Dragon,
and also the very year wherein he began his persecution, as also in
all probability, the first martyr of the Gentile Church of Christ, which
I take to be the Apostle Paul, and that for these Reasons, Viz., . . .
I shall in the next place discover the originall of the Beast which
was to act the second part of that Christian tragedy, begun by the
aforesaid Nero, and continued during the ten persecutions (viz.)
from the aforesaid Claudius Nero, unto Constantius Magnus, in
whose dayes aforesaid ten Persecutions had their period.

Who seeing the aforesaid Emperors his Predecessors frustrated of
their expectation (viz.) of a totall Extirpation of the Primitive
Church and frame of Gospel-government from off the earth, and
that notwithstanding all their bloudie Massacres, and killing courses,
whereby many thousands were oft-times slain in a day, resolved to
take a more subtile course, and that by practising another design to
the same effect, which was by giving a seat and power, and great
authority unto such silly soules as he could by that means delude
and insnare; To the end he might doe that by craft and subtiltie,
which his Predecessors could not doe by force and violence. To

which purpose I say it doth plainly appear that the said Constantius etc. called the great Councel of Nice, in which Diet the aforesaid Constantius, and they decreed, that like as the King of the Romans was then call'd Emperor above other Kings, so the Bishop of the same Citie, should be called Pope, above other Bishops. And to the more specious carrying on of the aforesaid design, he likewise erected many sumptious Temples or Churches, decking them with Jewels, and costly Ornaments; And to the end he might further procure his ends therein, he gave likewise to the Priests of them times (whom he had so insnared under the pretence of advancing and promoting religion) worldly power and great riches, that they might more freely mannage his design. And to carry it on yet further, he likewise pretended to have seen the Sign of the Crosse in the air, and thereby took occasion to set up Imagerie and Idolatry of Crosses and Saints reliques. . . .

All which doth clearly demonstrate the aforesaid Constantius to be the very Man, or Dragon, who gave his power unto the Beast, as Rev. 13.

Having thus discovered the place where, the time when, and the manner how the Dragon, and the Beast took their first rise, I shall in the next place compute the time of the aforesaid 1260 yeares, (which was assigned to be the time of the hiding of the Primitive Church, etc. in its Wilderness-condition) from the rise of the Beast or Papacie, To which purpose, it is very remarkable, that bewixt the Birth of Constantius, and the death of Luther, is fully expired the aforesaid number of years, Constantius being born in the year 283, and Luthers death happening in the year, 1546 from which latter number if you deduct, the former, the remainder will be 1263 years as by comparing of Eusebius with Mr. Fox in his Book of Martyrs, upon the life and death of the aforesaid Constantius and Luther will appear: So that it is probable the aforesaid Primitive Church etc. came out of its wilderness condition, about three years before the death of Luther.

Now that it came forth as aforesaid, not by the meanes of Luther, but rather contrary to his desire, will clearly appear by this insuing Storie of Spanhemus,[39] Professor of Leiden in his Historicall Narrative of the Church of Christ in Germany, which that Enemy of the Truth there stileth, by the scandalous name of Anabaptists, in which storie contrary to his intended desire he testifieth the visibility of the aforesaid true Church in Luthers time, as the aforesaid storie will

clearly manifest.* Where speaking out of ignorance, by way of
contempt against three famous Champions of the Primitive Church
of Jesus Christ (which was at that very instant making its first
approach out of its Wilderness-condition, in its morning dress) useth
these following expressions, by way of narration, viz.

That when God raised up Luther, Melancton, Zuinglius, and
divers other Worthies, to be Reformers of his Church, at the same
time the enemy of mankind raised up the Anabaptists to be the
disturbers of his Church: That Thomas Muntzer their great Anti-
signanus, etc. when he could not get Luther to joyn with him, etc.
began to thunder against Luther himself, crying out, that Luther was
as much in fault as the Pope of Rome, yea, and more, yea, that
Luther, and those of his party, favoured nothing but of the flesh,
vaunting indeed, that they had cut off some of the leaves of Antichrist, but the tree and the root remained still untouched, which
(said Muntzer, Storch, and Becold) must be cut down, and which
cut down they would.[40]

So that the Papacy, Prelacy, and Presbytery, may fitly be compared to three families under one roofe, striving to supplant each
other, witnesse the continuall conflicts betwixt the old Strumpet and
her aforesaid daughters, and that as it were in a battell Royall, both
by Word and Sword, to subvert each others Hyerarchies, which they
have already done in a great measure in this Nation, the full accomplishment whereof I hope in a short time to see effected both in this
Nation and elsewhere, which the Lord in much mercy hasten, that
the truth of his Promises may be fulfilled in these our dayes, which
was written by his Servant John, Rev. 13:10, viz. That such as have
and would lead the Primitive Church of Christ captive, may be led

---

* Reader, take notice that this story of the Anabaptists (scandalously so
called) was written by an utter adversary to the Truth, as I shall hereafter
make appear. Or otherwise, through his ignorance of the Truth. Take notice
also that the aforesaid Champions of the Truth, (viz.) Muntzer, etc.
appeared at the same time that Luther, etc. began to oppose the Pope, so
that when there was but the least way made for the Church of Christ to
appear, it had its Champions to publish it to the world, as by their expressions
to Luther did appear, wherein they spake nothing but the very truth, for
without all controversie, Luther etc. was no other then Romish Sectaries, yea,
such as made only a division in Rome, but was not from Rome, and so
consequently, such as was never of the true Church of Jesus Christ, and
therefore the Papists may boldly, and justly, question the Prelates, where
their Religion was before Luther, as also the Presbyterians before Calvin, in
as much as they are no other then the Daughters of that grand Harlot, Rev.
17.5. witnesse their Nationall Churches, their Popish institution of Preists,
and baptizing of infants, which are infallible characters, to prove them
Harlots like their Mother.

themselves into captivity, and that such as have killed them with the
Sword, etc. may be killed by the Sword, etc. Rev. 18:6, 7, 8. Psal.
149:6, 7, 8, 9 and that the true Primitive Church may be restored to
such a latitude, as to spread it self over the face of the whole earth,
as in Dan. 7:18, 27. . . .

Having thus clearly proved, that all the aforesaid societies of
people, are neither Churches or Ministers of Jesus Christ (albeit
their separations as aforesaid) it must of necessity follow, that the
Church, or society of People (now scandalously termed Anabaptists) was ever kept distinct and separate from Antichrist, and that
to all ends and purposes whatsoever, whether in essentials, substantials, and circumstantials, so that the aforesaid Primitive Church
and frame of Gospel-government, was never totally destroyed in her
externals by the aforesaid red Dragon, or Beast, or Antichrist
(maugre all their malice and indeavours to doe the same) much
lesse in her internals, but contrarywise preserved and continued unto
this present time; and therefore it will be needlesse to answer to
your third assertion, viz. That the Gospel-frame of Gospel-government is to be restored by some one man, etc. . . .

So like wise when the aforesaid Primitive Church, was penned up
into Mountaines, Dens, Desarts, and Caves of the earth, and when,
as it is likely, not above eight or ten persons might meet in one
place together, what need had they of Evangelists, Pastors, Teachers,
Elders, Deacons, etc. when one or two of them might supplie the
place of them all (so farre as there was need of them) and so likewise in relation to the rest of the Ordinances, what need was there
of any other then of private teachings, prophesying, prayer, bap-
tisme, breaking of bread, which I have fully cleared to all rationall
men, might be then performed by the aforesaid Church in its then
condition, where I compared it with the present Condition of the
Popish Synagogue in this nation: And without which it had been
impossible it should have subsisted for so long a time as 1260 years,
(which that it did, I have also cleared by the aforesaid instances of
Muntzer, Storch, and Becold, in their addresses to Luther, when the
aforesaid time was expired, albeit the said Luther was ignorant
therof, supposing (as yet you do) that the aforesaid Primitive
Church had been devolved into the then Antichristian estate, of
which he then conceived himself a Reformer, (the contrary to which
I thinke I have clearly proved) however I am confident that the then
poor distressed Saints, had as much respect to observe all the commands of Jesus Christ, as possibly were then in their power to

prosecute, during their aforesaid wilderness-condition, in the afore-said Mountains, Dens, Desarts, and Caves of the earth, whereunto they were confined, and in which they were preserved. . . .

I shall further prove from Scripture, where Jesus Christ promiseth to be with it to the end of the world, Matth. 28:20. Ergo, It was to have a continuance unto the end of the world, And if so, then during the aforesaid time of 1260 yeares. Again, It continued a Church, then in all the Essentials, Substantials, and Circumstantials that appertained unto it, (so far as there was need of, in its then condi-tion) as aforesaid. Again, I would gladly know any one Church (in that which we now call Christendome) that can produce the like hidden condition, as the Church now scandalously termed Anabap-tists. And much more in that it is so clearly discovered to be so near, yea even one and the same with the Pattern of the first Church that was erected by the commands of Jesus Christ, and the practice of the Apostles. And as to the place where it was so preserved, It may be probably conjectured to be in Germanie, in as much as the aforesaid Muntzer, etc. did there discover themselves at the time aforesaid.

Redeem the time therefore which you have hitherto spent in op-posing so plain a truth (as hath been declared) by disclaiming that Error, as you have done many more, (viz. your sprinkling and ordi-nation, etc.) in doing of which, you will have the benefit, I my desire, and God the Glory.

FINIS.

Editor's note

The Quakers or Society of Friends continued the Puritan revolution in a stable form, just as the Mennonites and Hutterites provided a peaceful alternative to violent Anabaptist revolt. The Friends were more spiritualistic than the Mennonites, although both groups rejected oaths and war. At the same time, George Fox (1624–1691) and his friends did not withdraw from society like the Mennonites.[41] Closely related to the Ranters, a group claiming possession of the Holy Spirit and tending toward lawlessness, the early Friends also sympathized with the millennial Fifth Monarchists, expecting an imminent reign of Christ to begin upon earth.[42] Like both Spirit- and Christ-centered millennialists, Fox interrupted church services and angrily denounced those identified as God's enemies. Early Quakers enraged their contemporaries by refusing hat honor, by using the familiar "thou" in addressing everyone, and by denouncing "steeple-houses" and "hireling priests." Fox's attack upon tithes and his insistence upon fair prices, his appeal to the poorer classes as well as his demand for equality of sex and his repudiation of slavery gave the movement a radical thrust from the beginning.

The Quakers were quite willing to attack wordly social ills, even after their original apocalyptic expectations of the Lord's coming waned in the late 1650s. Not as quiet as their descendants, Fox's followers in the north of England gave religious sanctions to an economic complaint— namely, church tithes exacted by landlords from impoverished tenants. What mattered above all to Fox and his descendants was personal renewal through the Holy Spirit. The Friends sublimated the revolutionary thrust of Puritan constitutions and providences into a religion of the heart, finding truth in the inner voice of God speaking to the soul. Yet the Friends knew that the "Lamb" still had a war to fight. Their continuing existence and influence carried forward Anabaptist and Puritan revolutionary principles in quiet, socially oriented religious forms, complementing the secular gains in modern democracy and the achievement of religious liberty, for which the radicals laid a cornerstone.

A Summary of Quaker
Teaching and Preaching
(c. 1655)

Teaching:

Now, when the Lord God and his son Jesus Christ, did send me
forth into the world, to preach his everlasting gospel and kingdom,
I was . . . commanded to turn people to that inward light, spirit and
grace . . . even that divine Spirit which would lead them into all
Truth. . . . I was to bring people off from all their own ways to
Christ . . . and from their churches, which men had made and
gathered, to the Church in God. . . . And I was to bring people off
. . . from men's inventions . . . with their schools and colleges for
making ministers of Christ . . . and from all their images and
crosses, and sprinkling of infants, with all their holy days (so called).
. . . I was moved to declare against them all.

Moreover, when the Lord sent me forth into the world, he for-
bade me to put off my hat to any, high or low; and I was required
to "thee" and "thou" all men and women, without any respect to
rich or poor, great or small. And as I travelled up and down, I was
not to bid people "good morrow" or "good evening." . . . About
this time, I was . . . exercised in going to their courts to cry for
justice, and in speaking and writing to judges and justices . . . and
in testifying against their wakes or feasts, their May-games, sports,
plays and shows. . . . In fairs also, and in markets, I was made to
declare against their cheating and cozening, warning all to deal
justly, to speak the truth, to let their "yea" be "yea" and their "nay"
be "nay" . . . and forewarning all of the great and terrible day of
the Lord which would come upon them all. . . . [43]

Preaching:

The Lamb . . . hath called us to make War in righteousness for his
name's sake, against Hell and death, and all the powers of darkness.
. . . And they that follow the Lamb shall overcome, and get the
victory over the beast, and over the Dragon, and over the gates
of Hell. . . . [44]

Put on your Armour, and gird on your Sword . . . and prepare
your selves to battel, for the Nations doth defie our God. . . . Arise,
arise, and sound forth the everlasting word of war and judgment in
the ears of all Nations. . . . Wound the Lofty, and tread under foot

the Honourable of the earth. . . . And the Lamb shall get the victory. . . . [45]

The Lamb's War YOU must know, before you can witness his kingdom. . . . The *Lamb wars* . . . in whomsoever he appears, and calls them to join with him herein . . . with all their Might . . . that he may form a new Man, a new Heart, new Thoughts, and a new Obedience . . . and *there is his Kingdom*. . . . Do you deny your selves of your pleasures, profits, ease and liberty, that you may hold forth a chaste . . . life of gentleness, faithfulness and truth. . . . Is this your War, and these your Weapons? . . . [46]

Notes

Notes

Introduction

1. For reflections on the nature of revolution, see Perez Zagorin, "Theories of Revolution in Contemporary Historiography," *Political Science Quarterly*, LXXXVIII (1973), 23–52; Issac Kramnick, "Explanations for Revolution," *History and Theory*, XI (1972), 26–63, and Lawrence Stone, "Theories of Revolution," in *The Causes of the English Revolution, 1529–1642* (New York, 1972), pp. 3–25. Chalmers Johnson in *Revolution and the Social System* (Hoover Institution Studies, vol. III; Stanford, Calif., 1964), defined revolution as violence directed toward a change in government, regime, or society. Our definition is based upon Thomas Kuhn's notion that scientific revolutions occur when ruling paradigms are replaced because of anomalies (see *The Structure of Scientific Revolutions* [Chicago, 1962]). Anabaptist and Puritan radicals may be seen to result from aspirational deprivation during the Reformation, when the old and new clergy could not satisfy rising lay expectations of spiritual zeal (see Ted R. Gurr, *Why Men Rebel* [Princeton, N.J., University Press, 1970]).

2. By the term Second Reformation, we refer to groups called "Fanatics" (Schwaermer) by Luther (see Karl Holl, "Luther und die Schwaermer," in *Luther* (Gesammelte Aufsaetze zur Kirchengeschichte, vol. I; Tuebingen, 1923), or "Left-wing Reformers" by Roland H. Bainton (The Left Wing of the Reformation," *Journal of Religion*, XXI [1941], 125), and "Radical Reformers" by George H. Williams (*The Radical Reformation* [Philadelphia, 1962]). For continental radical and left-wing bibliography, see Hans J. Hillerbrand, *A Bibliography of Anabaptist History, 1520–1630* (Elkhart, Ind., 1962).

By First Reformation, we refer to established reformers and revolutionary Catholics who remained close to Rome in sacramental theory, church organization, and church-state relations—the "Magisterial Reformers" of Williams, *Radical Reformation*.

3. In the introduction to his *Deutsche Messe und Ordnung des Gottesdiensts* of 1526, Luther outlined a possibility for a "third form" of the church (congregationalist pattern), where earnest Christians would center on the Word of God and practice discipline according to Matthew 18 (Luther, *D. Martin Luthers Werke: Gesammtausgabe* [Weimar, 1883 ff.], XIX, 44–114 [hereafter *WA*]).

263

4. Zwingli died on the battlefield as a Reformed chaplain and martyr only six years after Muentzer's defeat and death as a revolutionary heretic—yet their social ideals for Reformation were not widely separated. Calvin's introduction of lay elders and fenced communion services closely resembled Anabaptist practices, although he wrote bitterly against soul-sleepers, Libertines, Anabaptists, Nicodemites, and Anti-Trinitarians, which Calvin never distinguished clearly.

5. In *Spiritual and Anabaptist Writers*, (Library of Christian Classics, vol. XXV; Philadelphia, 1957), intro. (hereafter *SAW*).

6. See Steven Ozment, *Mysticism and Dissent: Religious Ideology and Social Protest in the Sixteenth Century* (New Haven, Conn., 1973), in general, and on Muentzer, H.-J. Goertz, *Innere und Aeussere Ordnung in der Theologie Thomas Muentzers* (Studies in the History of Christian Thought, vol. II; Leiden, 1967).

7. Frederick G. Heymann, Revolution and the German Peasants' War: An Historical Comparison," in *Medievalia et Humanistica*, I (Cleveland, 1970), 141–59.

8. For documentation on unrest in Germany, see Gerald Strauss, *Manifestations of Discontent in Germany on the Eve of the Reformation* (Bloomington, Ind., 1971). The standard work on the Peasants' War is Guenther Franz, *Der deutsche Bauernkrieg* (6th ed. rev.; Darmstadt, 1962). For sources, see Guenther Franz, *Quellen zur Geschichte des Bauernkrieges* (Darmstadt, 1963).

9. Claus-Peter Clasen, *Anabaptism: A Social History, 1525–1618 Switzerland, Austria, Moravia, South and Central Germany* (Ithaca, N.Y., 1972), pp. 152–57, points out the clear differences between Peasant and Anabaptist aims, but he notes that at least thirty-two Anabaptists are known to have taken part in the peasant uprising. See also Clasen's discussion of revolutionary Anabaptists: John Roemer in Thuringia, John Hut in Franconia, and a group in Esslingen (pp. 157–72).

10. Muentzer's theology is sympathetically discussed in Walter Elliger, *Thomas Muentzer* (Berlin, 1960); in Goertz, *Innere und Aeussere Ordnung*; in Thomas Nipperdey, "Theologie und Revolution bei Thomas Muentzer," in *Archiv fuer Reformationsgeschichte*, LIV (1963), 173; and in Eric W. Gritsch, *Reformer without a Church: The Life and Thought of Thomas Muentzer, 1488?–1525* (Philadelphia, 1967). See also Carl Hinrichs, *Luther und Muentzer: Ihre Auseinandersetzung ueber Obrigkeit und Widerstandsrecht* (Berlin, 1952) and Manfred Bensing, *Thomas Muentzer und der Thueringer Aufstand, 1525* (Berlin, 1966).

11. Franklin H. Littell, *The Anabaptist View of the Church* (2d ed.; Boston, 1958).

12. For a recent sociological study of Muenster, see Otthein Rammstedt, *Sekte und sociale Bewegung: Soziologische Analyse der Taeufer in Muenster, 1534–35* (Cologne, 1966). For a Marxist view, see Gerhard Brendler, *Das Taeuferreich zu Muenster, 1534/35* (Berlin, 1966). Muenster is discussed by Cornelius Krahn, *Dutch Anabaptism: Origin, Spread, Life, and Thought, 1450–1600* (The Hague, 1968), pp. 135–64. For sources, see Klemens Loeffler, *Die Wiedertaeufer zu Muenster, 1534–35* (Jena, 1923).

13. Documents for the Wittenberg disturbances of 1521–22 are presented in Nikolaus Mueller, *Die Wittenberger Bewegung, 1521 und*

1522 (Leipzig, 1911). Gordon Rupp, *Patterns of Reformation* (Philadelphia, 1969), discusses the Zwickau prophets in ch. 6.

Besides works on Muentzer referred to above in note 10, see Ozment, *Mysticism and Dissent*; Rupp, *Patterns of Reformation*, pp. 157–353; M. M. Smirin, *Die Volksreformation des Thomas Muentzer und der grosse Bauernkrieg* (Berlin, 1956); and James M. Stayer, *Anabaptists and the Sword* (Lawrence, Kan., 1972), pp. 73–90. For sources, see Thomas Muentzer, *Schriften und Briefe*, ed. Guenther Franz (Guetersloh, 1968).

14. For fifth monarchy dependence on Muentzer and Muenster, see Document 51.

15. *Anabaptists and the Sword*, pp. 329–37.

16. Discussed by Stayer, *Anabaptists and the Sword*, pp. 99–103. See Fritz Blanke, *Brothers in Christ: The History of the Oldest Anabaptist Congregation, Zollikon, near Zurich, Switzerland* (Scottdale, Pa., 1961). The documents can be found in L. von Muralt and W. Schmid, *Quellen zur Geschichte der Taeufer in der Schweiz* (Zuerich, 1952).

17. Torsten Bergsten, *Balthasar Hubmaier: Seine Stellung zu Reformation und Taeufertum, 1521–1528* (Kassel, 1961), pp. 277–301. Henry C. Vedder, *Balthasar Hubmaier* (New York, 1905). See Clasen, *Anabaptism*, pp. 152–53.

18. Peter Kawerau, *Melchior Hofmann als religioeser Denker* (Haarlem, 1954); Fr. Otto zur Linden, *Melchior Hofmann, ein Prophet der Wiedertaeufer* (Haarlem, 1885). Hofmann is discussed in Krahn, *Dutch Anabaptism*, pp. 80–117, and Stayer, *Anabaptists and the Sword*, pp. 211–26.

19. See note 12.

20. Menno Simons, *The Complete Writings*, ed. John C. Wenger (Scottdale, Pa., 1956); Harold S. Bender, *Conrad Grebel, 1498–1526, Founder of the Swiss Brethren* (Goshen, Ind., 1950); John C. Wenger, tr., "The Schleitheim Confession of Faith," *Mennonite Quarterly Review*, XIX (1945), 243–53; Robert Friedmann, *Hutterite Studies: Essays by Robert Friedmann*, ed. Harold S. Bender (Goshen, Ind., 1961).

21. On the Lutheran resisters, see Oliver K. Olson, "Theology of Revolution: Magdeburg, 1550–1551," *Sixteenth Century Journal*, III (1972), 56–79. For Luther's theory, see Heinz Scheible, ed., *Das Widerstandsrecht als Problem der deutschen Protestanten, 1523–1546* (Goettingen, 1969), and Gunther Wolf, ed., *Luther und die Obrigkeit in Wege der Forschung*, vol. LXXV (Darmstadt, 1970), for sources; for a discussion, see Hermann Doerries, *Wort und Stunde: Beitraege zum Verstaendnis Luthers* (Goettingen, 1970), III, 195–270, and Eric W. Gritsch, "Martin Luther and Violence: A Reappraisal of a Neuralgic Theme," *Sixteenth Century Journal*, III (1972), 37–55.

22. Michael Walzer, in *The Revolution of the Saints* (Cambridge, Mass., 1965), argued that the Puritans formed the first political parties as a result of their revolutionary ideology. J. W. Allen, *A History of Political Thought in the Sixteenth Century* (New York, 1957; orig. pub. 1928), noted the break from Calvin's prohibition of armed resistance by lesser magistrates at Magdeburg in Germany, by John Knox in Scotland, and by the Marian exiles Christopher Goodman and John Ponet. More recently, Robert Kingdon ("The First Expression of Theodore Beza's

Political Ideas," *Archiv fuer Reformationsgeschichte*, XLVI [1955],
88–100) and Irmgard Hoess ("Zur Genesis der Widerstandslehre Bezas,"
Archiv fuer Reformationsgeschichte, LIV [1963], 198–214) have argued
that Beza, Calvin's successor, transmitted the Magdeburg teaching about
the rights of lesser magistrates to resist tyranny by force of arms to the
French Huguenots when they were seeking legitimate reasons to oppose
royal persecution.

23. Sources: Stuart E. Prall, *The Puritan Revolution: A Documentary
History* (Garden City, N.Y., 1968); W. C. Abbot, *The Writings and
Speeches of Oliver Cromwell* (4 vols.; Cambridge, Mass., 1937–47).
Biographies: Robert S. Paul, *The Lord Protector: Religion and Politics in
the Life of Oliver Cromwell* (Grand Rapids, Mich., 1965); Christopher
Hill, *God's Englishman: Oliver Cromwell and the English Revolution*
(New York, 1970).

24. Like the French Protestants, Cardinal Robert Bellarmine, an
Italian Jesuit, wrote that an infidel prince may rightly be deposed by
force (in a *Responsio* of 1587 to Belloy's *Apologie*, under the name of
Franciscus Romulus). In 1598, Bellarmine's teacher at Rome, the
Spanish Jesuit Juan de Mariana, stated in his *De Rege et regis institu-
tione* that the will of the people is sufficiently expressed by a majority
and that if a prince overstep his authority he may rightfully be restrained
by force, warred upon, deposed, and killed (see Allen, *History of
Political Thought*, 360–66); Mariana's treatise is in George A. Moore, tr.,
Mariana: The King and the Education of the King (Washington, D.C.,
1948). Cardinal William Allen published *A True, Sincere, and Modest
Defense of English Catholics* (reissued at Menston, Eng., 1971) in 1584,
fully documenting English Catholic resistance theory from Protestant
sources (see Allen, *History of Political Thought*, pp. 203–8). Robert M.
Kingdon recounts "William Allen's Use of Protestant Political Argu-
ment" in Charles H. Carter, ed., *From the Renaissance to the Counter-
Reformation* (New York, 1965), pp. 164–76.

25. See note 23 above. On Puritan millennialism, see Norman Cohn,
The Pursuit of the Millennium (London, 1970), pp. 321–78; William
Lamont, *Godly Rule: Politics and Religion, 1603–60* (New York, 1969);
John F. Wilson, *Pulpit in Parliament: Puritanism during the English Civil
Wars, 1640–1648* (Princeton, N.J., 1969); and B. S. Capp, *The Fifth
Monarchy Men: A Study in Seventeenth Century English Millenarianism*
(London, 1972). On religion, consult William Haller, *The Rise of
Puritanism* (New York, 1938). For causes, see Stone, *Causes of the
English Revolution*. For a Marxist study, see Christopher Hill, *Puritanism
and Revolution* (New York, 1962). On the political aspects: Perez
Zagorin, *A History of Political Thought in the English Revolution* (New
York, 1966). On the sects: H. N. Brailsford, *The Levellers and the
English Revolution* (Stanford, Calif., 1961); Hugh Barbour, *The Quakers
in Puritan England* (New Haven, Conn., 1964). On the radicals:
Christopher Hill, *The World Turned Upside Down: Radical Ideas during
the English Revolution* (New York, 1972).

26. "Emergence of the Concept of Revolution," tr. Heinz Lubasz, in
Revolutions in Modern European History (New York, 1966).

27. *Revolution and the Social System.*

28. *Causes of the English Revolution*, p. 7.

The Peasants' War: South
Germany, Austria, and
Switzerland

1. The standard secondary work on the Peasants' War is by Guenther
Franz, *Der deutsche Bauernkrieg* (6th ed. rev.; Darmstadt, 1962).
Eyewitness accounts are found in Otto H. Brandt, *Der grosse Bauernkrieg: Zeitgenoessische Berichte, Aussagen und Aktenstuecke* (Jena,
1926). The standard source collection is by Guenther Franz, ed., *Quellen
zur Geschichte des Bauernkrieges* (Darmstadt, 1963).

2. On Hubmaier, see Document 16 below.
The Spiritualizer Carlstadt has been treated most fully and sympa-
thetically in Herman Barge, *Andreas Bodenstein von Karlstadt* (2 vols.;
Leipzig, 1905; reissued by B. de Graaf [Nieuwkoop, 1968]). See also
E. G. Rupp, *Patterns of Reformation* (Philadelphia, 1969); Hans J.
Hillerbrand, "Andreas Bodenstein of Carlstadt, Prodigal Reformer,"
Church History, XXXV (1966), 379–98; and Ronald J. Sider, *Andreas
Bodenstein von Karlstadt* (Leiden, 1974). Luther's elder colleague at
Wittenberg, and an important influence on Swiss Reformed and
Anabaptist sacramental views, Carlstadt died as a professor in Basel
in 1541.

On Muentzer, see Document 9 below.

3. Guenther Franz has discussed the authorship and background of
the Twelve Articles in "Die Entstehung der 'Zwoelf Artikel' der
deutschen Bauernschaft," *Archiv fuer Reformationsgeschichte*, XXXVI
(1939), 193–213.

4. Luther wrote three treatises in response to the Peasants' War: the
first chided the nobles and warned the peasants ("Admonition to Peace:
A Reply to the Twelve Articles of the Peasants in Swabia" [1525], in
Luther's Works, XLVI [Amer. ed.; Philadelphia and St. Louis, 1967],
17–43 [*WA*, XVIII, 291–334]); a second, written after the war had
begun, advised slaughter of rebellious peasants ("Against the Robbing
and Murdering Hordes of Peasants," *Luther's Works*, pp. 49–55 [WA,
XVIII, 357–61]); the third sought to justify his polemic outburst after
the rebellion had been suppressed ("An Open Letter on the Harsh Book
against the Peasants," *Luther's Works*, pp. 59–85 [WA, XVIII, 384–
401]).

5. The Twelve Articles were published in March 1525 by Sebastian
Lotzer of Memmingen. Balthasar Hubmaier admitted under torture in
1528 that he had approved and help revise the articles for the peasants.
The critical edition of the text is in Franz, ed., *Quellen zur Geschichte
des Bauernkrieges*, pp. 174–79. The translation is from Hans J.
Hillerbrand, ed., *The Protestant Reformation* (New York: Harper
Torchbook, 1968), pp. 64–66; reprinted by permission.

6. *Die Volksreformation des Thomas Muentzer und der grosse
Bauernkrieg* (Berlin, 1956; tr. of 1955 Russian 2d ed.).

7. Copies of the Article-Letter and the Constitutional Draft of the
peasants were found among Hubmaier's papers at Waldshut. Under
torture in Vienna, Hubmaier admitted that he had "expanded and interpreted articles that came to him from members of the peasant army" and
that he had taught that these demands should be accepted as "Christian

and just" (text in Franz, *Quellen zur Geschichte des Bauernkrieges*, pp. 231–34). Yet these articles come closer to Muentzer's political views than to those of Hubmaier, whose radicalism was the least separatist among the Anabaptists (see Torsten Bergsten, *Balthasar Hubmaier: Seine Stellung zu Reformation und Taeufertum, 1521–1528* [Kassel, 1961], pp. 281–301).

8. The critical edition of the Article-Letter is in Franz, ed., *Quellen zur Geschichte des Bauernkrieges*, pp. 235–36; my translation.

9. See reference to Gaismayr in George H. Williams, "The Two Social Strands in Italian Anabaptism, ca. 1526–ca. 1565," in Lawrence P. Buck and Jonathan W. Zophy, eds., *The Social History of the Reformation* (Columbus, Ohio, 1972), pp. 166–68. Walter Klaassen is writing a study on "The Religious Views of Michael Gaismair."

10. *Die Tiroler Bauernkrieg und Michael Gaismair* (Berlin, 1965), tr. from Czech into German by Eduard Ullman.

11. See Claus-Peter Clasen, *Anabaptism: A Social History, 1525–1618* (Ithaca, N.Y., 1972), pp. 295–97, for an evaluation of the community life of the Hutterites.

12. The critical edition of Gaismayr's "Plan of Reform" is in Franz, ed., *Quellen zur Geschichte des Bauernkrieges*, pp. 285–90. The translation is from Jacob Salwyn Schapiro, *Social Reform and the Reformation* (New York: Columbia University Press, 1909), pp. 147–51.

13. Siegfried Rother, *Die religioesen und geistigen Grundlagen der Politik Huldrych Zwinglis* (Erlangen, 1956); Robert C. Walton, *Zwingli's Theocracy* (Toronto, 1967); G. W. Locher, *Die Theologie Huldrych Zwinglis im Lichte seiner Christologie*, I: *Die Gotteslehre* (Zuerich, 1952); Joachim Rogge, *Zwingli und Erasmus: Der Friedensgedanken des jungen Zwingli* (Berlin, 1962).

14. The critical edition of Zwingli's "Plan for a Military Campaign" is in E. Egli, G. Finsler, and W. Koehler, eds., *Huldreich Zwinglis Saemtliche Werke*, III (Leipzig, 1914), 551, 562–63; my translation.

Conflict with Luther: Zwickau Prophets and Thomas Muentzer

1. See Paul Wappler, *Thomas Muentzer in Zwickau und die Zwickauer Propheten* (2d ed.; Guetersloh, 1966); see also documents in Nikolaus Mueller, *Die Wittenberger Bewegung, 1521 und 1522* (Leipzig, 1911), and discussion in Gordon Rupp, *Patterns of Reformation* (Philadelphia, 1969), ch. 6.

2. Luther, *Invocavit Sermons*, March 9–16, 1522, in *Luther's Works*, LI (Amer. ed.; Philadelphia and St. Louis, 1959), 70–100 (WA, X, 10^{III}, 1–64).

3. Luther, *A Sincere Admonition by Martin Luther to All Christians to Guard against Insurrection and Rebellion*, in *Luther's Works*, XLV (Amer. ed.; Philadelphia and St. Louis, 1962), 57–74 (WA, VIII, 676–87).

4. The critical edition of Hausmann's "Report Concerning the Zwickau Prophets" is in Wappler, *Thomas Muentzer in Zwickau*, pp. 81–86. The translation is by Eric W. Gritsch, from *Reformer without a*

Church (Philadelphia: Fortress Press, 1967), pp. 25–26; reprinted by permission.

5. See the discussion of Muentzer's piety, within a mystical context, in Steven Ozment, *Mysticism and Dissent* (New Haven, Conn., 1973).

6. On Muentzer in Prague, see Vaclav Husa, *Thomas Muentzer a Cechy* (Rozpravy Ceskoslovenske Akademie Ved, vol. LXVII, no. 11; Prague, 1957).

7. The critical edition of Muentzer's *Prague Manifesto* is in Thomas Muentzer, *Schriften und Briefe*, ed. Guenther Franz (Guetersloh, 1968), pp. 491–511. The translation is by Gordon Rupp, from *Patterns of Reformation* (Philadelphia: Fortress Press, 1969), pp. 175–78; reprinted by permission.

8. The medieval interpretation of Daniel 2, which confined the millennium to the work of the church on earth (Augustine) was challenged by the reformers. Flacius Illyricus and John Foxe both agreed that the pope was the Antichrist and that chaotic conditions indicated the end of the present age. Muentzer's millenarianism was also continued by such groups as the Puritan Fifth Monarchy Men, who claimed that after the four historical empires had run their course, the fifth monarchy would bring in the eschatological kingdom of God together with the millennial rule of the saints on earth. See the discussion in B. S. Capp, *The Fifth Monarchy Men: A Study in Seventeenth Century English Millenarianism* (London, 1972), pp. 23–45.

By relating the fifth monarchy to the fallen church in existence since the postapostolic generation, Muentzer heightened hopes that the latter-day church would soon realize through violence Christ's universal mission, which even the apostolic church had failed to achieve (in Franz, ed., *Schriften und Briefe*, p. 311).

9. The critical edition of Muentzer's *Sermon before the Princes on Daniel Two* is in Franz, ed., *Schriften und Briefe*, pp. 241–63. The translation is by George H. Williams: From SPIRITUAL AND ANA-BAPTIST WRITERS, The Library of Christian Classics, Volume XXV, edited by George Huntston Williams and Angel M. Mergal. Published in the U.S.A. by The Westminster Press, 1957. Used by permission.

10. Luther, *Letter to the Princes of Saxony Concerning the Rebellious Spirit*, in *Luther's Works*, XL (Amer. ed.; Philadelphia and St. Louis, 1958), 49–59 (WA, XV, 210–21).

11. Muentzer: "In the face of usury, taxes, and rents no one can have faith" (Franz, ed., *Schriften und Briefe*, p. 303). Muentzer confessed under torture that he had aimed for an egalitarian social order in which there were neither rich nor poor (see Document 9, article 8). Yet Muentzer also expressed doubts about the obedience to God of the common people as well as the rulers.

12. In July 1524, Muentzer wrote to his followers in Sangerhausen that "more than thirty alliances and covenants of the elect have been arranged. The game will be played in all lands" (Franz, ed., *Schriften und Briefe*, p. 408).

13. The critical edition of Muentzer's "Highly Provoked Defense [against Luther]" is in Franz, ed., *Schriften und Briefe*, pp. 321–43. The translation is by Hans J. Hillerbrand in *The Mennonite Quarterly Review*, XXXVIII (1964), 24–25, 27–28, 30–36; reprinted by permission.

14. In March 1524, under Muentzer's influence, the Allstedt towns-people had destroyed a shrine devoted to the Virgin Mary.

15. Laurentius of Nordhausen is Justus Jonas, the Wittenberg reformer, who was born at Nordhausen. St. Lawrence, a martyr of the early church, had been burned alive.

16. *Thomas Muentzer und der Thueringer Aufstand, 1525* (Berlin, 1966).

17. See George H. Williams, *The Radical Reformation* (Philadelphia, 1962), pp. 237–41; Horst W. Schraepler, *Die rechtliche Behandlung der Taeufer in der deutschen Schweiz, Sueddeutschland und Hessen, 1525–1618* (*Schriften zur Kirchen-und Rechtsgeschichte*, vol. IV; Tuebingen, 1957); Ethelbert Stauffer, "Anabaptist Theology of Martyrdom," *Mennonite Quarterly Review*, XIX (1945), 179–214; Franklin H. Littell, *Landgraf Philipp und die Toleranz* (Bad Nauheim, 1957).

18. *Anabaptism: A Social History, 1525–1618* (Ithaca, N.Y., 1972), pp. 427, 437.

19. The critical edition of Muentzer's Confession is in Franz, ed., *Schriften und Briefe*, pp. 544–48, translated by myself. The critical edition of Muentzer's Recantation is in Franz, ed., *Schriften und Briefe*, p. 550. The translation is by Hans J. Hillerbrand, from *The Reformation* (New York: Harper & Row, 1964), pp. 227–28; reprinted by permission.

Conflict with Zwingli: Swiss and South German Anabaptists

1. In E. Egli, G. Finsler, and W. Koehler, eds., "Welche Ursach gebend zu ufruren," *Huldreich Zwinglis Saemtliche Werke*, III (Leipzig, 1914), 63–64, 404.

2. The critical edition of The Second Zuerich Disputation is in E. Egli, G. Finsler, and W. Koehler, eds., *Huldreich Zwinglis Saemtliche Werke*, II (Leipzig: Me. Heinsius Nachfolger, 1908), 783–92. The translation is by Donald L. Ziegler: From Donald L. Ziegler, ed., *Great Debates of the Reformation* (New York: Random House, Inc., 1969), pp. 58–62; reprinted by permission. Additional passages have been translated and added by myself from Egli.

3. Emil Egli, ed., *Actensammlung zur Geschichte der Zuercher Reformation in den Jahren 1519–33* (Zurich, 1879), I, 72.

4. The critical edition of Grebel's Letter to Thomas Muentzer is in Leonhard von Muralt and Walter Schmid, *Quellen zur Geschichte der Taeufer in der Schweiz* (Zurich, 1952), pp. 13–21; the translation is revised from Walter Rauschenbusch, *The American Journal of Theology*, IX (1905), 91–99, by George H. Williams: From SPIRITUAL AND ANABAPTIST WRITERS, The Library of Christian Classics, Volume XXV, edited by George Huntston Williams and Angel M. Mergal. Published in the U.S.A. by The Westminster Press, 1957. Used by permission.

5. *Von dem Touff, vom Widertouff, und vom Kindertouff*, in E. Egli, G. Finsler, and W. Koehler, eds., *Huldreich Zwinglis Saemtliche Werke*, IV (Leipzig, 1927), 188–337, tr. by G. W. Bromiley, in *Zwingli and Bullinger* (Philadelphia, 1953), pp. 129–75.

6. The critical edition of Mantz's "Protest and Defense" is in von Muralt and Schmid, *Quellen zur Geschichte der Taeufer in der Schweiz*,

pp. 23–28. The translation is partly by Harold S. Bender, from *Conrad Grebel* (Goshen, Ind.: The Mennonite Historical Society, 1950), pp. 287–88, with additions from von Muralt translated by myself; reprinted by permission.

7. Heinrich Bullinger's *Reformationsgeschichte nach dem Autographen*, ed. J. J. Hottinger and H. H. Voegeli (3 vols.; Frauenfeld, 1838–1840). See Heinold Fast, *Heinrich Bullinger und die Taeufer* (Weierhof, 1959), for a discussion of the negative effect of Bullinger's writing upon the interpretation of Anabaptism.

8. The first edition of Bullinger's *History of the Reformation* was by Hottinger and Voegeli (see preceding note). The translation is by Hans J. Hillerbrand in *The Reformation* (New York: Harper Torchbook, 1964), pp. 228–29; reprinted by permission.

9. See note 5 above.

10. For a discussion of the first Anabaptist congregation at Zollikon, see Fritz Blanke, *Brothers in Christ* (Scottdale, Pa., 1961).

11. From the *Hutterite Chronicle*. A critical edition of the *Hutterite Chronicle* is in A. J. F. Ziegelschmid, *Die Aelteste Chronik der Hutterischen Brueder* (Philadelphia, 1943), pp. 44–48. The translation is by George H. Williams: From SPIRITUAL AND ANABAPTIST WRITERS, The Library of Christian Classics, Volume XXV, edited by George Huntston Williams and Angel M. Mergal. Published in the U.S.A. by The Westminster Press, 1957. Used by permission.

12. See Lowell H. Zuck, "Anabaptism: Abortive Counter-Revolt within the Reformation," *Church History*, XXVI (1957), 1–16.

13. For a discussion of Sattler's teaching on separatist nonresistance, see James M. Stayer, *Anabaptists and the Sword* (Lawrence, Kan., 1972), pp. 117–31.

14. The critical edition of the *Schleitheim Confession of Faith* is in Beatrice Jenny, *Das Schleitheimer Taeuferbekenntnis, 1527* (*Schaffhauser Beitraege zur vaterlaendischen Geschichte*, vol. XXVIII; Schaffhausen, 1951), pp. 9–18). The translation is by John C. Wenger in *The Mennonite Quarterly Review*, XIX (1945), 243–53; reprinted by permission.

15. For a recent discussion of Hubmaier's early years, see Torsten Bergsten, *Balthasar Hubmaier: Seine Stellung zu Reformation und Taeufertum, 1521–1528* (Kassel, 1961).

16. The critical edition of Hubmaier's *On the Sword* is in Balthasar Hubmaier, *Schriften*, ed. Gunnar Westin and Torsten Bergsten (Guetersloh, 1962), pp. 432–57; the translation is by Henry C. Vedder in *Balthasar Hubmaier* (New York: G. P. Putnam's Sons, 1905), pp. 302–7.

The Kingdom of Muenster: North German and Dutch Anabaptism

1. See discussions of Hofmann in Cornelius Krahn, *Dutch Anabaptism: Origin, Spread, Life, and Thought, 1450–1600* (The Hague, 1968), pp. 80–117; James M. Stayer, *Anabaptists and the Sword* (Lawrence, Kan., 1972), pp. 211–26; and George H. Williams, *The Radical Reformation* (Philadelphia, 1962), pp. 259–64, 307–9. The most recent

book about Hofmann is by Peter Kawerau, *Melchior Hofmann als Religioeser Denker* (Haarlem, 1954).

2. John of Batenburg, a bastard son of Dutch nobility, became an Anabaptist militant and tried unsuccessfully to complete the Muenster revolutionary program after that city had fallen (see Williams, *Radical Reformation*, pp. 381–86). David Joris mediated as a Spiritualizer between belligerent Batenburgers and pacific Obbenites at Bocholt in 1536. Thinking of himself as "the third David" (compare the third age of the Spirit of Joachim), Joris gathered messianic followers, but he died respectably in Basel as a disguised religious refugee. See Roland H. Bainton, *David Joris: Wiedertaeufer und Kaempfer fuer Toleranz* (Leipzig, 1937), and Bainton's brief essay on Joris in his *Travail of Religious Liberty* (Philadelphia, 1951), pp. 125–48.

3. The critical edition of Hofmann's *The Ordinance of God* is in Samuel Cramer and F. Pijper, eds., *Bibliotheca Reformatoria Neerlandica* (The Hague, 1909), V, 148–67. The translation is by George H. Williams: From SPIRITUAL AND ANABAPTIST WRITERS, The Library of Christian Classics, Volume XXV, edited by George Huntston Williams and Angel M. Mergal. Published in the U.S.A. by The Westminster Press, 1957. Used by permission.

4. In allusion to II Esdras 5:4 ("After the third period . . . you will see confusion everywhere"), Hofmann echoed Joachim of Flora's belief in the third age of the Spirit and also emphasized that great suffering was about to happen to the saints, after which the end would come.

5. Hofmann regarded the "Key of David" as his scriptural interpretative principle (Isaiah 22:22: "What he opens [using the key of David] no man shall shut, and what he shuts no man shall open"). The key's "clovenness," Hofmann taught, indicates the oneness of the Old and New Testaments, with Old Testament images corresponding to New Testament events.

6. Robert Stupperich introduces Rothmann in his source collection, *Die Schriften Bernhard Rothmanns*, I (Muenster, 1970), x–xxiv. See also Stayer, *Anabaptists and the Sword*, pp. 239–52, and Jack W. Porter, "Bernhard Rothmann 1495–1535, Royal Orator of the Muenster Anabaptist Kingdom" (unpub. Ph.D. diss., University of Wisconsin, 1964).

7. On the two Johns, see Krahn, *Dutch Anabaptism*, pp. 133–45, and Williams, *Radical Reformation*, pp. 368–75.

8. For the shift from peaceful to violent Anabaptism at Muenster, see Karl-Heinz Kirchhoff, "Was There a Peaceful Anabaptist Congregation in Muenster in 1534?" in *Mennonite Quarterly Review*, XLIV (1970), 357–70.

On communism at Muenster, see Hans von Schubert, *Der Kommunismus der Wiedertaeufer in Muenster und seine Quellen* (Heidelberg, 1919), and Otthein Rammstedt, *Sekte und sociale Bewegung: Sociologische Analyse der Taeufer in Muenster 1534–35* (Cologne, 1966), and from a Marxist perspective Gerhard Brendler, *Das Taeuferreich zu Muenster, 1534/35* (Berlin, 1966).

On polygamy at Muenster, see Roland H. Bainton, "Interpretations of the Immoralities of the Patriarchs," *Early and Medieval Christianity* (*The Collected Papers in Church History*, vol. I; Boston, 1962), p. 128, and George H. Williams, *Radical Reformation*, pp. 511–13.

9. The critical edition of Rothmann's *Confession of Faith and Life of the Church of Christ of Muenster* is in Stupperich, ed., *Schriften Rothmanns*, I, 195–208; my translation.

10. For the history of the concept of the heavenly flesh of Christ, see Hans Joachim Schoeps, *Vom Himmlischen Fleisch Christi* (Tuebingen, 1951). Schoeps noted (pp. 25–47) that although Caspar Schwenckfeld's version of the heavenly flesh doctrine was more moderate than that of Melchior Hofmann, Hofmann's view was passed on to Rothmann.

11. For the distinctive position of Anabaptists on faith, works, and sanctification see George H. Williams, "Sanctification in the Testimony of Several So-Called Schwaermer," in Ivar Asheim, ed., *The Church, Mysticism, Sanctification, and the Natural in Luther's Thought* (Philadelphia, 1967), pp. 194–211.

12. On Anabaptist baptism, see Rollin S. Armour, *Anabaptist Baptism: A Representative Study* (Scottdale, Pa., 1966).

13. Rothmann here recalled the climax of the struggle for control of Muenster among Catholics, the Lutheran party in the council, and Rothmann's followers. Rothmann was permitted to stay after his Second Reformation party showed willingness to defend itself and the Lutherans attempted to balance Catholic attacks against the radicals with an effort to maintain the Reformation in Muenster.

14. Rothmann noted the transition of the Second Reformation party to crusading militarism after they discovered a plot against them on February 9. Having already shown willingness to defend themselves in November, the Anabaptists now became advocates of a Christian magistracy resistance doctrine against their combined Catholic and Protestant enemies.

15. Under siege, the Muenster Anabaptists moved beyond a resistance doctrine to a spirit of apocalyptic urgency. The escape of the Anabaptists from military disaster on February 10 was regarded as a divine miracle. The sword was now used both for internal discipline and against the besieging enemy. Late in February, Knipperdolling restrained John of Leiden from his intention to kill all the uncovenanted godless (cf. Thomas Muentzer) within the city, and the nonbelievers quickly left Muenster. See the article by Karl-Heinz Kirchhoff, "Was There a Peaceful Anabaptist Congregation?" and Stayer, *Anabaptists and the Sword*, pp. 255–80.

16. C. A. Cornelius, ed., *Die Geschichtsquellen des Bisthums Muenster* (Muenster, 1965; reprint of 1853 ed.), pp. 83, 87, 277.

17. Hans Ritschl, *Die Kommune der Wiedertaeufer in Muenster* (Bonn, 1923), pp. 29–32.

18. Rammstedt, *Sekte und sociale Bewegung*.

19. The critical edition of *Thirteen Statements of the Order of [Private] Life* is in Heinrich Detmer, ed., *Hermanni a Kerssenbroch: Anabaptistici furoris Monasterium . . . evertentis historica narratio* (Muenster, 1899–1900), p. 577; my translation. A selection by Kerssenbroch is given by Klemens Loeffler, ed., *Die Wiedertaeufer zu Muenster, 1534/5* (Jena, 1923), pp. 81–83.

20. The critical edition of the *Code for Public Behavior* is in Loeffler, ed., *Die Wiedertaeufer zu Muenster*, pp. 83–86. The translation is by Hans J. Hillerbrand in his *The Reformation* (New York: Harper & Row, 1964), pp. 257–59; reprinted by permission.

21. "Primitivismus," in Littell and Hans Hermann Walz, eds.,
Weltkirchenlexikon: Handbuch der Oekumene (Stuttgart, 1960), cols.
1182–87. See also Franklin H. Littell, *The Origins of Sectarian
Protestantism* (New York, 1964).

22. The critical edition of Rothmann's *Restitution . . . of Christian
Teaching, Faith, and Life . . . through the Church of Christ at Muenster*
is in Stupperich, ed., *Schriften Rothmanns*, pp. 208–84; the translation
is by myself.

23. The critical edition of Rothmann's *Concerning Revenge* is in
Stupperich, ed., *Schriften Rothmanns*, pp. 284–97; the translation is by
myself. A convenient copy of the work may be found in Heinold Fast,
ed., *Der linke Fluegel der Reformation* (Bremen, 1962), pp. 342–60.

The Peaceable Kingdom:
Mennonite and
Hutterite Reaction

1. On Obbe Philips, see the article by N. van der Zijpp in *The
Mennonite Encyclopedia* (Scottdale, Pa., 1959), IV, 9–11.

2. The critical edition of Obbe Philips's *Confession* is in Samuel
Cramer and F. Pijper, eds., *Bibliotheca Reformatoria Neerlandica* (The
Hague, 1910), VII, 121–38. The translation is by Christiaan Theodoor
Lievestro: From SPIRITUAL AND ANABAPTIST WRITERS, The
Library of Christian Classics, Volume XXV, edited by George Huntston
Williams and Angel M. Mergal. Published in the U.S.A. by The
Westminster Press, 1957. Used by permission.

3. Three hundred militant Anabaptists en route to Muenster under
John van Geelen were besieged in the Old Cloister monastery near
Bolsward, the Netherlands, and were crushed in April 1535. A nearby
priest, Menno Simons, was deeply affected by this tragedy, in which
Peter Simons, perhaps his brother, died. See Document 22 and
Cornelius Krahn, *Dutch Anabaptism: Origin, Spread, Life and Thought,
1450–1600* (The Hague, 1968), p. 152.

4. On Simons, see Cornelius Krahn, *Menno Simons (1496–1561)*
(Karlsruhe, 1936). See also Krahn, *Dutch Anabaptism*, pp. 150–55,
169–77; George H. Williams, *The Radical Reformation* (Philadelphia,
1962), pp. 387–94; and James M. Stayer, *Anabaptists and the Sword*,
(Lawrence, Kans., 1972), pp. 309–28.

5. On Bouwens, see the article by Karel Vos in *The Mennonite
Encyclopedia*, III, 305; Krahn, *Dutch Aanabaptism*, pp. 229–33; and
Williams, *Radical Reformation*, pp. 493–99.

6. The critical edition of Menno Simons's *Conversion, Call, and
Testimony* is in H. Jz. Herrison, ed., *Opera Omnia Theologica*
(Amsterdam, 1681), fols. 225–324. The translation is by Leonard
Verduin (from Menno's *Reply to Gellius Faber*): Reprinted by per-
mission from *The Complete Writings of Menno Simons*, John C.
Wenger, editor, copyright 1956 by Mennonite Publishing House,
Scottdale, Pa. 15683.

7. The critical edition of Menno Simons's *Reply to False Accusations*
is in Herrison, ed., *Opera Omnia Theologica*, fols. 491–516. The
translation is reprinted by permission from *The Complete Writings of*

Menno Simons, John C. Wenger, editor, copyright 1956 by Mennonite Publishing House, Scottdale, Pa. 15683.

8. On Jakob Hutter, see Hans Fischer, *Jacob Hutter: Leben, Froemmigkeit, Briefe* (Mennonite Historical Series, no. 4; Newton, Kan., 1956), and Robert Friedmann, *Hutterite Studies*, ed. Harold S. Bender (Goshen, Ind., 1961). See also the article by Johann Loserth in *The Mennonite Encyclopedia*, II, 851–54, and Williams, *Radical Reformation*, pp. 417–25.

9. On Peter Riedemann, see the article by Robert Friedmann in *The Mennonite Encyclopedia*, IV, 326–28, and Williams, *Radical Reformation*, pp. 425–28.

10. On the biblical basis for Hutterite community of goods, see Victor Peters, *All Things Common: The Hutterian Way of Life* (Minneapolis, 1965), and Lydia Mueller, *Der Kommunismus der maehrischen Wiedertaeufer* (Leipzig, 1927). Also see D. Sommer, "Peter Ridemann and Menno Simons on Economics." *Mennonite Quarterly Review*, XXVIII (1954), 205–23; Peter James Klassen, *The Economics of Anabaptism, 1525–1560* (London, 1964); Claus-Peter Clasen, *Anabaptism: A Social History* (Ithaca, N.Y., 1972), pp. 210–97; and Robert Friedmann, "The Christian Communism of the Hutterite Brethren," *Archiv fuer Reformationsgeschichte*, XLVI (1955), 196–209.

11. The original edition of Peter Riedemann's *Concerning Community of Goods* of 1565 is entitled *Rechenschaft unserer Religion, Leer and Glaubens Von den Bruedern so man die Hutterischen nennt aussgangen*. There is a copy in the University of Chicago Library. The translation is by Kathleen E. Hasenberg in Peter Riedemann, *Account of Our Religion, Doctrine and Faith* (London, 1950), pp. 102–21, reprinted in Hans J. Hillerbrand, *The Protestant Reformation* (New York, 1968), pp. 143–46. Reprinted by permission of the Plough Publishing House. See the discussion by Friedmann in *Hutterite Studies*, pp. 224–28.

Revolution: Protestant Resistance in Germany, Scotland, France, and the Netherlands

1. On Luther and resistance, see the discussion by Hermann Doerries, *Wort und Stunde: Beitraege zum Verstaendnis Luthers* (Goettingen, 1970), III, 195–270; Eric W. Gritsch, "Martin Luther and Violence: A Reappraisal of a Neuralgic Theme," *The Sixteenth Century Journal*, III (1972), 37–55; Oliver K. Olson, "Theology of Revolution: Magdeburg, 1550–1551," *Sixteenth Century Journal*, III (1972), 56–79; and Lowell C. Green, "Resistance to Authority and Luther," *Lutheran Quarterly*, V (1954), 338–48. Sources: Heinz Scheible, ed., *Das Widerstandsrecht als Problem der deutschen Protestanten, 1523–1546* (Goettingen, 1969), and Gunther Wolf, ed., *Luther und die Obrigkeit in Wege der Forschung*, vol. LXXV (Darmstadt, 1970).

2. Analyzed by Doerries, *Wort und Stunde*, pp. 215–64, and Green, "Resistance to Authority," pp. 344–45. Text in Scheible, ed., *Das Widerstandsrecht*, no. 15, pp. 63–66.

3. The critical text of the letter of Luther to Lazarus Spengler in Nuernberg, March 18, 1531, is in the Weimar edition Briefwechsel (W-Br), VI (Weimar, 1935), 56. The translation is from *What Luther Says*, Vol. II, by Ewald Plass, copyright 1959 by Concordia Publishing House, St. Louis, Mo. Used by permission.

4. The critical text of Luther's *Disputation Concerning the Right to Resist the Emperor*, May 8–9, 1539, is in the WA, XXXIX (Weimar, 1932), ii, 55–56, 65–66, 77. The translation is by Lowell C. Green, from "Resistance to Authority and Luther," in *Lutheran Quarterly*, V (1954), 346; reprinted by permission.

5. The original Latin edition of the Magdeburg Confession is entitled *Confessio et Apologia Pastorum et reliquorum Ministrorum Ecclesiae Magdeburgensis* (Magdeburg, 1550). A microfilm copy is in the Center for Reformation Research, St. Louis. The translation is from *The Age of the Reformation* by Roland H. Bainton, © 1956. Reprinted by permission of D. Van Nostrand Company. Although often attributed to Nicholas Amsdorf, the 1550 Confession appears to have been written primarily by Superintendent Nicolaus Gallus of Ratisbon. Friedrich Huelsse, "Beitraege zur Geschichte der Buchdruckerkunst in Magdeburg," *Geschichtsblaetter fuer Stadt und Land Magdeburg*, XV–XVII (Magdeburg, 1880–82), 27, reprinted in *Bibliographie Reconditae* (Amsterdam, 1966), I, 346–738, reports a gloss in the handwriting of Johann Wigand in the copy of the Confession in the Wolfenbuettel Library attributing the authorship to Gallus. See also Olson, "Theology of Revolution," pp. 56–79.

6. For introduction to Calvin, the *Institutes*, and his work in Geneva, see François Wendel, *Calvin: The Origins and Development of His Religious Thought* (London, 1963); E. W. Monter, *Calvin's Geneva* (New York, 1967); Robert W. Kingdon, *Geneva and the Coming of the Wars of Religion in France, 1555–1563* (Geneva, 1956); and G. L. Hunt, *Calvin and the Political Order* (Philadelphia, 1965).

7. From Calvin's *Institutes*, bk. 4, ch. 20, paras. 29, 31, and 32. The critical text of the *Institutes* is in *Johannis Calvin Opera Selecta*, ed. Peter Barth and Wilhelm Niesel (Munich, 1928–36); the 1559 edition of the *Institutes* is in volumes 3–5. The translation is by Ford Lewis Battles: From CALVIN: INSTITUTES OF THE CHRISTIAN RELIGION, Volume XXI, edited by John T. McNeill, translated by Ford Lewis Battles. Copyright © MCMLX, W. L. Jenkins. Used by permission of The Westminster Press.

8. For Beza, see Paul-F. Geisendorf, *Theodore de Beze* (Geneva, 1967), and Henry M. Baird, *Theodore Beza: The Counsellor of the French Reformation* (New York, 1899). See also Robert M. Kingdon, "The First Expression of Theodore Beza's Political Ideas," in *Archiv fuer Reformationsgeschichte*, XLVI (1955), 88–100 (hereafter *ARG*); Irmgard Hoess, "Zur Genesis der Widerstandslehre Bezas," *ARG*, LIV (1963), 198–214; and Sebastian Castellio, *Concerning Heretics*, ed. *Roland H. Bainton* (New York, 1935), pp. 107–9.

9. For Hotman, see Donald R. Kelley, *François Hotman: A Revolutionary's Ordeal* (Princeton, N.J., 1973), and Document 34; for Amboise, see Kingdon, *Geneva*, pp. 68–78.

10. Copies of the Latin text of Beza's *De Haereticis a Civili Magistratu Puniendis . . .* (Geneva, 1554) can be found in the library

of Roland H. Bainton, Yale University, and in the Munich Staatsbibliothek. The translation is by Robert M. Kingdon in "The First Expression of Theodore Beza's Political Ideas," *ARH*, XLVI (1955), 89–92; reprinted by permission.

11. For Ponet, see Winthrop S. Hudson, *John Ponet (1516?–1576): Advocate of Limited Monarchy* (Chicago, 1942), and Christina Hallowell Garrett, *The Marian Exiles: A Study in the Origins of Elizabethan Puritanism* (Cambridge, Eng., 1938; reprinted 1966), pp. 253–58.

12. Garrett, *Marian Exiles*. For a denial of Garrett's view that Ponet directed an Anglican conspiracy from Strassburg against Knox at Frankfurt see Ronald J. Vander Molen, "Anglican against Puritan: Ideological Origins during the Marian Exile," *Church History*, XLII (1973), 45–57. See also J. W. Allen, *A History of Political Thought in the Sixteenth Century* (New York, 1957), pp. 118–20.

13. A facsimile reproduction of Ponet's *A Shorte Treatise of Politike Power* (1556) appears in Winthrop S. Hudson, *John Ponet*, pp. 111–12, 117–18, 125–26, 47–48, 79–81.

14. For Goodman, see Garrett, *Marian Exiles*, pp. 162–64, and Allen, *History of Political Thought*, pp. 116–18.

15. A facsimile reproduction of Goodman's *How Superior Powers Oght to be Obeyd* (Geneva, 1558; copy at Union Theological Seminary, New York) is in an edition by the Facsimile Text Society (New York, 1931), pp. 179–82, on microfilm at the Center for Reformation Research, St. Louis.

16. For Knox, see Jasper Ridley, *John Knox* (New York, 1968), and W. Stanford Reid, "The Coming of the Reformation to Edinburgh," *Church History*, XLII (1973), 27–44.

17. Knox's *The First Blast of the Trumpet against the Monstrous Regiment of Women* is in David Laing, ed., *The Works of John Knox* (Edinburgh, 1855; reprinted New York, 1966), IV, 349–422.

18. The full text of Knox's *The Appelation from the Sentence Pronounced by the Bishops and Clergy: Addressed to the Nobility and Estates of Scotland* (1558) is in Laing, ed., *Works of John Knox*, IV, 496–98.

19. The full text of Knox's *The Interview with Mary Queen of Scots* (1561) is in Laing, ed., *Works of John Knox*, II, 277–79, 281–84, 286.

20. The full text of Knox's *Debate with Lethington* (1564) is in Laing, ed., *Works of John Knox*, II, 452–54, 456–58.

21. For Buchanan, see P. Hume Brown, *George Buchanan: Humanist and Reformer* (Edinburgh, 1890); Allen, *History of Political Thought*, pp. 336–42; and J. N. Figgis, *Political Thought from Gerson to Grotius: 1414–1625* (New York, 1960), pp. 167–72.

22. A facsimile reproduction of Buchanan's *De jure regni apud Scotos* (Edinburgh, 1579) appears in a volume with the same title (New York, 1969); the translation is by Charles F. Arrowood, ed., *The Powers of the Crown in Scotland* (Austin, Tex.: The University of Texas Press, 1949), pp. 92–95, 141–48.

23. For Hotman, see Kelley, *François Hotman*.

24. The critical edition of Hotman's *Francogallia* (Geneva, 1573) is translated by J. H. M. Salmon, with notes on the Latin text by Ralph E.

Giesey (Cambridge, Eng.: Cambridge University Press, 1972), pp. 295–99, 519, 523–25.

25. Ansegius, Abbot of Fontenelle (d. 833), *Capitularia regum Francorum*, ed. A. Boret (*Monumenta Germaniae historica, Libelli de lite*, vol. II; Berlin, 1879), p. 3.

26. Cicero, *De legibus*, ed. C. W. Keyes (London, 1928), p. 464.

27. *Corpus iuris civilis* (compiled in the sixth century), ed. P. Krueger, T. Mommsen, R. Schoell, and G. Kroll (Berlin, 1954), p. 231.

28. *The Politics*, ed. H. Rackham (New York, 1932), p. 263.

29. *Corpus iuris canonica* (compiled in the twelfth century), ed. E. Friedberg (Leipzig, 1879–81; new ed., Graz, 1955), I, 22.

30. *Ibid.*, II, 265.

31. J. H. Elliott, "Revolution and Continuity in Early Modern Europe," *Past and Present*, XLII (1969), 35–36, reprinted in Lawrence and Carol Kaplan, eds., *Revolutions: A Comparative Study* (New York, 1973), p. 52.

32. For Beza, see references in note 8 above, and also A. A. van Schelvan, "Beza's De Iure Magistratuum in Subditos," in *Archiv fuer Reformationsgeschichte*, XLV (1954), 62–83.

33. The critical edition of Beza's *De iure magistratuum* (Lyon, 1580) is edited by Klaus Sturm (Neukirchen-Vluyn, 1965) and is similar to the 1576 Latin translation; the critical edition of the original French version, *Du Droit des Magistrats* (1574, without place or publisher), is introduced and edited by Robert M. Kingdon (Geneva, 1970). The translation is by H. L. Gonin, in A. H. Murray, ed., *Beza: Concerning the Rights of Rulers over Their Subjects and the Duty of Subjects towards Their Rulers* (Capetown: Hollandsch Afrikaansche Uitgevers Maatschappij, 1956), pp. 33–86; reprinted by permission.

34. Biblical references to revolts against Jehoram and Amaziah are in II Kings 8:22 and II Kings 14:19.

35. On Du Plessis-Mornay, see Figgis, *Political Thought*, 174–79, and Ralph E. Giesey, "The Monarchomach Triumvirs: Hotman, Beza and Mornay," *Bibliotheque d'Humanisme et Renaissance*, XXXII (1970), 41–76. On Languet, see G. t'van Isselsteyn, "L'auteur de l'ouvrage 'Vindiciae contra Tyrannos'," *Revue historique*, CLXVII (1931), 46–59. Johan Junius, councillor to William of Orange and Elector Frederick III, has also been suggested as the author (Derek Visser, "Junius: The Author of the 'Vindiciae contra Tyrannos,'" *Tijdschrift voor Geschiednis*, LXXXIV [1971], 510–25).

36. For Bodin, see Julian H. Franklin, *Jean Bodin and the Rise of Absolutist Theory* (New York, 1973).

37. The original edition, *Vindiciae contra tyrannos* (Edinburgh [Basel?], 1579), gave the author as Junius Brutus. An English translation was made by William Walker, *A Defence of Liberty against Tyrants* (London, 1648). Laski republished Walker's translation with an historical introduction (Harold J. Laski, ed., *A Defense of Liberty against Tyrants* [Gloucester, Mass., 1963], pp. 111–12, 117, 212–13, 215, 227–29). Frederick S. Carney promises a new translation (Frederick S. Carney, "Associational Thought in Early Calvinism," in

Voluntary Associations, D. B. Robertson, ed. [Richmond, Va., 1966],
p. 397).

38. II Kings 11:17–20.

39. I Kings 13:1–10.

40. For Theudas see Acts 5:36.
Bar Kochba led a second Jewish revolt against Rome in 132 to
135 A.D. He was thought to be the messianic star out of Jacob (Num.
24:17).
The Anabaptist Kingdom of Muenster fell in 1535 (Documents 17
through 21).

41. For William of Orange, see C. V. Wedgwood, *William the Silent*
(London, 1960), and for his wife see "Charlotte de Bourbon," in
Roland H. Bainton, *Women of the Reformation in France and England*
(Minneapolis, 1973), pp. 89–111.

42. Originally published in French, William's *Apologie* was published
the same year (1581) in translations into Dutch, German, Latin, and
English. The original English translation, *The Apologie or Defence of
the Most Noble Prince William, by the Grace of God Prince of Orange
. . .* (Delft, 1581), has been edited and reprinted by H. Wansink
(Leiden, 1969), pp. 14, 16–17, 74, 78–79, 88–89, passages modernized
here.

43. The *Act of Abjuration* (Declaration of Independence) of the
Estates General of the United Netherlands, July 26, 1581, is taken from
C. V. Wedgwood, *William the Silent* (London: Jonathan Cape, 1944),
p. 224; reprinted by permission.

44. The *Formula of Abjuration* of the Estates General of the United
Netherlands, July 29, 1581, is taken from John L. Motley, *The Rise of
the Dutch Republic* (New York: John B. Alden, 1899), IV, 652. See
also J. W. Smit, "The Netherlands Revolution," in Robert Forster and
Jack P. Greene, eds., *Preconditions of Revolution in Early Modern
Europe* (Baltimore, 1970), pp. 19–54.

Roman Catholic Resistance in
England and Spain

1. William Cecil, Lord Burghley, *The Execution of Justice in England*
(London, 1583).

2. On Cardinal Allen, see Robert M. Kingdon, "William Allen's Use
of Protestant Political Argument," in Charles H. Carter, ed., *From the
Renaissance to the Counter-Reformation* (New York, 1965), pp. 164–76,
and Garrett Mattingly, "William Allen and Catholic Propaganda in
England," *Aspects de la propagande religieuse* (Geneva, 1957), pp.
333–38.

3. For canonization of the forty English Catholic martyrs, see Thomas
H. Clancy, "Are Martyrs Relevant?" *America,* CXXIII (Oct. 24, 1970),
320, and Peter Hebblethwaite, "Forty More Saints," *America,* CXXIII
(Nov. 14, 1970), 399–400.

4. A facsimile edition of William Allen, *A True, Sincere and Modest
Defence of English Catholics* (1584), from the original in the Bodleian

Library, is in the series *English Recusant Literature, 1558–1640*, LXVIII, sel. and ed. D. M. Rogers (Menston, Eng., 1971), 77–84.

5. Allen is quoting from the 1555 *Commentaries* of the German Lutheran historian of the Reformation, John Sleidan (*De statu religionis et reipublicae, Carolo quinto, Caesare, Commentarii* [Geneva, 1559]). Sleidan cites Calvin's 1561 commentary on Daniel (see William Baum et al., eds., *Ioannis Calvini Opera* [*Corpus Reformatorum*] [Braunschweig, 1889], XLI, 25–26).

6. Beza's version of the New Testament appeared in 1565.

7. The quotation is from the French Reformed *Confession of Faith* of 1559, in Philip Schaff, *Creeds of the Evangelical Protestant Churches* (New York, 1877), pp. 356–82.

8. The Zwingli quotation is from a letter to Konrad Sam and Simpert Schenk of Ulm and Memmingen in August 1530, in E. Egli, G. Finsler, and W. Koehler, eds., *Huldreich Zwinglis Saemtliche Werke*, XI (Leipzig, 1905), 68–70.

9. Goodman praised the abortive revolt of Sir Thomas Wyatt against Mary Tudor in 1554 in his *How Superior Powers Oght to be Obeyd* (Geneva, 1558); there is a facsimile edition introduced by Charles H. McIlwain (New York, 1931), p. 204.

10. The quotation is from Knox's *Appellation* of 1558, in David Laing, ed., *The Works of John Knox* (Edinburgh, 1855; reprinted New York, 1966), IV, 540.

11. The Luther quotation was made at a conference of lawyers held in Torgau in 1530 (see Heinz Scheible, ed., *Das Widerstandsrecht als Problem der deutschen Protestanten, 1523–1546* [Guetersloh, 1969], p. 67). The Hessian-Saxon manifesto was issued on September 2, 1546. The summary from Sleidan is of the 1550 Magdeburg Confession (*Confessio et Apologia Pastorum . . . Magdeburgensis* [Magdeburg, 1550]; microfilm copy in the Center for Reformation Research, St. Louis).

12. For Mariana, see J. W. Allen, *A History of Political Thought in the Sixteenth Century* (New York, 1957), pp. 360–66, and G. P. Gooch, *English Democratic Ideas in the Seventeenth Century* (New York, 1959), pp. 21–25.

13. For Bellarmine, see James Broderick, S.J., *Robert Bellarmine* (Westminster, Md., 1961), and John C. Murray, "St. Robert Bellarmine on the Indirect Power," *Theological Studies*, IX (1948), 491–535.

14. The original edition was entitled *De Rege et regis institutione* (Toledo, 1599); the translation is from an edition by George Albert Moore, ed., *Mariana: The King and the Education of the King* (Washington, D.C.: The Country Dollar Press, 1948), pp. 135–49.

15. Mariana half approved of the recent assassination of King Henry III, who had opposed the revolutionary Catholic League. When King Henry IV was murdered in 1610, the Jesuits condemned Mariana's teaching on tyrannicide.

16. Mariana noted that Athens and Rome honored their historic tyrannicides. Thrasybulus, a Greek statesman, overthrew the thirty Spartan tyrants over Athens in 403 B.C. The despotic Roman emperor Domitian, persecuter of the Christians, was assassinated in 96 A.D. The emperor Elagabalus, who reintroduced worship of the sun god, was murdered in 222 A.D. in a Pretorian uprising.

Puritan Religious Revolution
in England

1. On Foxe, see William Haller, *The Elect Nation: The Meaning and Relevance of Foxe's Book of Martyrs* (New York, 1963); J. F. Mozley, *John Foxe and His Book* (New York, 1940); and V. Norskov Olsen, *John Foxe and the Elizabethan Church* (Berkeley, Calif., 1973).

2. On Brightman, see B. G. Cooper, "The Academic Re-discovery of Apocalyptic Ideas in the Seventeenth Century," *Baptist Quarterly*, XVIII (1959–60), 352–56, and Peter Toon, ed., *Puritans, the Millennium and the Future of Israel* (Greenwood, S.C., 1970), pp. 26–32.

3. On Mead and Alsted, see Toon, ed., *Puritans*, pp. 56–65; Olsen, *John Foxe*, pp. 84–85, and Robert G. Clouse, "Johann Heinrich Alsted and English Millennialism," *Harvard Theological Review*, LXII (1969), 189–207. On Napier, see Robert G. Clouse, "John Napier and Apocalyptic Thought," *Sixteenth Century Journal*, V (1974), 101–14.

4. The critical edition of Foxe's Preface from the *Acts and Monuments* (1570) is in Leonard J. Trinterud, ed., *Elizabethan Puritanism* (New York, 1971), pp. 53–66; Trinterud's edition is taken from Stephen Reed Cattley and George Townsend, eds., *The Acts and Monuments of John Foxe* (London, 1843), corrected by Trinterud from the original editions of 1563 and 1570.

5. On the effects of Puritan preaching, see John F. Wilson, *Pulpit in Parliament: Puritanism during the English Civil Wars, 1640–1648* (Princeton, N.J., 1969), and Paul S. Seaver, *The Puritan Lectureships: The Politics of Religious Dissent, 1560–1662* (Stanford, Calif., 1970). The standard history is by Patrick Collinson, *The Elizabethan Puritan Movement* (London, 1967), together with two works by William Haller, *The Rise of Puritanism* (New York, 1957) and *Liberty and Reformation in the Puritan Revolution, 1640–1649* (New York, 1955).

6. For an introduction to the English Puritan Revolution, see Austin Woolrych, "The English Revolution, 1640–1660," in E. W. Ives, ed., *The English Revolution* (New York, 1971), pp. 1–33 (reprinted in Lawrence and Carol Kaplan, eds., *Revolutions: A Comparative Study* [New York, 1973], pp. 77–111), and also Lawrence Stone, *The Causes of the English Revolution, 1529–1642* (New York, 1972). On radical revolutionaries, see Christopher Hill, *The World Turned Upside Down: Radical Ideas during the English Revolution* (New York, 1972); on conservative revolutionaries, see David Underdown, *Pride's Purge: Politics in the Puritan Revolution* (Oxford, Eng., 1971).

7. See A. D. Lindsay, *The Essentials of Democracy* (Philadelphia, 1929).

8. The critical edition of the Root and Branch Petition is in Henry Gee and William John Hardy, eds., *Documents Illustrative of English Church History* (London, 1910), pp. 537–45; Gee and Hardy's edition is based upon John Rushworth, *Historical Collections of Private Passages of State . . . 1618–1648* (London, 1680–1701 and 1721–22), IV, 93. William M. Lamont, in *Godly Rule: Politics and Religion, 1603–60* (New York, 1969), p. 95, maintains that the main influence upon "root and branch" Puritans was the apocalyptic prophecy of Thomas Brightman.

9. On millenarian preaching, see Wilson, *Pulpit in Parliament*, p. 195.

10. Statistics on millenarian preachers are given in B. S. Capp, *The Fifth Monarchy Men: A Study in Seventeenth Century English Millenarianism* (London, 1972), p. 38.

11. On Hanserd Knollys, see Haller, *Rise of Puritanism*, pp. 270–72.
On Thomas Goodwin, one of the "Dissenting Brethren" of the Westminster Assembly, see Haller, *Rise of Puritanism*, pp. 75–79, 94–96. Goodwin's autobiography, "The Life of Dr. Thomas Goodwin," appeared in *The Works of Thomas Goodwin* V, (London, 1704).

12. The original edition of *A Glimpse of Sions Glory, or The Churches Beauty Specified* was printed anonymously in London by William Larner in 1641. It has also been attributed to Hanserd Knollys (by Haller) and Jeremiah Burroughes (by H. M. Dexter), but it was probably a sermon preached first in Holland by Thomas Goodwin (see John F. Wilson, "A Glimpse of Syons Glory," *Church History*, XXXI [1962], 66–73, and A. R. Dallison in Toon, ed., *Puritans*, pp. 131–36). A critical selection from the text is in A. S. P. Woodhouse, ed., *Puritanism and Liberty, Being the Army Debates, 1647–49* (Chicago, 1965), pp. 233–41.

13. For narratives on the Great Rebellion, see C. V. Wedgwood, *The King's Peace, 1637–1641* (London, 1955) and *The King's War, 1641–1647* (London, 1958). A power struggle between king and Parliament figured prominently, as did religious divisions between Anglicans and Puritans. Social division appears to have been less important; although the aristocracy was largely royalist, the gentry was split (but see Hill, *World Turned Upside Down*, for a Marxist view).

14. Recent biographies of Cromwell include Robert S. Paul, *The Lord Protector: Religion and Politics in the Life of Oliver Cromwell* (Grand Rapids, Mich., 1964); Christopher Hill, *God's Englishman: Oliver Cromwell and the English Revolution* (New York, 1970); and Antonia Fraser, *Cromwell: The Lord Protector* (New York, 1974).

15. The Solemn League and Covenant was prepared by Alexander Henderson, modeled on the Scottish national covenant of 1638. The critical edition is in Henry Gee and Hardy, eds., *Documents Illustrative of English Church History*, pp. 569–74; their edition is based upon John Rushworth, *Historical Collections of Private Passages of State . . . , 1618–1648* (London, 1721–22), V, 478.

16. On Samuel Rutherford, see the article in the *Dictionary of National Biography* (London, 1909), XVII, 496–98 (hereafter *DNB*), and G. P. Gooch, *English Democratic Ideas in the Seventeenth Century* (New York, 1961), pp. 98–99.

17. The original title was *Lex Rex: The Law and the Prince. A Dispute for the Just Prerogative of King and People* (London: Printed for John Field . . . , Octob. 7, 1644), reprinted in Woodhouse, ed., *Puritanism and Liberty*, pp. 199–200, 211–12; text modernized.

18. Roland H. Bainton, "Congregationalism and the Puritan Revolution from the Just War to the Crusade," *Andover Newton Bulletin*, XXXV (1943), 1–20, reprinted in Roland H. Bainton, *Studies on the Reformation* (*Collected Papers in Church History*, ser. 2; Boston, 1963), pp. 248–74.

19. On Ram, see the article in *DNB*, XVI, 669–70.

20. The selection from Ram's *Souldiers Catechism* is reprinted from Bainton, *Studies on the Reformation*, p. 273.

21. Besides biographies of Cromwell by Paul, Hill, and Fraser (note 14), see Sir Charles H. Firth, *Cromwell's Army* (London, 1921), and Leo F. Solt, *Saints in Arms: Puritanism and Democracy in Cromwell's Army* (Stanford, Calif., 1959), as well as H. R. Trevor-Roper, "Oliver Cromwell and His Parliaments," in R. Pares and A. J. P. Taylor, eds., *Essays Presented to L. B. Namier* (London, 1956).

22. On Puritan radicals, see Hill, *World Turned Upside Down*. Leveller tracts have been edited by William Haller and Godfrey Davies, *The Leveller Tracts, 1647–1653* (New York, 1944). Leveller manifestos have been edited by Don M. Wolfe, *Leveller Manifestoes of the Puritan Revolution* (New York, 1969). Digger tracts have been edited by George H. Sabine in *The Works of Gerrard Winstanley* (Ithaca, N.Y., 1941). For the Fifth Monarchists, see Capp, *Fifth Monarchy Men*.

23. The letter of Oliver Cromwell from Bristol, September 14, 1645, is from W. C. Abbot, ed., *The Writings and Speeches of Oliver Cromwell* (4 vols.; Cambridge, Mass., 1937–47), I, 377. It can also be found in Stuart E. Prall, ed., *The Puritan Revolution: A Documentary History* (Garden City, N.Y., 1968), pp. 119–25.

24. On Lilburne and the Levellers, see Howard Shaw, *The Levellers* (New York, 1968); H. N. Brailsford, *The Levellers and the English Revolution* (Stanford, Calif., 1961); and D. B. Robertson, *The Religious Foundations of Leveller Democracy* (New York, 1951).

25. Lilburne's Agreement of the People of October 28, 1647, is from S. R. Gardiner, ed., *Constitutional Documents of the Puritan Revolution* (3d ed.; Oxford, Eng., 1968), pp. 333–35; text modernized. Also in G. R. Elton, *Renaissance and Reformation, 1300–1648* (New York, 1963), pp. 208–9.

26. For Milton's dialogue with the radicals, see Hill, *World Turned Upside Down*, pp. 320–36. Also see Don M. Wolfe, *Milton in the Puritan Revolution* (New York, 1943); Michael Fixler, *Milton and the Kingdoms of God* (Evanston, Ill., 1964); and William Empson, *Milton's God* (rev. ed.; London, 1965).

27. Milton's *The Tenure of Kings* (1649) is in volume V of F. A. Patterson, ed., *The Works of John Milton* (18 vols.; New York, 1931–38), and in Prall, ed., *Puritan Revolution*, pp. 35–41; text modernized. See David Masson, *The Life of John Milton* (New York, 1946), V, 1649–54.

28. Claude de Seyssel, a former minister of King Louis XII, published his commentary on French political thought, *Le Grant Monarchie de France*, in 1518.

29. Matthew of Paris, an English monk and chronicler, died in 1259. His *Chronica maiora* criticized the policies of King Henry III.

30. Peter Martyr Vermigli (1500–1562), a refugee Italian Protestant theologian, was invited by Thomas Cranmer to become professor of divinity at Oxford in 1547.
Sir Thomas Smith (1513–77), secretary of state under Queen Elizabeth I, wrote the most important description of the government of England in the Tudor age.

31. Gildas (516?–570) was the earliest British historian. His history of Britain, *Gildae Sapientis de excidio et conquestu Britanniae*, was published by Polydore Vergil in 1525.

32. Milton's Sonnet XVI, "To the Lord General Cromwell," was written in 1652 and first published in 1694. It can be found in E. A. J. Honigmann, *Milton's Sonnets* (New York, 1966), pp. 145–52. Addressing Cromwell, Milton warned against "new foes" who advocated a state-supported church limiting religious toleration, which was contrary to the views of both Milton and Cromwell.

33. On Winstanley, see Sabine, *Works of Winstanley*; Hill, *World Turned Upside Down*, pp. 90–103; D. W. Petegorsky, *Left-Wing Democracy in the English Civil War: A Study in the Social Philosophy of Gerrard Winstanley* (London, 1940); and Winthrop S. Hudson, "The Economic and Social Thought of Gerrard Winstanley," *Journal of Modern History*, XVIII (1946), 1–26, and "Gerrard Winstanley and the Early Quakers," *Church History*, XII (1943), 177–94.

34. Selections from the original edition of Winstanley et al., *The True Levellers' Standard Advanced* (London, 1649), are reprinted in Woodhouse, ed., *Puritanism and Liberty*, pp. 379–85.

35. *The Diggers' Mirth or Certain Verses Composed and Fitted to Tunes, for the Delight and Recreation of All Those Who Dig . . .* (London, 1650) is reprinted from Woodhouse, ed., *Puritanism and Liberty*, pp. 385–86.

36. On the Fifth Monarchy Men, see Capp, *Fifth Monarchy Men*.

37. On John More, see Capp, *Fifth Monarchy Men*, p. 256. On Spittlehouse, see Capp, p. 263, and *DNB*, XVIII, 814.

38. John Spittlehouse and John More, *A Vindication of the Continued Succession of the Primitive Church . . .* (London, 1652); a photocopy of the original is in the American Baptist Historical Society, Rochester, N.Y., title, pp. 10–16, 27–30. I have retained the spelling of the original, which is especially colorful.

39. The reference is to Friedrich Spanheim the Younger (1632–1701), a Calvinist theologian of Leiden famous for his *Summa historiae ecclesiasticae* of 1689.

40. Becold is John of Leiden, king of the Anabaptists in Muenster.

41. On George Fox, see Norman Penney, ed., *The Journal of George Fox, 1694* (London, 1927); William C. Braithwaite, *The Beginnings of Quakerism* (2d ed.; Cambridge, Eng., 1955); and Hugh S. Barbour, comp., *Early Quaker Writings, 1650–1700* (Grand Rapids, Mich., 1973).

42. On the Ranters, see A. L. Morton, *The World of the Ranters* (London, 1970), and Hill, *World Turned Upside Down*, pp. 163–85.

43. George Fox, *The Journal of George Fox, 1694*, ed. John L. Nickalls (Cambridge, Eng., 1952), pp. 34–38.

44. Edward Burrough, in his Epistle to the Reader, introducing George Fox, *The Great Mistery of the Great Whore Unfolded* (London, 1659).

45. Edward Burrough and Francis Howgill, *To the Camp of the Lord in England* (London, 1655), p. 9.

46. James Naylor, *Works: A Collection of Sundry Books, Epistles and Papers . . .* (London, 1716), pp. 385, 391–92; the selections are from *The Lamb's War against the Man of Sin* (London, 1658). Quotations 193–96 are given in Hugh Barbour, *The Quakers in Puritan England* (New Haven, Conn., 1964), pp. 39–41.

Selected
Bibliography

Selected Bibliography

Christianity and Revolution

Guenther Lewy has recently published seventeen case studies on *Religion and Revolution* (New York: Oxford University Press, 1974), including chapters 5 and 6 (pp. 102–53) on revolutionary millenarianism during the German Reformation and on the Puritan Revolution and the Fifth Monarchy Men. Lewy's case studies are more impressive as history than is his theory that religion becomes revolutionary when millenarian revolts occur, when militant religious nationalism arises, when religious leaders support revolution, or when individual theologians or laymen aid revolutionary movements.

Isaac Kramnick opts for a political explanation for revolution in "Explanations for Revolution," *History and Theory*, XI (1972), 26–63, although he also allows for economic, sociological, and psychological causes. Four useful historical approaches to revolutionary theory are Perez Zagorin, "Theories of Revolution in Contemporary Historiography," *Political Science Quarterly*, LXXXVIII (1973), 23–52; Lawrence Stone, *The Causes of the English Revolution, 1529–1642* (New York: Harper and Row, 1972), pp. 3–25; H. G. Koenigsberger, "Early Modern Revolutions: An Exchange [with Lawrence Stone]," *Journal of Modern History*, XLVI (1974), 99–110; and Martha Ellis François, "Revolts in Late Medieval and Early Modern Europe: A Social Model," *Journal of Interdisciplinary History*, V (1974), 19–43.

The definition of revolution used in this book is borrowed from Thomas Kuhn's notion that scientific revolutions occur when ruling paradigms are replaced because of anomalies (*The Structure of Scientific Revolutions* [Chicago: University of Chicago Press, 1962]) and from Ted R. Gurr's *Why Men Rebel* (Princeton, N.J.: Princeton University Press, 1970), which argues that Anabaptist and Puritan radicalism resulted from aspirational deprivation during the Reformation, when the old and new clergy could not satisfy rising lay expectations of spiritual zeal.

Other important general works on revolution include Chalmers A. Johnson, *Revolution and the Social System* (Hoover Institution Studies, vol. III; Stanford, Calif.: The Institution, 1964); Samuel P. Huntington, *Political Order in Changing Societies* (New Haven, Conn.: Yale University Press, 1968); Neil L. Smelser, *The Theory of Collective Behavior* (New York: Free Press of Glencoe, 1964); C. Crane Brinton, *The Anatomy of Revolution* (rev. ed.; New York: Vintage, 1965); Hannah Arendt, *On Revolution* (New York: Viking, 1965); Eugen Rosenstock-Huessy, *Out of Revolution* (Norwich, Vt.: Argo, 1969); and Jacques Ellul, *Autopsy of Revolution* (New York: Knopf, 1971).

Anabaptist and Puritan Sources and Works of General Interest

The traditional (Lutheran) definition of Anabaptists as "fanatics" (Schwaermer) has been continued by Karl Holl in "Luther und die Schwaermer," *Gesammelte Aufsaetze zur Kirchengeschichte*, vol. I: *Luther* (Tuebingen: J. C. B. Mohr, 1923). Favorable definitions, from a theological perspective of Anabaptists as "Left-wing Reformers" and "Radical Reformers," have been presented by Roland H. Bainton, "The Left Wing of the Reformation," *Journal of Religion*, XXI (1941), 125, and by George H. Williams, *The Radical Reformation* (Philadelphia: Westminster, 1962). A recent sociological study of Anabaptism by Claus-Peter Clasen, *Anabaptism: A Social History, 1525–1618: Switzerland, Austria, Moravia, South and Central Germany* (Ithaca, N.Y.: Cornell University Press, 1972), concludes from statistical evidence that the movement was numerically unimportant.

Publication of Anabaptist sources proceeds steadily. Since 1930, thirteen volumes (often regional Germanic court documents) have appeared in the *Quellen zur Geschichte der Taeufer series* (Leipzig-Guetersloh). The Hesse *Wiedertaeuferakten 1521–1626* have been edited by Guenther Franz (Marburg: N. G. Elwert, 1951). One of three volumes of *Quellen zur Geschichte der Taeufer in der Schweiz* (Zurich: S. Hirzel, 1952) has been published. Three volumes of Dutch Anabaptist sources (vols. II, VII, and X) have appeared in the *Bibliotheca Reformatoria Neerlandica*, ed. Samuel Cramer and F. Pijper (The Hague: Martinus Nijhoff, 1903–14). A new Dutch series, *Documenta Anabaptistica Neerlandica*, has been announced. Hutterite, Mennonite, and Muensterite source collections will be referred to below.

The most useful Anabaptist source book in English is George H. Williams, ed., *Spiritual and Anabaptist Writers*, which is volume XXV in the Library of Christian Classics (Philadelphia: Westminster, 1957), cited as *SAW* in the notes. A basic bibliography is Hans J. Hillerbrand, ed., *A Bibliography of Anabaptist History, 1520–1630* (Elkhart, Ind.: Institute of Mennonite Studies, 1962). The most comprehensive textbook treatment, including Spiritualist and Unitarian movements as well, is George H. Williams's *Radical Reformation*. For biographical and place references, see Harold S. Bender et al., *The Mennonite Encyclopedia* (4 vols.; Scottdale, Pa.: Mennonite Publishing House, 1955–59).

For English Puritan documents and commentaries, see J. P. Kenyon, ed., *The Stuart Constitution* (Cambridge, Eng.: Cambridge University Press, 1966), along with similar older collections by S. R. Gardiner, G. W. Prothero, and J. R. Tanner. For the earlier Tudor period, see G. R. Elton, ed., *The Tudor Constitution* (Cambridge, Eng.: Cambridge University Press, 1962). A convenient brief source collection is Stuart E. Prall, ed., *The Puritan Revolution: A Documentary History* (Garden City, N.Y.: Anchor, 1968). A helpful collection of essays introducing the social context of the Civil War is edited by E. W. Ives—*The English Revolution, 1600–1660* (New York: Harper Torchbook, 1971). Valuable bibliographical guides include Conyers Read, *Bibliography of British History: Tudor Period, 1485–1603* (2d ed.; Oxford, Eng.: Oxford University Press, 1959); A. W. Pollard and G. R. Redgrave, *A Short-Title Catalogue of Books Printed in England, Scotland, and Ireland, and of English Books Printed Abroad, 1475–1640* (London: Bibliographical Society, 1926); and Donald G. Wing, *A Short-Title Catalogue of Books Printed in England, Scotland, Ireland, Wales, and British America, and of English Books Printed in Other Countries, 1641–1700* (3 vols.; New York: Modern Language Association, 2d ed., 1972; 1st ed., 1945–51). L. Stephen and S. Lee, eds., *Dictionary of National Biography* (63 vols.; London: Smith, Elder, 1885–1909), is indispensable for biographical references.

The best one-volume history of the Puritan Revolution is Ivan Roots, *The Great Rebellion, 1642–1660* (London: Batsford, 1966). A fuller narrative can be found in two books by C. V. Wedgwood: *The King's Peace, 1637–1641* and *The King's War, 1641–1647* (London: Collins, 1955 and 1958). The great standard work is S. R. Gardiner's *History of England from the Accession of James I to the Outbreak of the Civil War, 1603–1642* (10 vols.; London: Longmans, Green, 1884–86), *History of the Great Civil War, 1642–1649* (4 vols.; London: Longmans, Green, 1898–1901), and *History of the Commonwealth and Protectorate, 1649–1656* (4 vols.; New York, Longmans, Green, 1903). On Oliver Cromwell, see W. C. Abbot, ed., *The Writings and Speeches of Oliver Cromwell* (4 vols.; Cambridge, Mass.: Harvard University Press, 1937–47), and biographies by Robert S. Paul (*The Lord Protector: Religion and Politics in the Life of Oliver Cromwell* [Grand Rapid, Mich.: Eerdmans, 1965]), for a religious orientation, and by Christopher Hill (*God's Englishman: Oliver Cromwell and the English Revolution* [New York: Dial, 1970], for a Marxist orientation.

For Puritan religious thought, consult Patrick Collinson, *The Elizabethan Puritan Movement* (London: Cape, 1967), along with M. M. Knappen, *Tudor Puritanism* (Chicago: University of Chicago Press, 1939); William Haller, *The Rise of Puritanism* (New York: Harper Torchbook, 1938), and its sequel *Liberty and Reformation in the Puritan Revolution* (New York: Columbia University Press, 1963); Christopher Hill, *Society and Puritanism in Pre-Revolutionary England* (New York: Schocken, 1964), which emphasizes nontheological aspects; and Michael Walzer, *The Revolution of the Saints* (Cambridge, Mass.: Harvard

University Press, 1965), which traces how modern politics developed from Puritan religious ideology. Puritan millennialism is examined in Norman Cohn, *The Pursuit of the Millennium* (New York: Harper Torchbook, 1961), in William M. Lamont, *Godly Rule: Politics and Religion, 1603–60* (New York: St. Martin's, 1969), in John F. Wilson, *Pulpit in Parliament: Puritanism during the English Civil Wars, 1640–1648* (Princeton: Princeton University Press, 1969), and in B. S. Capp, *The Fifth Monarchy Men: A Study in Seventeenth Century English Millenarianism* (London: Faber and Faber, 1972). Two helpful political histories are J. W. Allen, *A History of Political Thought in the Sixteenth Century* (New York: Barnes and Noble, 1957), and Perez Zagorin, *A History of Political Thought in the English Revolution* (New York: Humanities, 1966). Radical ideas in the Puritan Revolution are masterfully discussed by Christopher Hill, *The World Turned Upside Down: Radical Ideas during the English Revolution* (New York: Viking, 1972). The best introduction and documentary collection on the idea of liberty in Puritanism is A. S. P. Woodhouse, ed., *Puritanism and Liberty, Being the Army Debates (1647–9) from the Clarke Manuscripts with Supplemental Documents* (Chicago: University of Chicago Press, 1965; originally published 1938).

The Peasants' War

Bax, E. Belfort. *The Peasants' War in Germany*. London: Swan Sonnenschein, 1899.

Brandt, Otto H. *Der grosse Bauernkrieg, Zeitgenoessische Berichte, Aussagen und Aktenstuecke*. Jena: Eugen Diedrichs, 1926.

Engels, Friedrich. *The German Revolutions: The Peasant War in Germany and Germany: Revolution and Counter-Revolution*. Ed. Leonard Krieger. Chicago: University of Chicago Press, 1967.

Franz, Guenther. "Die Entstehung der 'Zwoelf Artikel' der deutschen Bauernschaft," *Archiv fuer Reformationsgeschichte*, XXXVI (1939), 193–213.

———. *Der deutsche Bauernkrieg*. 6th ed. Darmstadt: Wissenschaftliche Buchgesellschaft, 1962.

———. *Quellen zur Geschicte des Bauernkrieges*. Darmstadt: Wissenschaftliche Buchgesellschaft, 1963.

Heymann, Frederick G. "The Hussite Revolution and the German Peasants' War: An Historical Comparison." In *Medievalia et Humanistica*, vol. I, ed. Paul M. Clogan, pp. 141–59. Cleveland: Western Reserve University Press, 1970.

Macek, Josef. *Die Tiroler Bauernkrieg und Michael Gaismair*. Tr. from Czech into German by Eduard Ullman. Berlin: Deutscher Verlag der Wissenschaften V E B, 1965.

Schapiro, Jacob Salwyn. *Social Reform and the Reformation*. New York: Columbia University Press, 1909.

Sessions, Kyle C., ed. *Reformation and Authority: The Meaning of the Peasants' Revolt*. Lexington, Mass.: Heath, 1968.

Strauss, Gerald. *Manifestations of Discontent in Germany on the Eve of the Reformation*. Bloomington, Ind.: Indiana University Press, 1971.

Zwickau Prophets and Thomas Muentzer

Bensing, Manfred. *Thomas Muentzer und der Thueringer Aufstand, 1525.* Berlin: Deutscher Verlag der Wissenschaften V E B, 1966.

Ebert, Klaus. *Theologie und politisches Handeln: Thomas Muentzer als Modell.* Stuttgart: W. Kohlhammer, 1973.

Elliger, Walter. *Thomas Muentzer.* Berlin: Wichern, 1960.

Franz, Guenther, ed. *Thomas Muentzer: Schriften und Briefe.* Guetersloh: Gerd Mohn, 1968.

Goertz, H.-J. *Innere und Aeussere Ordnung in der Theologie Thomas Muentzers. Studies in the History of Christian Thought,* vol. II. Leiden: E. J. Brill, 1967.

Gritsch, Eric W. *Reformer without a Church: The Life and Thought of Thomas Muentzer, 1488?–1525.* Philadelphia: Fortress, 1967.

Hinrichs, Carl. *Luther und Muentzer: Ihre Auseinandersetzung ueber Obrigkeit und Widerstandsrecht.* Berlin: Walter de Gruyter, 1952.

Mueller, Nikolaus. *Die Wittenberger Bewegung, 1521 und 1522.* Leipzig: M. Heinsius Nachfolger, 1911.

Nipperdey, Thomas. "Theologie und Revolution bei Thomas Muentzer," *Archiv fuer Reformationsgeschichte,* LIV (1963), 145–81.

Ozment, Steven. *Mysticism and Dissent: Religious Ideology and Social Protest in the Sixteenth Century.* New Haven, Conn.: Yale University Press, 1973.

Rupp, Gordon. *Patterns of Reformation.* Philadelphia: Fortress, 1969.

Smirin, M. M. *Die Volksreformation des Thomas Muentzer und der grosse Bauernkrieg.* Berlin: Dietz, 1956. Trans. of Russian 2d ed. of 1955.

Wappler, Paul. *Thomas Muentzer in Zwickau und die Zwickauer Propheten.* 2d ed. Guetersloh: Gerd Mohn, 1966.

Zuck, Lowell H. "Fecund Problems of Eschatological Hope, Election Proof, and Social Revolt in Thomas Muentzer." In *Reformation Studies: Essays in Honor of Roland H. Bainton,* ed. Franklin H. Littell, pp. 239–50. Richmond, Va.: John Knox, 1962.

Swiss and South German Anabaptists

Armour, Rollin S. *Anabaptist Baptism: A Representative Study.* Scottdale, Pa.: Herald, 1966.

Bender, Harold S. *Conrad Grebel, 1498–1526, Founder of the Swiss Brethren.* Goshen, Ind.: Mennonite Historical Society, 1950.

Bergsten, Torsten. *Balthasar Hubmaier: Seine Stellung zu Reformation und Taeufertum, 1521–1528.* Kassel: J. G. Oncken, 1961.

Blanke, Fritz. *Brothers in Christ: The History of the Oldest Anabaptist Congregation, Zollikon, near Zurich, Switzerland.* Scottdale, Pa.: Herald, 1961.

Egli, Emil, ed. *Actensammlung zur Geschichte der Zuercher Reformation in den Jahren 1519–1533.* 2 vols. Zurich: Meyer and Zeller, 1879.

Fast, Heinold. *Heinrich Bullinger und die Taeufer.* Weierhof:
Mennonitischen Geschichtsverein, 1959.

Gratz, Delbert. *Bernese Anabaptists.* Scottdale, Pa.: Herald, 1961.

Hillerbrand, Hans J. "The Origins of Sixteenth Century Anabaptism:
Another Look," *Archiv fuer Reformationsgeschichte,* LIII (1962),
152–80.

Jenny, Beatrice. *Das Schleitheimer Taeuferbekenntnis, 1527.* From the
"Schaffhauser Beitraege zur vaterlaendischen Geschichte," XXVIII
(1961), 9–18.

Klassen, William. *Covenant and Community: The Life, Writings and
Hermeneutic of Pilgram Marpeck.* Grand Rapids, Mich.: Eerdmans,
1968.

Littell, Franklin H. *The Origins of Sectarian Protestantism.* New York:
Macmillan, 1964. A new edition of *The Anabaptist View of the
Church.*

Muralt, Leonhard von, and Walter Schmid, eds. *Quellen zur Geschichte
der Taeufer in der Schweiz.* Zurich: S. Hirzel, 1952.

Peachey, Paul. *Die soziale Herkunft der Schweizer Taeufer in der
Reformationszeit.* Karlsruhe: Heinrich Schneider, 1954.

Stayer, James M. *Anabaptists and the Sword.* Lawrence, Kan.: Coronado,
1972.

Vedder, Henry C. *Balthasar Hubmaier.* New York: G. P. Putnam's Sons,
1905.

Walton, Robert C. *Zwingli's Theocracy.* Toronto: University of Toronto
Press, 1968.

Yoder, John H., ed. and tr. *The Legacy of Michael Sattler.* Scottdale,
Pa.: Herald, 1973. First published volume of Classics of the Radical
Reformation.

Zuck, Lowell H. "Anabaptism: Abortive Counter-Revolt Within the
Reformation," *Church History,* XXVI (1957), 1–16.

The Kingdom of Muenster

Bainton, Roland H. *David Joris: Wiedertaeufer und Kaempfer fuer
Toleranz.* Leipzig: M. Heinsius Nachfolger, 1937.

Brendler, Gerhard. *Das Taeuferreich zu Muenster, 1534/35.* Berlin:
Deutscher Verlag der Wissenschaften V E B, 1966.

Cohn, Norman. *The Pursuit of the Millennium.* Rev. ed. London:
Granada, 1970.

Cornelius, C. A., ed. *Die Geschichtsquellen des Bisthums Muenster.*
Muenster: Aschendorffsche Verlagsbuchhandlung, 1965. Reprint of an
1853 edition.

Detmer, Heinrich, ed. *Hermanni a Kerssenbroch: Anabaptistici furoris
Monasterium . . . evertentis historica narratio.* Muenster: Theissing,
1899–1900.

Kawerau, Peter. *Melchior Hofmann als religioeser Denker.* Haarlem:
DeErven F. Bohn N V, 1954.

Kirchhoff, Karl-Heinz. "Was There a Peaceful Anabaptist Congregation
in Muenster in 1534?" *Mennonite Quarterly Review,* XLIV (1970),
357–70.

Rammstedt, Otthein. *Sekte und sociale Bewegung: Sociologische Analyse der Taeufer in Muenster 1534–35.* Cologne: Westdeutscher, 1966.

Ritschl, Hans. *Die Kommune der Wiedertaeufer in Muenster.* Bonn: Kurt Schroeder, 1923.

Schubert, Hans von. *Der Kommunismus der Wiedertaeufer in Muenster und seine Quellen.* Heidelberg: Carl Winter, 1919.

Stayer, James. "The Muensterite Rationalization of Bernhard Rothmann," *Journal of the History of Ideas,* XXVIII (1967), 179–92.

Stupperich, Robert. *Die Schriften Bernhard Rothmanns.* Vol. I. Muenster: Aschendorffsche Verlagsbuchhandlung, 1970.

Wray, Frank J. "The 'Vermahnung' of 1542 and Rothmann's 'Bekenntnisse,' " *Archiv fuer Reformationsgeschichte,* XLVII (1956), 243–50.

Mennonites and Hutterites

Durnbaugh, Donald F., ed. *Every Need Supplied: Mutual Aid and Christian Community in the Free Churches, 1525–1675.* Documents in Free Church History, ed. Franklin H. Littell and George H. Williams. Philadelphia: Temple University Press, 1974.

Dyck, Cornelius J., ed. *An Introduction to Mennonite History.* Scottdale, Pa.: Herald, 1967.

———. *A Legacy of Faith: The Heritage of Menno Simons.* Newton, Kan.: Faith and Life, 1962.

Fischer, Hans. *Jacob Hutter: Leben, Froemmigkeit, Briefe.* Mennonite Historical Series, no. 1. Newton, Kan., 1956.

Friedmann, Robert. "The Christian Communism of the Hutterite Brethren," *Archiv fuer Reformationsgeschichte,* XLVI (1955), 196–209.

———. *Hutterite Studies: Essays by Robert Friedmann.* Ed. Harold S. Bender. Goshen, Ind.: Mennonite Historical Society, 1961.

Hillerbrand, Hans J. "Menno Simons: Sixteenth Century Reformer," *Church History,* XXXI (1962), 387–99.

Horsch, John. *The Hutterian Brethren, 1528–1931: A Story of Martyrdom and Loyalty.* Goshen, Ind.: Mennonite Historical Society, 1931.

Horst, Irvin B. *The Radical Brethren: Anabaptism and the English Reformation to 1558.* Nieuwkoop: B. de Graaf, 1972.

Keeney, William E. *The Development of Dutch Anabaptist Thought and Practice from 1539–1564.* Nieuwkoop: B. de Graaf, 1968.

Klassen, Peter James. *The Economics of Anabaptism, 1525–1560.* The Hague: Mouton, 1964.

Krahn, Cornelius. *Menno Simons (1496–1561).* Karlsruhe: Schneider, 1936.

———. *Dutch Anabaptism: Origin, Spread, Life, and Thought, 1450–1600.* The Hague: Martinus Nijhoff, 1968.

Littell, Franklin H. *A Tribute to Menno Simons.* Scottdale, Pa.: Herald, 1961.

Mueller, Lydia. *Der Kommunismus der maehrischen Wiedertaeufer.* Schriften des Vereins fuer Reformationsgeschichte, vol. XLV. Leipzig: The Society, 1927.

Oyer, John S. *Lutheran Reformers against Anabaptists.* The Hague: Martinus Nijhoff, 1969.

Peters, Victor. *All Things Common: The Hutterian Way of Life.* Minneapolis: University of Minnesota Press, 1965.

Riedemann, Peter. *Account of Our Religion, Doctrine and Faith.* London: Hodder and Stoughton, 1950.

Verheyden, A. L. E. *Anabaptism in Flanders, 1530–1650.* Scottdale, Pa.: Herald, 1961.

Wenger, John C., ed. *The Complete Writings of Menno Simons.* Scottdale, Pa.: Herald, 1956.

Zeman, Jarold K. *The Anabaptists and the Czech Brethren in Moravia, 1526–1628.* The Hague: Mouton, 1969.

Zieglschmid, A. J. F. *Die aelteste Chronik der Hutterischen Brueder.* Ithaca, N.Y.: Cayuga, 1943.

Protestant Resistance: German, Scottish, French, and Dutch

Allen, J. W. *A History of Political Thought in the Sixteenth Century.* New York: Barnes and Noble, 1957; originally published 1928.

Brown, P. Hume. *George Buchanan: Humanist and Reformer.* Edinburgh: D. Douglas, 1890.

Doerries, Hermann. *Wort und Stunde: Beitraege zum Verstaendnis Luthers.* Goettingen: Vandenhoeck und Ruprecht, 1970.

Elliot, J. H. "Revolution and Continuity in Early Modern Europe," *Past and Present,* XLII (1969), 35–56. Reprinted in Lawrence and Carol Kaplan, eds., *Revolutions: A Comparative Study* (New York: Vintage, 1973).

Figgis, J. N. *Political Thought from Gerson to Grotius: 1414–1625.* New York: Harper Torchbook, 1960; originally published 1907.

Franklin, Julian H. *Jean Bodin and the Rise of Absolutist Theory.* New York: Cambridge University Press, 1973.

Garrett, Christina Hallowell. *The Marian Exiles: A Study in the Origins of Elizabethan Puritanism.* Cambridge, Eng.: Cambridge University Press, 1938. Reprinted 1966.

Geyl, Pieter. *The Revolt of the Netherlands, 1555–1609.* 2d ed. New York: Barnes and Noble, 1958.

Giesey, Ralph E. "The Monarchomach Triumvirs: Hotman, Beza and Mornay," *Bibliotheque d'Humanisme et Renaissance,* XXXII (1970), 41–76.

Green, Lowell C. "Resistance to Authority and Luther," *Lutheran Quarterly,* V (1954), 338–48.

Gritsch, Eric W. "Martin Luther and Violence: A Reappraisal of a Neuralgic Theme," *Sixteenth Century Journal,* III (1972), 37–55.

Hoess, Irmgard. "Zur Genesis der Widerstandslehre Bezas," *Archiv fuer Reformationsgeschichte,* LIV (1963), 198–214.

Hotman, François. *Francogallia.* With notes on the Latin text by Ralph E. Giesey; trans. J. H. M. Salmon. Cambridge, Eng.: Cambridge University Press, 1972.

Hudson, Winthrop S. *John Ponet (1516?–1576): Advocate of Limited Monarchy.* Chicago: University of Chicago Press, 1942.

Kelley, Donald R. *François Hotman: A Revolutionary's Ordeal.* Princeton, N.J.: Princeton University Press, 1973.

Kingdon, Robert M. "The First Expression of Theodore Beza's Political Ideas," *Archiv fuer Reformationsgeschichte,* XLVI (1955), 88–100.

————. *Geneva and the Coming of the Wars of Religion in France, 1555–1563.* Geneva: Droz, 1956.

Kingdon, Robert M., and Robert D. Linder. *Calvin and Calvinism: Sources of Democracy?* Lexington, Mass.: Heath, 1970.

Koenigsberger, H. G. "Organization of Revolutionary Parties in France and the Netherlands during the Sixteenth Century," *Journal of Modern History,* XXVII (1955), 335–51.

Laing, David, ed. *The Works of John Knox.* Edinburgh: Printed for the Bannatyne Club, 1855. Reprinted New York: A M S, 1966.

Laski, Harold J., ed. *A Defense of Liberty against Tyrants.* Gloucester, Mass.: Peter Smith, 1963. Original edition: *Vindiciae contra tyrannos* (Edinburgh [Basel?], 1579).

Molen, Ronald J. Vander. "Anglican against Puritan: Ideological Origins during the Marian Exile," *Church History,* XLII (1973), 45–57.

Olson, Oliver K. "Theology of Revolution: Magdeburg, 1550–1551," *Sixteenth Century Journal,* III (1972), 56–79.

Reid, W. Stanford. "The Coming of the Reformation to Edinburgh," *Church History,* XLII (1973), 27–44.

Ridley, Jasper. *John Knox.* New York: Oxford University Press, 1968.

Scheible, Heinz, ed. *Das Widerstandsrecht als Problem der deutschen Protestanten, 1523–1546.* Goettingen: Vandenhoeck und Ruprecht, 1969.

Schelvan, A. A. van. "Beza's De Iure Magistratuum in Subditos," *Archiv fuer Reformationsgeschichte,* XLV (1954), 62–83.

Smit, J. W. "The Netherlands Revolution." In *Preconditions of Revolution in Early Modern Europe,* ed. Robert Forster and Jack P. Greene, pp. 19–54. Baltimore: Johns Hopkins Press, 1970.

Walzer, Michael. *The Revolution of the Saints.* Cambridge, Mass.: Harvard University Press, 1965.

Wedgwood, C. V. *William the Silent.* London: Jonathan Cape, 1944.

William of Orange. *The Apologie or Defence of the Most Noble Prince William, by the Grace of God Prince of Orange. . . .* Ed. H. Wansink. Leiden: E. J. Brill, 1969.

Wolf, Gunther, ed. *Luther und die Obrigkeit in Wege der Forschung.* Darmstadt: Wissenschaftliche Buchgesellschaft, 1970.

Roman Catholic Resistance: English and Spanish

Allen, William. *A True, Sincere and Modest Defence of English Catholics* (1584). Ed. D. M. Rogers. Menston, Yorks., Eng.: Scolar Press, 1971.

Bossy, John. "The Character of Elizabethan Catholicism." In *Crisis in Europe, 1560–1660*, ed. Trevor Aston, pp. 235–60. Garden City, N.Y.: Anchor, 1967.

Broderick, James S.J. *Robert Bellarmine*. Westminster, Md.: Newman, 1961.

Clancy, Thomas H. "Are Martyrs Relevant?" *America*, CXXIII (1970), 320.

Gooch, G. P. *English Democratic Ideas in the Seventeenth Century*. New York: Harper Torchbook, 1959.

Haile, Martin. *An Elizabethan Cardinal: William Allen*. St. Louis: B. Herder, 1914.

Kingdon, Robert M. "William Allen's Use of Protestant Political Argument." In *From the Renaissance to the Counter-Revolution*, ed. Charles H. Carter, pp. 164–76. New York: Random House, 1965.

Laures, John. *The Political Economy of Juan de Mariana*. New York: Fordham University Press, 1928.

Mattingly, Garrett. "William Allen and Catholic Propaganda in England." In *Aspects de la propagande religieuse*, pp. 333–38. Geneva: Droz, 1957.

Moore, George Albert, ed. *Mariana: The King and the Education of the King*. Washington, D.C.: Country Dollar, 1948.

Murray, John C. "St. Robert Bellarmine on the Indirect Power," *Theological Studies*, IX (1948), 491–535.

Nuttall, Geoffrey. "The English Martyrs of 1535–1680," *Journal of Ecclesiastical History*, XXII (1971), 191–97.

English Puritan Revolution

See also Anabaptist and Puritan Sources

Bainton, Roland H. "Congregationalism and the Puritan Revolution from the Just War to the Crusade," *Andover Newton Bulletin*, XXV (1943), 1–20. Reprinted in Roland H. Bainton, *Studies on the Reformation* (Collected Papers in Church History, ser. 2; Boston: Beacon, 1963), pp. 248–74.

Barbour, Hugh. *The Quakers in Puritan England*. New Haven, Conn.: Yale University Press, 1964.

Barbour, Hugh, and Arthur O. Roberts, comps. *Early Quaker Writings, 1650–1700*. Grand Rapids, Mich.: Eerdmans, 1973.

Barker, Arthur E. *Milton and the Puritan Dilemma, 1641–60*. Toronto: University of Toronto Press, 1942.

Brailsford, H. N. *The Levellers and the English Revolution*. Stanford, Calif.: Stanford University Press, 1961.

Braithwaite, William C. *The Beginnings of Quakerism*. 2d ed. Cambridge, Eng.: Cambridge University Press, 1955.

Christianson, Paul. "From Expectation to Militance: Reformers and Babylon in the First Two Years of the Long Parliament," *Journal of Ecclesiastical History*, XXIV (1973), 225–44.

Clouse, Robert G. "Johann Heinrich Alsted and English Millenialism," *Harvard Theological Review*, LXII (1969), 189–207.

———. "John Napier and Apocalyptic Thought," *The Sixteenth Century Journal*, V (1974), 101–14.

Empson, William. *Milton's God*. Rev. ed. London: Chatto and Windus, 1965.

Firth, Sir Charles H. *Cromwell's Army*. London: Methuen, 1921.

Fixler, Michael. *Milton and the Kingdoms of God*. Evanston, Ill.: Northwestern University Press, 1964.

Fox, George. *The Journal of George Fox* (1594). Ed. John L. Nickalls. Cambridge, Eng.: Cambridge University Press, 1952.

Fraser, Antonia. *Cromwell, the Lord Protector*. New York: Knopf, 1974.

Gee, Henry, and William John Hardy, eds. *Documents Illustrative of English Church History*. London: Macmillan, 1910.

Hudson, Winthrop S. "Gerrard Winstanley and the Early Quakers," *Church History*, XII (1943), 177–94.

———. "The Economic and Social Thought of Gerrard Winstanley," *Journal of Modern History*, XVIII (1946), 1–26.

Lindsay, A. D. *The Essentials of Democracy*. Philadelphia: University of Pennsylvania Press, 1929.

Morton, A. L. *The World of the Ranters*. London: Lawrence and Wishart, 1970.

Mozley, J. F. *John Foxe and His Book*. New York: Macmillan, 1940.

Olsen, V. Norskov. *John Foxe and the Elizabethan Church*. Berkeley: University of California Press, 1973.

Petegorsky, D. W. *Left-Wing Democracy in the English Civil War: A Study in the Social Philosophy of Gerrard Winstanley*. London: Gollancz, 1940.

Robertson, D. B. *The Religious Foundations of Leveller Democracy*. New York: Columbia University Press, 1951.

Sabine, George H., ed. *The Works of Gerrard Winstanley*. Ithaca, N.Y.: Cornell University Press, 1941

Seaver, Paul S. *The Puritan Lectureships: The Politics of Religious Dissent, 1560–1662*. Stanford, Calif.: Stanford University Press, 1970.

Shaw, Howard. *The Levellers*. New York: Harper and Row, 1968.

Solt, Leo F. *Saints in Arms: Puritanism & Democracy in Cromwell's Army*. Stanford, Calif.: Stanford University Press, 1959.

Toon, Peter, ed. *Puritans, the Millennium and the Future of Israel*. Greenwood, S.C.: Attic, 1970.

Trevor-Roper, H. R. "The General Crisis of the Seventeenth Century." In *Crisis in Europe, 1560–1660*, ed. Trevor Aston, pp. 63–102. Garden City, N.Y.: Anchor Books, 1967.

Trinterud, Leonard J., ed. *Elizabethan Puritanism*. New York: Oxford University Press, 1971.

Underdown, David. *Pride's Purge: Politics in the Puritan Revolution*. Oxford, Eng.: Oxford University Press, 1971.

Wilson, John F. "A Glimpse of Syons Glory," *Church History*, XXXI (1962), 66–73.

Wolfe, Don M. *Milton in the Puritan Revolution*. New York: Humanities, 1943.

Indexes

Index of Persons, Places, and Topics

Index of Biblical References